ETHNOGRAPHIC S[...]

Volume 39

PEOPLES OF THE CENTRAL CAMEROONS (TIKAR. BAMUM AND BAMILEKE. BANEN, BAFIA, AND BALOM.)

PEOPLES OF THE CENTRAL CAMEROONS (TIKAR. BAMUM AND BAMILEKE. BANEN, BAFIA, AND BALOM.)

Western Africa
Part IX

MERRAN MCCULLOCH,
MARGARET LITTLEWOOD
AND I. DUGAST

Routledge
Taylor & Francis Group

LONDON AND NEW YORK

First published in 1954 by the International African Institute

This edition first published in 2017
by Routledge
2 Park Square, Milton Park, Abingdon, Oxon OX14 4RN

and by Routledge
711 Third Avenue, New York, NY 10017

Routledge is an imprint of the Taylor & Francis Group, an informa business

© 1954 International African Institute

British Library Cataloguing in Publication Data
A catalogue record for this book is available from the British Library

ISBN: 978-1-138-23217-4 (Set)
ISBN: 978-1-315-30463-2 (Set) (ebk)
ISBN: 978-1-138-23951-7 (Volume 39) (hbk)
ISBN: 978-1-138-23952-4 (Volume 39) (pbk)
ISBN: 978-1-315-29573-2 (Volume 39) (ebk)

Publisher's Note
The publisher has gone to great lengths to ensure the quality of this reprint but points out that some imperfections in the original copies may be apparent.

Disclaimer
The publisher has made every effort to trace copyright holders and would welcome correspondence from those they have been unable to trace.

Publisher's note

Due to modern production methods, it has not been possible to reproduce all the charts which appeared in the original book. Please go to www.routledge.com/Ethnographic-Survey-of-Africa/Forde/p/book/9781138232174 to view them.

ETHNOGRAPHIC SURVEY OF AFRICA

EDITED BY DARYLL FORDE

WESTERN AFRICA

PART IX

PEOPLES OF
THE CENTRAL CAMEROONS

TIKAR

By MERRAN McCULLOCH

BAMUM and BAMILEKE

By MARGARET LITTLEWOOD

BANEN, BAFIA, and BALOM

By I. DUGAST

LONDON

INTERNATIONAL AFRICAN INSTITUTE

1954

This study is one section of the Ethnographic Survey of Africa which the International African Institute is preparing with the aid of a grant made by the Secretary of State, under the Colonial Development and Welfare Acts, on the recommendation of the Colonial Social Science Research Council.

PRINTED IN ENGLAND BY
HAZELL, WATSON & VINEY, LTD
LONDON AND AYLESBURY

FOREWORD

THE International African Institute has, since 1945, been engaged on the preparation and publication of an Ethnographic Survey of Africa, the purpose of which is to present in a brief and readily comprehensible form a summary of available information concerning the different peoples of Africa with respect to location, natural environment, economy and crafts, social structure, political organization, religious beliefs and cults. While available published material has provided the basis for the Survey, a mass of unpublished documents, reports and records in Government files and in the archives of missionary societies, as well as field notes and special communications by anthropologists and others, have been generously made available and these have been supplemented by personal correspondence and consultation. The Survey is being published in a number of separate volumes, each of which is concerned with one people or a group of related peoples, and contains a comprehensive bibliography and specially drawn map.

A committee of the Institute was set up under the Chairmanship of Professor Radcliffe-Brown and the Director of the Institute has undertaken the organization and editing of the Survey. The generous collaboration of a number of research institutions and administrative officers in Europe and in the African territories was secured, as well as the services of senior anthropologists who have been good enough to supervise and amplify the drafts.

The work of the Survey was initiated with the aid of a grant from the British Colonial Development and Welfare Funds, on the recommendation of the Social Science Research Council, to be applied mainly though not exclusively to work relating to British territories. A further grant from the Sudan Government has assisted in the preparation and publication of sections dealing with that territory.

The Ministère de la France d'Outre-mer and the Institut Français d'Afrique Noire were good enough to express their interest in the project and through their good offices grants have been received from the Governments of French West Africa and the French Cameroons for the preparation and publication of sections relating to those areas. These sections have been prepared by French ethnologists with the support and advice of Professor M. Griaule of the Sorbonne and Professor Th. Monod, Director of I.F.A.N.

The collaboration of the Belgian authorities in this project was first secured by the good offices of the late Professor de Jonghe, who enlisted the interest of the Commission d'Ethnologie of the Institut Royal Colonial Belge. The collaboration of the Institut pour la Recherche Scientifique en Afrique Centrale has also been readily accorded. Work relating to Belgian territories is being carried out under the direction of Professor Olbrechts at the Centre du Documentation of the Musée du Congo Belge, Tervuren, where Mlle. Boone and members of her staff are engaged on the assembly and classification of the vast mass of material relating to African peoples in the Belgian Congo and Ruanda-Urundi. They work in close collaboration with ethnologists in the field to whom draft manuscripts are submitted for checking.

The International African Institute desires to express its very grateful thanks to those official bodies whose generous financial assistance has made the carrying out of this project possible and to the many scholars, directors of research organizations, administrative officers, missionaries and others who have collaborated in the work and, by granting facilities to our research workers and by correcting and supervising their manuscripts, have contributed so largely to whatever merit the various sections may possess.

FOREWORD

Since the unequal value and unsystematic nature of existing material was one of the reasons for undertaking the Survey, it is obvious that these studies cannot claim to be complete or definitive; it is hoped, however, that they will present a clear account of our existing knowledge and indicate where information is lacking and further research is needed.

In connection with the preparation of this volume, our thanks are especially due to the following: the Gouvernement du Cameroun Français for providing a financial contribution towards this and other studies relating to its territory; Dr. Phyllis Kaberry for her supervision of the Tikar, Bamum, and Bamileke sections and for the use of her unpublished material; Dr. M. D. W. Jeffreys for the use of material on some of the Tikar peoples; Pasteur Henri Martin for his assistance on various points, and the Director of Centrifan, Douala, for supplying population figures. Madame Dugast, in addition to being responsible for one section, has kindly supplied material for the others. We are also grateful to Miss Strizower, who translated some of the German material, and to Miss Madeline Manoukian, who translated the Banen, Bafia, and Balom sections from the French.

DARYLL FORDE,
Director,
International African Institute.

CONTENTS

vii

INTRODUCTION

The similarities in the political, economic, and social systems of the cluster of peoples which are described in this section of the Ethnographic Survey cannot be enumerated in their entirety in an introductory note. It may, however, be useful to indicate a few of the features which justify the inclusion of these peoples—Tikar, Bamum, Bamileke, Banen, and Bafia—in a single volume.

They inhabit a continuous stretch of territory which extends roughly between 4° 15′ and 7° N. and 9° 45′ and 11° 15′ E. The history of the area is one of a long series of struggles, raids, and invasions, involving mass migrations, contacts, and conflicts between different ethnic groups. Thus each of these peoples has at some period come into contact with one or more of the others, either in the course of migrations or through invasions or warfare. Often the presence of resemblances is the result of an obvious historical connection between the peoples concerned, such as the adoption by the invading Bamum of the language of the Bamileke whom they found living in the area. Moreover, the ruling group of Bamum are alleged to be of Tikar origin and, according to tradition, were the fellow travellers of the Nsaw during their southward migrations 200 to 300 years ago.

With the exception of certain isolated groups of Banen and Bafia, all these peoples are organized in chiefdoms of varying scale. The figures show that small-scale chiefdoms are found among the Banen, Bafia, and Bamileke. Within the last group there is a wide variation in the size of the chiefdoms; for example, the Bandeng chiefdom has an area of approximately 6 square miles and a population of 458, while that of Baleng has an area of approximately 117 square miles and a population of 11,196. Moving farther north, chiefdoms range in scale from that of Nsaw, with an area of 720 square miles and a population of 59,464, to Bamum, 2,812 square miles and a population of 79,850.

Throughout the area, with the exception of the Banen and Bafia, men's associations are an important feature of the political and social organization. Thus the *mandjong* or *mandjon* society, to which all adult males automatically belong and whose functions in the past were largely military, is found both among the Nsaw and the Bamileke. The members of many of the existing associations have police duties, as in the *mouinngou* society of the Bamum, the *kuentaŋ* of the Bamileke, and the *ngwirong* of the Nsaw. Qualifications for admittance to the Bamum *ngirri*, the Bamileke *nia*, and the Nsaw *ŋgiri* are also similar. In the first two of these membership is limited to the sons of the *fon*, the king or chief, while in the last it is confined to the *fon's* close male relatives.

A ranking and title-holding system exists throughout the area, excluding the Banen and Bafia. In many cases the holding of a title is dependent upon appointment to a particular political office. A striking point of resemblance among the Bamileke, Bamum, and Tikar is that the queen mother holds a special position and a title is always conferred upon her. She commands great respect and may take part in council deliberations and judicial affairs.

All the peoples, with a few exceptions among the Tikar and Banen, are patrilocal and patrilineal, and it appears that throughout most of the area the basis of the social organization is the localized patrilineage. Belief that the ancestors live on after death and watch over the living members of the lineage is widespread, and sacrifices and offerings are regularly made to them. This belief is strongly developed among the Bamileke, where paternal and maternal skulls form the object of a cult. A cult of ancestral skulls also exists among the Bamum.

The notion of the sacredness of the king or chief is general, and the concurrent identification of the chief with the leopard and python is discussed in the text. Everywhere he has important ritual duties; among the Banen, for example, he is the intermediary between his people and the forces of nature, while among the Tikar he performs the major annual sacrifices to God and the ancestors.

Divination by the earth spider is practised by all the peoples in the area, with certain differences in the diviners' techniques. Similarly they all share a common attitude to the birth of twins, who are always welcomed and honoured and never deliberately angered. Special names are given to one or both, and among the Bamum both are adopted by the king; among the Bamileke and the Tikar the chief is entitled to only one. There is, finally, the cicatrization of women found among the Bamum, Bamileke, Banen, and Bafia, with only minor variations in pattern.

Although they show certain similarities with the three other peoples, the Banen and Bafia are less conveniently grouped with them. One of the factors favouring their inclusion was the availability of a large body of field data, much of which has been collected by Madame Dugast, who was herself able to complete this part of the volume.

Since very few comprehensive studies of peoples in French Cameroons territory have been made, it is probable that some whose cultural affinities would have justified their inclusion in this section of the Survey have inevitably been left out. It is because of this lack of available material that the Bali people, for instance, have received only a brief mention.

LOCATION AND DISTRIBUTION

LOCATION

The people known as Tikar number about 170,000 and form the largest ethnic group in Bamenda Province of the British Cameroons. A further 10,500 live in adjacent districts of the French Cameroons, mostly along the Mbam and Kim river valleys. Their neighbours are: to the north-west and north, the peoples of Benue Province in Nigeria, the Mbembe group[1] in Bamenda, and the Mambila of Adamawa Province; to the east, the Fulani, Wute, and Bamum in the French Cameroons; to the south-east, the Bamileke, also in the French Cameroons; and to the south-west and west, the Bali, Widekum, and Aghem groups in Bamenda.

GROUPING

(a) Administrative

Bamenda is organized into 23 Native Authority Areas, 22 of which have, since 1949, been federated into four groups, each with its own central treasury and council.[2] Neither the Federations nor the Native Authorities coincide entirely with ethnic boundaries. In the following list areas inhabited mainly by Tikar are italicized:

Federation

North-western:	*Fungom, Bum, Kom,* Aghem, Beba-Befang, Esimbi.
North-eastern:	Mbembe, Mfumte, Misaje, *Mbem, Mbaw, Wiya, War, Tang.*
South-western:	Ngwo, Ngie, Ngemba, Meta, Mogamaw.
South-eastern:	*Banso* [*Nsaw*], *Ndop,* and *Bafut.*

(b) Ethnic[3]

Taking as criteria their traditions of origin and migration, and broad linguistic and cultural similarities, the people of Bamenda fall into five main groups: Tikar, Widekum, Mbembe, Aghem, and Bali. To these should be added the Hausa and Bororo (Pastoral) Fulani, who have entered the country in increasing numbers since the advent of British rule. The former tend to congregate in large market villages, while the latter pasture cattle on the hilltops of the plateau, especially in Nsaw, Nsungli, Kom, Bafut, and Fungom (all Tikar areas), and in Ngwo.

The Bali (or Bani) who numbered approximately 23,231 in 1953, are reputed to be a branch of the Chamba-Leko of Adamawa. Owing to increasing Fulani pressure at the beginning of the last century, they left Koncha under their leader Gawebe and journeyed south to Tibati. From there they proceeded to make war upon the Bamum and eventually reached Bamenda from Bagam. Some were mounted on horseback and harried Bafueng, Bande, and Bafut before passing on to what is now Bali-Nyonge, some 16 miles to the west of Bamenda Station. They established a chiefdom, similar in organization to many of the small patrilineal Tikar chiefdoms to the east. Owing to the paucity of information available in this country they are not discussed in this volume.[4]

The Tikar are grouped into a number of independent chiefdoms, differing in size, language, political structure, and kinship organization. Of the predominantly

---

[1] i.e., Mbembe, Misaje, Mfumte.
[2] The remaining area, Bali, is independent.
[3] Kaberry, 3, 1952, pp. 2–4.
[4] There is a brief account of the Bali in Kaberry, op. cit., *passim.*

11

Tikar authorities listed above, it is only in Nsaw, Kom, and Bum, where consolidated chiefdoms were formed prior to the arrival of Europeans, that the existing boundaries correspond fairly closely with traditional organization. Ndop Authority is made up of 12 small chiefdoms which are neither linguistically nor culturally homogeneous, and which include one non-Tikar chiefdom.[5] Fungom Authority contains a number of small Tikar chiefdoms differing in dialect, culture, and origin, and several groups of Mbembe and Zumper peoples. Bafut contains Widekum settlements; Mbaw, small bands of Mambila origin. The " Nsungli " group of Tikar is contained in three Native Authorities—War, Tang, and Wiya—but the villages which belong to any one of these units do not occupy a continuous stretch of territory but are inter-digitated among villages belonging to the other two units.

Tikar in the French Cameroons[6] are divided into seven independent chiefdoms: Bamkim, north of the Mbam River, and Bang-Heng, Ina, Oue, Yakong, Ngambe, Ngoume, and Ditam, to the south and south-east. In addition there is a large group of Tikar in the northern part of Bamum country.

Nomenclature

There is considerable confusion in the spelling of names of Bamenda tribes, owing partly to differences in French, German, and English versions, and partly to the adoption of terms used by the tribes in speaking of each other. For instance, the *Ba*-prefixes before many names are of Bali origin; Bali versions were largely adopted by the Germans. Most villages have several alternative and not always recognizable names, and in the more heterogeneous areas groups are usually referred to in the literature by village names and not those of the areas. Alternative village names are for convenience given in a later section; the following are collective names :

(a) *Tikar* (*Tikari, Tikali, Tikare, Tika, Tiker*) is a collective term used both by these tribes in referring to themselves, and by neighbouring tribes in identi-fying them. Tikar tribes recognize relations with one another mainly on grounds of origin and general linguistic similarity. The name is still used in French inventories and maps; in British literature separate Tikar groups are usually referred to by name.

(b) *Nsungli* (*Nsungni, Ndzungli, Zungle*) derives from the Lamnso (Nsaw—see below) word for " chatterers," and is a collective term used by the Nsaw in referring to the War (Wa, Mbwat, Wat, Wot), the Tang (Taŋ), and the Wiya (Ndu, Ndum, Wimbu) tribes. The term Nsungli is not used by the three tribes concerned, but since they present marked similarities in culture and dialect, in contrast to neighbouring peoples, the term has been used for convenience by Kaberry and other writers and, until very recently, in administrative reports.[7] Alternative names given above for War and Wiya are those of leading villages (Mbwat and Ndu respectively), some-times used to refer to the whole group.

(c) A third collective term is *Kaka-Ntem* (*Tem*), formerly a Native Authority now broken into Mfumte, Mbaw, and Mbem.[8]

(d) *Nsaw*[8A] (*Bansaw, Banso, Nso*) is the name of a Native Authority and is one of the largest of the consolidated chiefdoms in Bamenda. The language of Nsaw is called Lamnso.

(e) The *Kom* are also known as *Bikom* or *Bamekom*, their language as *Nkom*; like the Nsaw, they migrated into Bamenda as a group, built up a central-

---

[5] Bali-Kumbat, a Bali (Chamba) chiefdom.
[6] Dugast, 1949, p. 129.
[7] Kaberry, op. cit., p. 2. Nsungli was formerly one Native Authority Area.
[8] See Jeffreys, 1942, p. 49.
[8A] Nsaw represents a phonetic *Nsɔ*. Administrators and modern maps generally use the spelling Banso.

ized chiefdom incorporating several stranger groups, and have given their name to a Native Authority.

(*f*) *Bafut* (*Fut, Bufu, Fu*) is the name of the village which claims seniority in the Authority now known by that name.

(*g*) *Ndop* (*Bandop, Ndob, Ndobo*) is the name of a former Tikar area in French territory which most of the Bamenda groups claim as their place of origin. It is used as a name for an Authority which, as noted above, is really a congeries of independent chiefdoms.

(*h*) *Fungom* is the name of a village which has been adopted as a Native Authority name; Fungom village, however, did not traditionally claim superiority over other villages in the area.

(*i*) *Bum*, like Kom and Nsaw, is the name of a Tikar group who built up a centralized chiefdom in what is now Bum Authority. *Bafumbum*[9] is the Hausa version of the name of the clan of the chief of Bum, and is used in some of the German literature for the whole group.[10]

---

[9] Talbot (1926, vol. IV, pp. 95–6) refers to the " Bafumbum-Bansaw " as a linguistic group.
[10] Bridges, 1933.

DEMOGRAPHY

(a) Bamenda Province: Total Population, 1944–50[1]

1944: 286,000	1948: 301,000
1945: 289,400	1949: 287,300
1946: 285,300	1950: 286,200
1947: 287,000	1953: 429,038

(b) Predominantly Tikar Authorities: Density, Area, and Estimated Population (1947–48)

The following figures are based on figures for adult taxable males in Tikar groups for 1947:[2]

Native Authority	Density per Square Mile	Area in Square Miles	Estimated Population 1947
Nsaw	40	720	33,950
Kom	62	280	17,178
Bum	14	347	4,322
Bafut	60	340	19,110
Ndop	69	510	38,846
Wiya	7	100(?)	6,608
Tang	40	150	6,790
War	68	125	9,541
Mbem	44	292	12,873
Mbaw	10	216	2,845
Fungom	20	1,088	17,636
Total, 1947			**169,699**
Total Tikar in Bamenda			169,699[3]
Tikar chiefdoms in French Cameroons			8,863[4]
Tikar in Bamum territory, French Cameroons			1,660[5]
Total Tikar			**180,222**

The figures for 1953 show a marked increase and are as follows:

Native Authority	Population 1953
Nsaw	59,464
Kom	26,663
Bum	5,155
Bafut	33,998
Ndop	44,084
Wiya	9,875
Tang	12,734
War	13,375
Mbem	2,130
Mbaw	3,328
Fungom	20,702
Total, 1953	**231,418**[5A]

[1] Report to U.N.O., 1951.
[2] Kaberry, written communication. Kaberry gives 175,000 as the estimated population of Tikar groups in Bamenda in 1948 (3, 1952, p. 3). The estimated population for Bamenda as a whole was then 301,000. As the estimated population for 1949 and 1950 is closer to the estimated population for 1947, Kaberry has suggested that the 1947 figures for adult taxable males in Tikar groups be used for this Survey.
[3] Kaberry, loc. cit.   [4] Dugast, 1949, p. 130.   [5] Ibid.
[5A] The 1953 figure of 259,914 Tikar includes some groups which are not regarded as Tikar in this Survey.

(c) *Nsaw Native Authority*

Density.[6] The population is unevenly distributed; density in the area as a whole is about 40 to the square mile, but within a radius of some two hours' walking distance from the capital, Kimbaw[7] (which has a population of 4,800), density was probably well over 100 to the square mile in 1947–48.   In this area there are 17 villages with a total population of nearly 15,000, i.e., nearly half the total Nsaw population. Mbiami has today a total population of over 2,000.[8] Of the 47 villages recognized by the Administration as separate tax-paying units, 7 have a population of 1,000 to just over 2,000,[9] 15 have a population of 500 to just under 1,000, 21 have a population of some 200 to 500.

In the great majority of villages population ranges from 300 to 800.

Sex and Age Distribution.[10] The following figures for sex and age distribution date from 1933, but may be useful for comparison with subsequent estimates:

Nsaw Villages	Men	Women	Total Adults
Kimbaw-Gam (Gham)	656	745	1,401
Kimbaw-Ba (Baa)	473	387	860
Total Kimbaw	1,129	1,132	2,261
Ketiwum	474	403	877
Tabessob	514	490	1,004
Ngonsen (Ngonzen)	379	390	769
Kekaigwen (Kikai-Kengvenki)	351	347	698
Waikawbi (Vekovi)	321	311	632
Mbam	335	283	618
Melu (Meluf)	330	375	705
Melim	259	234	493
Kekai-Kelak (Kikai-Kilaki)	322	258	580

	Men	Women	Children	Total
i. Total Nsaw villages (including eight smaller ones)	5,594	5,304	7,862	18,760
ii. Mbiami	181	149	173	503
iii. Nine sub-villages	1,488	1,361	1,283	4,132
Total Nsaw Authority, 1933	7,263	6,814	9,318	23,395

[6] Kaberry, 1950, p. 309, and 3, 1952, pp. 9–10.

[7] Usually spelt Kumbo on maps.   The form Banso, by which name the town is known to all except Nsaw people, is also found.

[8] The 1947–48 estimate of the population of Mbiami includes Bamum, Hausa, and other strangers, while the 1933 figures given below probably exclude these.   But there has been a great deal of settlement in Mbiami owing to pressure of land around Kimbaw.   (Kaberry, personal communication.)

[9] Mbiami, Kikai-Kilaki, Kikai-Kengvenki, Vekovi, Mbam, Meluf, and Nkor.

[10] Bridges, 1934.

(d) *Ndop: Sex and Age Distribution, 1925, by Villages*[11]

The following figures were for 1925:

Village	Men	Women	Children	Total
Baba	338	452	461	1,251
Babungo (Bamungo)	562	620	639	1,821
Bafanji	390	529	509	1,428
Bamali (Bamale)	230	282	232	744
Bambalang	256	361	224	841
Bamunka	310	325	203	838
Bamumkumbit..	293	341	351	985
Bamessing (Nsei)	673	820	744	2,237
Bamessi	477	537	401	1,415
Bangola	366	409	284	1,059
Oku (sub-chiefdom)	903	871	896	2,670
Total	4,798	5,547	4,944	15,289

(e) *Kom: Sex and Age Distribution, 1927*[12]

The 1927 Assessment Report gives the following figures for 1926, when there were 35 hamlets and sub-towns:

Men	3,326
Women	4,764
Children	5,464
Total ..	13,554

Reliable figures for other areas are not available.

[11] Drummond-Hay, 1925.
[12] Evans, 1927.

LANGUAGE

Languages spoken in Bamenda have usually been classified as belonging to the Benue-Cross-River (or semi-Bantu) group, and the Tikar placed in the Bafumbum-Bansaw sub-group.[1] Greenberg, however, has suggested that Bali, Bafut, and Ndop (and presumably other Tikar dialects) are Bantu.[2] Bruens holds that Nkom resembles both Bantu and Sudanic. The position should be clarified with the publication of the results of the linguistic field survey of the northern Bantu borderland recently carried out by the International African Institute.

At present the extent of the similarity between Tikar languages is not very clear; nor is the distinction between languages and dialects. So marked is the linguistic heterogeneity that villages only a few miles away from one another often speak languages which are not mutually intelligible, and this occurs within, as well as across, administrative boundaries. In such a situation it is only possible to note briefly what is known of languages spoken in the various Native Authority areas.[3]

(a) Nsaw

Lamnso (*lam* = language) is spoken throughout Nsaw Authority. Lamnso in a distinctive dialectal form is spoken by the Oku sub-tribe in Ndop Authority.

In the sub-villages of Din, Lassin, Mbinon, Dom, and Djottin-Vitum, in addition to Lamnso a language called *nooni* (or *nolli*) is used.

According to tradition these villages were founded by the Bum group of Tikar, and later conquered by the Nsaw. The Bum found earlier inhabitants in the area; *nooni* is presumably derived from the language of these people, whose descendants, according to Jeffreys,[4] live today in the Kabiim, Biim, and Fonfuka valleys.

Other groups conquered or incorporated by the Nsaw appear to have adopted Nsaw dialects. Jeffreys[5] gives a few notes on the now practically extinct language of one of these groups, the Nkat (Nkar).

(b) Kom

A study of Nkom has been made by Bruens, who refers to Tsan (a village in the extreme north-east of Kom N.A.) and Kidzem (spoken at Babanki and Babanki-Tungaw in Bafut N.A.) as dialects of Nkom; and to Mme, We, and Ye (of which the first two are village-names in Fungom N.A.) as languages closely related. Yum (either Wum or Aghem) is mentioned as another related language. Ndabe and Mekaf are referred to as other languages spoken in or near the Kom Area, but differing somewhat from those already mentioned. Lamnso is also allied to Nkom.[6]

(c) Fungom

According to Meyer,[7] the most common speech in Fungom N.A. is We, of which a dialect is spoken at Esu. Jeffreys[8] notes that languages spoken in We, Isu (Esu), and Zoo (Jua or Zhoa) are very similar, and that they are understood also in Mme, Kuk, and Fungom villages and in Kom and Aghem.[9] A " different language " (probably Badji or Jukun) is spoken in northern Fungom.[10]

---

[1] See, e.g., Talbot, loc. cit.
[2] Greenberg, 1949, pp. 5–7.
[3] See Westermann and Bryan, 1952, pp. 123–6, for summaries of the known characteristics of individual Tikar languages.
[4] MS. notes.
[5] 4, 1945.
[6] Bruens, 1942–45, pp. 828, 830, 839.
[7] 1942, p. 275.
[8] MSS.
[9] Kaberry adds that kinship terms in Fungom village, Mme, Kom, and Aghem are very similar.
[10] Richardson, quoted by Westermann and Bryan, op. cit., p. 124.

(d) War, Tang, and Wiya

These are three related dialects. According to Carpenter[11] and Jeffreys[12] they bear little resemblance to other Tikar languages. But Kaberry notes[13] that some terms are related to Lamnso words.

(e) Mbem and Mbaw

From Jeffreys's notes it would appear that the language of Mbem and Mbaw is called Ntem, and that it is related to the Nsungli group. The inhabitants of Rom (or Lom) village-area in Mbem speak a Nsungli dialect. In another context, however, Jeffreys notes that the Rom are bilingual, learning first Kaka (Ntem), and later a Nsungli dialect, apparently Ndum (the Wiya dialect).[14]

(f) Bum

Jeffreys[15] states that Nama, the language of the Bum, is spoken in all the villages which they conquered except Ngong, which retains its own language. Nama is said to be closer to Nkom than to either the Nsungli dialects or Lamnso. Bum and Kom have a common boundary, trade and intermarry.

(g) Bafut

Many Widekum have been absorbed by the peoples of Bafut, who, according to Talbot,[16] now speak a Widekum dialect. Jeffreys has a note to the effect that the language of Babanki (Kijom Kitingo) village is not the same as was once spoken at Ndobo, and that the Babanki people understand neither Lamnso nor Lammum.[17] Bruens, however, holds that the language of Babanki is a dialect of Nkom.

(h) Ndop

According to Jeffreys's notes (quoted from the Bamunka chief), the people of Bamungo (Babungo), Babessi (Bamessi), Bamali (Bamale), Bambalang, Baba, Bamessing (Nsei), and Bamunka speak mutually intelligible dialects. According to Schmidt, however, the language of Nsei would be understood only by two neighbouring villages, and resembles Lammum.[18]

(i) Tikar in French Territory

Dugast quotes a statement by Charbin[19] that the original Tikar language was " Sudanese," but that Tikar have adopted the language of the people they conquered. According to Richardson,[20] two main Tikar dialects are spoken in French territory, north and south of the River Mbam respectively. The southern dialect is called Ngembi.

Literature in Tikar Languages

The Roman Catholic Mission has produced an unpublished Lamnso grammar and a mimeographed catechism in Nkom.[21]

[11] MS. notes.
[12] MSS.
[13] Kaberry, written communication.
[14] This fact was also noted by Migeod (1925, p. 134).
[15] MS.
[16] Quoted by Westermann and Bryan, op. cit., p. 127.
[17] *Lam* = language. Lammum is the language of the Bamum.
[18] Schmidt, MS.
[19] Unpublished MS.
[20] Personal communication, see Westermann and Bryan, op. cit., p. 125.
[21] Westermann and Bryan, op. cit., p. 123.

Linguae Francae

Fulani is used as a *lingua franca* in Ntem and Mbaw, Lammum in southern Bamenda,[22] and Badji or Jukun in northern Fungom.[23] In addition, most adherents of the Basel Mission speak Bali and this mission has published a translation of the New Testament in Bali.[24]

[22] Carpenter, 1933.
[23] Richardson, quoted by Westermann and Bryan, op. cit., p. 124.
[24] The original language of the Bali was Mubakaw, but in Bamenda they adopted Mungaka, which is probably a fusion of Bati and Bamum dialects. (Kaberry, 3, 1952, p. 7, f.n. 1.)

TRADITIONS OF ORIGIN AND HISTORY

According to their own traditions, the various groups of Tikar came to Bamenda from places called Tibati, Banyo, Ndobo, and Kimi, north and north-east of present Tikar territory. Jeffreys identifies Kimi as present-day Bamkim, which is still in Tikar territory in the French Cameroons. It is suggested that they came to this area from Tibati, Banyo, or Ngaoundere, all in French territory,[1] and ultimately perhaps from Bornu (Lake Chad).[2] French ethnologists[3] incline to the view that the Tikar and the Mbum derived from the same stock, and that the separation took place many generations ago at a point somewhere between Ngaoundere and Tibati. The Tikar settled in the vast plain watered by the Mbam River and its tributaries, the Mape and the Kim.

About 300 years ago, increasing Chamba and Fulani pressure, internal dissension, and a desire for new land resulted in the splitting off of small bands of Tikar, who travelled west and south-west and eventually reached what is now Bamenda. The sequence of their migrations is, however, uncertain.

(a) Ndop

Among the earlier settlers were those coming from Ndobo to the Ndop Plain in the south of Bamenda Province, where small, politically autonomous villages were constituted some six to ten miles apart. These settlers appear to have come in two main waves. The first, according to Drummond-Hay, founded the villages of Bafanji, Bamessing (*Nsei*), Bamessi, and Bamale, from the last of which were founded Bambalang, Bamunka, and Bamumkumbat. Later immigrants founded Baba, Bamungo, and Bangola. None of these units was sufficiently strong to dominate the others; hostilities over land, murder, and slave-raids characterized their relations, and even further Fulani and Chamba raids in the last century failed to bring about any semblance of political unity or federation, although from time to time asylum was granted by one village to refugees from another.[4]

Traditions cited by Jeffreys[5] describe the settling in the Ndop area of a band of Bali. Having defeated a group of earlier inhabitants (apparently not of Tikar origin), they founded the village of Balikumbat (Bali in the Hills), and commenced attacks against other Ndop villages which continued until the end of the 19th century. Baba, Bamessing, Bafanji, Bambalang, and Bamale with its daughter villages were all at one time paying tribute to Balikumbat in the form of leopard skins; other villages were attacked but do not appear to have been tributary.[6]

Under German rule, Bamungo was responsible for collecting taxes from Baba, Bangola, and Bambalang, and from Oku, a Nsaw sub-tribe settled in the north of Ndop.[7] Under British rule, the 10 Ndop villages, with Balikumbat and Oku, were constituted a Native Authority.

(b) Mbem-Nsungli Group

Mbem, Mbaw, and the Nsungli area were also the scene of early Tikar migrations into Bamenda. Settlements were made below the escarpment in the area formerly known as Ntem; but at a later date, three main groups, whose descendants were to constitute the Wiya, War, and Tang groups (Nsungli) went up on to the plateau and founded a number of small villages. In each of the three groups one village-

[1] Kaberry, 3, 1952, p. 4.
[2] Jeffreys MS.
[3] Dugast, 1949.
[4] Kaberry, loc. cit.
[5] MS.
[6] Drummond-Hay, 1925.
[7] Ibid.

head claimed the title of *fon*[8] and supremacy over the others, but even before the arrival of the Germans his authority had been challenged by some of the component villages, intent on preserving their autonomy.[9]

Under the British, Mbem, Mbaw, Mfumte (together known as the Kaka-Ntem Area) were included as part of Nsungli Native Authority from 1923 till 1932.[10]

(I) *Mbem Authority* today contains the following villages: Mbem, Fam, Si, Nyong, Ntim, Sam, Ngung, Bom, Gom, Winkwa, and Lom (Rom). The last is closely related both linguistically and culturally to the Wiya of the Nsungli group.

(II) *Mbaw Authority* contains five communities of Tikar—Ntem, Ngu, Ngomkaw, Mbirikpa, and Nwat—and three Mambila villages (Nguron, Ngom, and Li).[11]

(III) *The Nsungli Authorities.* Wiya villages today include: Kawnchep, Kup, Nyar, Nkang, Lu, and Ndu, of which the last claims seniority and is the centre for the Native Court. Ndu is also used frequently as an alternative name for the Wiya as a whole or for their language.

Tang villages include: Tala, Binka, Tache (Touche), Taku, Tundip, Sina, and Ngapu. Settlers from Tang went to the north of Nsaw and became subjects of the Fon-Nsaw. Some of their descendants form part of the Tang clan in Nsaw, of which Sangfir, Kuila, and Ndzendzef are branches.

War villages include: Nkambe, Kungi (Kawngi), Mbinsua (Binshua), Njap, Tsup (Shup), Ntumbo (Tumbaw), Ndipji, and Mbwat, of which the last claims seniority.

At some time after the settlement of the Nsungli group, a large band split off from Mbwat (most senior of the War group) and travelled south into what is now Nsaw country, where they established the villages of Nkor and Djottin-Vitum, and their offshoots—Dom, Din, Mbinon, and Lassin. They are said to have found earlier settlers in the area whose descendants, according to Jeffreys, live today in the Fonfuka, Kabiim, and Biim valleys. Some of the migrants remained in these villages; others journeyed farther west and founded the centralized chiefdom of Bum.[12]

(c) Bum

According to Jeffreys,[13] citing traditions from Fonfuka and Bum villages, the first Bum village was at Ngunabum, where nine chiefs were buried. Because of the deaths in rapid succession of several preceding chiefs, the tenth chief decided to move to Sawe, and later Lagabum (Do), the residence of the present chief (the eleventh, i.e., the chief at the time of Jeffreys's visit). Earlier inhabitants were conquered in the villages of Sawe, Fonfuka, and Ngong, but of the three only Ngong retained its own language. Lagabum was built on an unoccupied site. In the reign of the tenth chief the Kom made two attacks on Bum but were defeated; a half-brother of the chief settled at Fonfuka.

Villages in the Bum Authority today are: Fonfuka, Bum Mungong (Ngong), Laabum (Lagabum), Sa (Sawe), Fat, Mbu, Ngon, Melung, Ngunakumbi, Ifum, Chan, Ngunabum, Bwabwa Su, and Sat.

(d) Bafut

Bafut, Nsaw, and Kom were probably among the last of the large-scale Tikar migrations to Bamenda. Bafut Authority contains seven village groups which before British rule appear to have remained autonomous: Bafut in the north-west

---

[8] The Nsaw term for " paramount chief," *fon* (pl. *afon*) is used by Kaberry for convenience for all Tikar paramount chiefs, and this usage is followed here. There are dialectal variants in other areas.
[9] Kaberry, loc. cit.
[10] Carpenter, 1933.
[11] Newton, 1936.
[12] Kaberry, loc. cit.; Jeffreys MS.
[13] Jeffreys MS.

of the area, where the country is undulating and more densely forested than elsewhere; Bambui and Bambili on the lower hill slopes; Babanki (Kijom Kitingo) and
its offshoot (Babanki-Tungaw), surrounded by ranges of hills; Bamenda to the south-
east, in flat country; and Bafreng on the plain at the foot of the escarpment.
Traditionally, predecessors of the Bafut, Babanki, Bafreng, and Bambili groups
formed the first migration from Ndobo; the Babanki were called Kijom in Ndobo
and the name is still sometimes used. A second migration, of a group known as
Baminyam, led to the founding of Bambui and Bamenda villages. Although the
villages were attacked by both Bali and Kom, they seem to have formed no
alliances among themselves.

On the arrival of the Germans fighting broke out, and Bafut was burnt
down in 1895. The seven villages were administered directly from Bamenda.[14]

(e) Kom

The Kom are said to have come from Ndobo by way of Bamessi (in Ndop
Authority). Three ruling families originally settled at Laakom, whence they spread
to other villages, including Mme, Kuk, Nyos, Fungom, and Kung, all in the Fungom
Authority. These villages, as well as the main Kom group, are matrilineal. The
Kom also defeated a number of patrilineal villages and made them tributary:
Nchang, Ake, Mejang, Mejung, and Basaw.[15] Today, the heads of these five groups,
together with chiefs of Ajung and Bassin Oku (Besanoku)[16] are the seven Govern-
ment sub-chiefs of Kom.[17]

No historical explanation of the Kom matrilineal descent system is given in the
literature.

(f) Fungom

Fungom, Mme, Kuk, and Nyos villages, referred to in the official report
(1936):
(a) Fungom village area:[18] *Fungom, Mme (Bafmen Me, Men), Nyos, Kuk (Ku),
Fang.* (b) We village area: *We (Kuwe), Jua (Zoo, Zhoaw),* and Munkap (Menkep,
Bunaghi). (c) Esu village area: *Esu (Isu),* Furu, Nkang-Nkang (Furuwa), Nser
(Nsa), and Badji (Zumperri). (d) Munken village area: Munken (Benchen), Belo
(Abar), Missong (Bijun), Mufu, Mandabi (Njan), and Mashi (Bupang). (e) Kung
village area: *Kung* and *Koshin.*

Fungom, Mme, Kuk, and Nyos villages, referred to in the official report
as " the Chap group," were traditionally settled by peoples who came from Banyo
in the French Cameroons at about the same time as the Kom and Bafut peoples.
They settled first at Ndewum near what is now Mme, whence they spread to form
the present villages. All are matrilineal and appear to be offshoots of Kom. Atshaf
(Chap) is the name of the clan of the chiefs of Fungom and Mme and has for this
reason become associated with the group of villages. An Atshaf family in Kom today
may be related. The Fungom village chief claims seniority in the area.[19]

Some reports suggest that patrilineal Fang village is also part of the Fungom-
Mme group; others that the people of Fang are of Widekum extraction. Possibly
Fang was a Widekum village conquered by this group of Tikar. Another version,
received by Kaberry from the Fang chief and council, is that Fang came with
Befang from Bafang in the French Cameroons, passed through Nsaw and fought

[14] Hawkesworth, 1926; Newton, 1934; Jeffreys MS.
[15] Jeffreys, 1951, p. 242, suggests that the power of the Kom was due to their mastery
of iron.
[16] An offshoot of the Oku sub-tribe of Nsaw. (Jeffreys MS.)
[17] Evans, 1927, and comments thereon by Hawkesworth.
[18] Those in italics are Tikar or mainly Tikar villages. Names in brackets are alternatives
given by Jeffreys in notes on the 1936 Report.
[19] Kaberry, written communication; 1936 Report.

with the Nyos people in Bum before the founding of Fungom village. Later they separated from Befang, who went to their present site south of Aghem.[20]

Isu (Esu) traditions suggest a close connection with the Fungom-Mme group. According to We tradition, their ancestors had already arrived in Fungom when Isu was founded. Today We and Isu speak the same dialect. The We chief claims that We and Zhoaw (Zua, Jua) were originally " brothers " and that later Zhoaw separated from We and went to its present site to the north.[21]

Of the non-Tikar groups in Fungom, Furu, Nser, Munkap, and Mashi appear to have a common place of origin, possibly Mbembe[22] or Kentu.[23] According to Kaberry,[24] Mashi and Munkap claim to derive from Bebe Jatto and Bebe Ketti (in Mbembe), but no longer follow matrilineal descent. Badji is a Zumper village. Mufu, Belo, Mundabi, and Missong are offshoots of Munken,[25] but their origin is not clear.

(g) Nsaw

Kaberry[26] describes how the Nsaw, according to their own traditions, left Tibati some 200 to 300 years ago and eventually reached Kovifem, having passed through Rifum in the French Cameroons, where they separated from their alleged fellow travellers, the Mbam[27] and the Bamum. At Kovifem, in the north-east of Nsaw, which was their first capital, the Fon-Nsaw was joined by small bands from Tikar who had settled in other parts of Bamenda—notably in Mbaw, Nsungli, Ndop, and Babanki. Many of their leaders, while they became the voluntary allies of the Fon-Nsaw, retained a semi-independent status as m'tar, in contrast to members of the Fon's own clan (wiri-e-Fon) on the one hand, and to members of the nshilaf (servant) class on the other. Others were assimilated into the Fon's own clan and assumed the status of duiy or distant clansmen. Three became founders of important sub-clans and were appointed senior councillors (vibai), namely Fai-o-Ndzendzef (from the Tang clan in the Nsungli area), Fai-o-Tankum (from Mbaw), and Fai-o-Luun (from Kiluun in the French Cameroons).

Some of the leaders and their kin settled in Kovifem, others in the surrounding area. As the size of their compounds extended, individuals moved out to form new settlements. These men, sometimes accompanied by their brothers, travelled south and south-west, where they found either unoccupied land or earlier settlers from other tribes from whom they " begged " arable land and residential sites.

The Fon-Oku and the Fon-Mbiami claim that their ancestors were sons of the Fon-Nsaw, but left him at Rifem and proceeded with their followers to the territories which they now occupy. The Fon of Oku succeeded in creating a small independent chiefdom in the range to the west of Nsaw; while many of the predecessors of the present Fon-Mbiami remained undisturbed in their title to land and political autonomy in the district lying some 15 miles to the east of Kimbaw until about five generations ago, when the Fon at Kovifem transferred his capital to Kimbaw and became Paramount Chief of all villages in Nsaw.[28]

This transfer of the capital was the result of Fulani raids on Kovifem during the last century. After the first raid, the Fon and some of his followers went south to Tauwvisa, a few miles from Kimbaw. Two afon died there, so the next Fon returned to Kovifem. But after a second large-scale Fulani raid he fled to Bamum,

[20] Kaberry, written communication.
[21] Ibid.
[22] Cantle, 1930.
[23] Smith, 1929.
[24] 3, 1952, p. 6, f.n. 2.
[25] Johnson, 1936.
[26] Op. cit., p. 5.
[27] The Nsaw spoke of the Mbam as their " brothers." They probably referred to the Tikar group now settled on the north of the Mbam River in the French Cameroons. (Kaberry, personal communication.)
[28] Kaberry, op. cit., pp. 10, 30–1.

and then to Baba territory in Ndop. From there he went to Oku, and finally reached Kimbaw where, after conquering the Fon-Nkar who claimed that territory, he made his capital. The Fon-Nkar was made a sub-chief and assisted the Fon-Nsaw in conquering the villages of Nsungli extraction in the north-west (Djottin-Vitum, Din, Dom, Lassin, Mbinon, Nkor, and Nser).[29]

(h) French Tikar

According to Dugast, the Tikar in French territory did not unite but remained in small groups, making continual attacks on each other. During the 19th century their country was invaded by the Fulani, who conquered one Tikar town after another. Instead of making further migrations, the Tikar formed various alliances among themselves. The *Lamido* of Tibati settled near Ngambe in a large military camp called Sanserni, having entered into good relations with the chief of Ngambe. The Fulani attacked Ngambe and laid siege to it for seven years; the town was not completely encircled and the Tikar and their Bamum allies sent in provisions and arms. The siege was not lifted until the arrival of the Germans in 1899, who sent the *Lamido* of Tibati home and re-established the authority of the Tikar chiefs. For many years the Tikar had been living in fortified towns; now they dispersed and settled in villages along the valleys.[30]

[29] i.e., Nser in Nsaw Authority. Another Nser village is in Fungom. Kaberry, op. cit., p. 5. See Jeffreys, 1945, for the Nkat (Nkar) version, which, apart from stating that the Nsaw while at Tauwvisa were vassals of the Nkat, does not differ in any important respect.
[30] Dugast, 1949, p. 129.

PHYSICAL ENVIRONMENT [1]

The dominant feature of Bamenda is the high grassy plateau which sweeps from the north-east and east over the centre of the Province at an average height of 4,500 feet above sea-level. Above this again hills and ranges rise another 1,000 to 2,500 feet, to culminate in Mount Oku at 7,000 feet.

Except for the forested slopes of Mount Oku, there is little timber on the plateau. At one time it probably fell within the belt of high forest, but local methods of cultivation have denuded the region of most of its trees. In the valleys woodland alternates with meadow; villages are overshadowed by groves of kola trees; plantations of raffia grow along the streams. In the north-west of the Province the plateau descends gradually to the orchard-bush of Fungom. The southern escarpment at Nsaw and Oku rises sharply from the Ndop Plain—a relatively low-lying area with an average elevation of some 3,000 feet above sea-level. This region is sparsely covered with small timber and scattered oil-palm, and punctuated by massive outcrops of basalt and granite. The Plain is broken by the Babanki Pass—a spur which runs out from Mt. Oku to link the central plateau with the high grasslands which lie beyond Bamenda Station and stretch south to the French Cameroons. Bamenda Station (the Administrative headquarters) is on the edge of the escarpment of this more southern range.

Bamenda Province is well watered: streams in the east—the Nun and the Mbam —flow into the Sanaga River in the French Cameroons; the Donga, Katsina Ala, and Metchem flow west to join the Benue in Nigeria. The rainfall varies from some 65 inches in Nsaw to 124 inches in Kom. The wet season begins about the end of March and finishes early in November, the heaviest precipitation occurring between August and mid-October. From December until March the harmattan from the north envelops the country in a dim red haze of dust.

Temperatures vary considerably. On the plateau temperature rarely rises above 84° F. in the shade, even in the hottest time of the year, although Bamenda is only some 6° north of the Equator. During the rains it often drops to 65° F. during the day and much lower at night. Mists drive down the valleys; gales carry away branches and beat down groves of plantain, and houses are frequently struck by lightning. In the low-lying forest areas and on the Plain temperatures are higher, soaring in the afternoons to 92° F.

The motor roads which serve Tikar country converge at Bamenda Station, linking it with Bafut, Kom, Ndop, Nsaw, Nsungli, Bum, and Fungom Authorities. Most Tikar villages can be approached only by native footpaths. The nearest railway is in French territory, terminating at Fumban. Apart from the administrative headquarters of the Province, Bamenda Station contains a school and a hospital; nearby the Roman Catholic and Cameroons Baptist Missions have their headquarters, and there is a U.A.C. store near the African market. In Nsaw there is a Roman Catholic Mission with European priests in charge, the headquarters being at Shishong (some two miles from Kimbaw), where there is also a maternity clinic run by the nuns. The Mission has a school at Shishong, and smaller ones at Kimbaw and other villages. The headquarters of the Basel Mission in Nsaw is at Kishong, where there is a European in charge. Like the Roman Catholic Mission, the Basel Mission has schools in many areas. In 1949 the hospital in Kimbaw was taken over by the Cameroons Baptist Mission. There are six villages, including Kimbaw, where markets are held every eighth day.[2]

[1] Summarized from Kaberry, op. cit., pp. 18–19.
[2] Kaberry, written communication.

25

MAIN FEATURES OF ECONOMY

Kaberry has made a detailed analysis of Bamenda economy, with particular reference to the Nsaw group of Tikar and to the role of women in the economy. Schmidt has published several articles, mostly concerned with agricultural rituals, on Nsei (Bamessing) village in Ndop N.A. Only brief references are available from other sources. The short outline given below is based on Kaberry's monograph unless otherwise stated.

AGRICULTURE

Tikar economy is based on subsistence agriculture, but the various groups are linked together by a network of trade.

Main Crops

Staple crops are maize and cocoyams; others include finger-millet, guinea-corn, yams, cassava, beans, groundnuts, gourds, plantains, and sugar-cane, but there is some variation in their relative importance in different areas. Native white carrots and sweet potatoes are important secondary foods, eking out resources during periods of scarcity. European vegetables (especially Irish potatoes) and fruit have been increasingly cultivated during the last few years, and brown rice is now grown in Kom. Castor seed and coffee (mainly *Arabica*) are increasing in importance as export crops. Kolas, which grow well in Nsaw, Nsungli, and Oku, tobacco, and livestock also provide cash income. Raffia plantations are important as a source of materials for house-building and weaving, and the trees are tapped for wine.[3]

Methods of Cultivation[4]

Plots are burned and cleared from about the beginning of December for planting with yams in February and maize in March, although a certain amount of planting takes place during other seasons. The main maize harvest is in August on the plateau. Shifting cultivation is practised, the length of time for which an area is worked varying with type of crop, fertility of soil, and availability of other land. In Laikom village in Kom, for example, ground is often left fallow after two years of cultivation, while in the more densely populated Kimbaw large farms may be worked for five or six years, and smaller ones for an even longer period.

Tools

A woman's chief implements are a short-handled hoe and a small knife. Men use a matchet for clearing and planting, and a small mattock for the weeding of raffia plantations.

DIVISION OF LABOUR

While most agricultural activities are the concern of women, the clearing of trees and heavy bush is done by men. For a large farm the men may organize a working team, consisting of the land-holder, his kinsmen, and friendly neighbours, recompense being given in food and beer or wine. A husband or son may work alone on a small plot. Men may also assist in the harvesting of maize, finger-millet, and guinea-corn, but in most areas their contribution to agriculture takes little of their time—Kaberry suggests for Nsaw not more than 10 days in the year.[5] In Mbem and Mbaw, however, men do more farm-work, and Sieber[6] confirms this

---

[3] Kaberry, op. cit., pp. 20–2.
[4] Ibid., pp. 53–61.
[5] Ibid., p. 55. See also Schmidt, 1951, p. 20.
[6] 1935.

for these areas and the neighbouring Tikar in French territory. He notes that here men do " most " of the farm-work, women helping only with hoeing, and suggests that the difference from usual Tikar practice is due to the prevalence of elephant grass, whose roots are too strong for women to remove. Schmidt[7] tabulates the division of agricultural and other tasks between the sexes in Nsei (Bamessing). Here men cut grass in preparing the fields, assist in harvesting and carrying home maize. Women are responsible for hoeing, planting, weeding, and for most of the harvesting.

DOMESTIC ANIMALS

Fowls, sheep, goats, and pigs are reared, but are killed as a rule only for sacrifices, ceremonies, house-building, or to honour a special visitor. Fulani pasture cattle and occasionally sell beasts to local butchers who retail the meat in the market.

HUNTING AND FISHING

Men and boys hunt during the dry season. Communal hunting groups may be formed to follow in the wake of fires lit to burn the fields in November. In Nsei and Mbem fishing is done by all women during January at the time of low-water in the streams.

CRAFTS

House-building[8]

This is mainly the work of men, but in Zhoaw and Mashi women help with the mudding. Houses have a framework of light poles obtained from raffia-palm mid-ribs. Houses are square structures of wattle and daub, surmounted by a pyramidal thatched roof, the usual size being between 12 and 15 feet square. An attic under the roof is used for storage. In villages near the motor-road Tikar are beginning to build in sun-dried brick, which does not require raffia poles.

Pottery[9]

Clay deposits are worked in Bamessi, Bamessing, Mbem, and some Fungom villages. Generally speaking, pottery is women's work except in Mbem and Munkap. Schmidt notes that 46 men of Nsei are potters. Men make clay pipes.

Smithing

Smithing is confined to certain villages, the most important being Bamungo, Oku, Isu, and some other Fungom villages. Today scrap iron instead of ore is generally used. Jeffreys[10] has published some notes on smithing in Isu; here foundry-working and blacksmithing are specialized crafts, although sometimes one man may be both smelter and smith.

Other Crafts

Other specialist occupations include the manufacture of caps, bags, baskets, mats, umbrellas, stools, hoe-handles, wooden dishes, mortars, fishing nets, etc., some tribes having a reputation for finer work than others and exporting a large quantity of their goods over the adjacent region. Little cloth is woven; men usually wear Hausa or European cloth, while most women wear only a pubic covering or a string fringe.[11]

[7] Op. cit., p. 24.
[8] Kaberry, op. cit., pp. 10 and 88. See also Dugast, 1949, p. 129, for French Tikar.
[9] Kaberry, op. cit., pp. 21 and 86.
[10] 1948.
[11] Kaberry, op. cit., p. 22.

TRADE[12]

Men who require cash for the purchase of clothes and household goods, as well as for marriage payments, are the main traders. Petty trade in foodstuffs is carried on by women, usually when they need cash for some specific purpose; but a few trade regularly.

Some foodstuffs—groundnuts, tobacco, and palm-oil—grow only in certain areas, and many tools and utensils are made by specialists in a few villages. Such goods are traded throughout the territory. Some plain-dwellers, especially those in Ndop N.A., are able to plant maize twice yearly and so have a small surplus for sale to other areas. Men who trade in maize or groundnuts buy small quantities from a number of individuals and sell in the large markets of Kimbaw, the Ndop villages, Bali, and Bamenda Station. The main imports from outside Bamenda Province are camwood, tobacco, rock salt, and, especially important, Hausa cloth, some of which is sold by Hausa traders, but much by local Africans who make journeys to Adamawa and Northern Nigeria, taking with them oil or kolas for exchange.

Schmidt mentions, but does not describe in detail, co-operative credit groups (" savings banks ") among the traders in Nsei. Eight such groups, each attended weekly by 20 to 30 men, existed in the sub-village in Nsei in which she worked.[13]

The need to accumulate marriage payment[14] was and still is one of the main incentives to economic activity on the part of the men. To get the necessary cash and goods, a man must either act as middleman or produce articles which he can sell.

---

[12] For a detailed description of modern Bamenda trade, see Kaberry, op. cit., chaps. II VII, VIII.

[13] 1948. See also Kaberry, op. cit., chap. 7.

[14] Kaberry, 1950, p. 24.

LOCAL AND KIN GROUPING

Detailed information on local and kin grouping is available only for the Nsaw; this is here summarized, similarities and differences in other Tikar areas being mentioned when they are known. The account is based on Kaberry's monograph.

Except in Kom and in the Fungom villages of Mme, Kuk, Nyos, Fungom, and Kung, the Tikar trace descent patrilineally and practise patrilocal marriage, the basis of social organization being the localized exogamous patrilineage.

PATRILINEAL TRIBES

The Household

In all areas each married woman generally has her own hut, which she occupies with her daughters and young sons. If her husband has only one wife, he may possess no special dwelling of his own, but he usually builds one when circumstances permit. Sons may share this with him till they reach adolescence, when they may take over a vacant hut; when a son marries he will build a hut for his bride, usually in the father's compound.

The Compound

The size of the compound varies widely. In Nsungli and Nsaw one which has been established for several generations may contain anything from 10 to 20 houses; while that of a senior councillor in Nsaw is often much larger (that of Fai-o-Ndzendzef, for example, has 103 houses and extends over some four acres of land). In other Tikar areas, compounds are often much smaller, being inhabited only by the compound head, his wives, married sons, and, more rarely, younger married brothers (with their wives and unmarried children). Dwellings and store huts usually face a central courtyard and nearby are small kitchen gardens. Where compounds are small, the male and unmarried female members of a number of adjacent compounds are usually related by agnatic ties and come under the authority of one of the compound heads who acts as lineage head.

In Nsungli and Nsaw, where compounds are larger, a compound may contain from 4 to 10 elementary families in huts grouped round a rectangular courtyard. "The elementary family emerges as a clearly defined residential, social, and economic unit, producing nearly all the food it requires and exercising a certain amount of control over its own affairs. But male members of these families, as well as unmarried females, are related to the compound head by patrilineal ties and may therefore be regarded as the main part of a co-residential patrilineage. The women, who at marriage go to live with their husbands, pay frequent visits, sometimes continue to work plots on the land of the lineage; and they may, in old age, or when widowed or divorced, return to live in the parental compound."[1]

The Village

Patrilineal groups of this kind which make up a village belong to different clans.[2] In Nsaw they are under the political authority of a village head (*tantee*, literally father of the village), who is usually a descendant of the first settler or of the senior man of a small band of settlers in the area. He is responsible for the maintenance of order, for the transmitting of the *Fon*'s orders, and, assisted by resident lineage heads, for settling minor disputes.[3] He has no rights over village land as a whole, but he is also head of a lineage centred in the village, and by virtue of this he administers and allocates among his dependants certain tracts of land in the village

---

[1] Kaberry, 3, 1952, pp. 10–12.
[2] See below, p. 31.
[3] Although there is right of appeal to the *Fon*'s court or, nowadays, to that of the N.A.

and its vicinity to which his ancestors laid claim in the past and which have been retained for the use of the lineage. Other lineage heads, usually those resident in the village,[4] have similar rights of administering tracts of village land.

Villages vary widely in size; in the majority, population ranges from 300 to 800.[5] Most villages are fairly compact clusters of compounds, although much depends on the lie of the land. Except in Ndop and Bafut,[6] villages are not sub-divided into wards.

The Patrilineage (Nsaw)

According to Bridges, there were about 420 *afai* (heads of lineages) in Nsaw N.A. in 1935. In Nsaw the average size of a lineage is difficult to compute, since it may number anything from 20 to 70 members. Frequently a *fai* or lineage head has under his direct surveillance (i.e., in his own compound) from 3 to 10 adult married males related agnatically to him. Sometimes a man may go to live in another part of the village or even in another village, because of shortage of building space or of good farm land, because of illness, constant misfortune or quarrels, or because of his desire to form his own compound and, ultimately, his own sub-lineage. But even if he builds his compound many miles away he still remains under the authority of his *fai* and is known merely as a compound-owner (*ngalaa*), whatever the number of his wives and children.

Sub-lineages (Nsaw)

If a compound prospers and at least two generations have lapsed since its foundation, the title of sub-lineage head, or *she*, may, with the consent of the *Fon* and of the *fai* of the parent lineage, be conferred on one of its members. The new *she* then has rights of inheritance to the property (including kolas and raffia) of the members of his compound, and arranges the marriages of the women. But he is expected to make a token gift of firewood each year to the *fai* of the parent lineage. After a lapse of four generations the title of *fai*, indicative of senior status, may be granted; after five generations, marriage is permitted between members of the two lineages.[7]

The Fai or Lineage Head (Nsaw)[8]

Character and not seniority in age is the main criterion for eligibility to any position of authority in Nsaw, although usually a married man is preferred. In choosing a *fai*, the opinion of members of the lineage is given special weight, but *afai* who live close by may be consulted and the final decision must be ratified by the *Fon*. Failing any suitable male candidates, the selection may be made from another lineage of the same clan or, more rarely, the first-born son of a woman of the lineage may be appointed. If none of the males has reached puberty, a woman may be temporarily appointed to act as trustee.

The *fai* settles minor disputes within the lineage and, as in all Bamenda tribes, is the intermediary between his dependants and their lineal ancestors. The latter function, Kaberry points out, is one of the main sanctions for his secular authority and an important factor in the cohesion of the lineage.

The *fai* has the following rights:

(a) He may call on all his dependants for assistance in the clearing and culti-vation of his farm, and in the construction of houses and bridges, and the clearing of paths.

---

[4] Sometimes the lineage head of a compound-owner may reside in another village—see below.
[5] See p. 15 above.
[6] See Kaberry, op. cit., p. 11.
[7] Ibid., p. 12.
[8] Kaberry, op. cit., pp. 13–14.

(b) He inherits, with minor exceptions, the raffia and kola trees planted by male members of the lineage, as well as livestock, guns, and money. He also inherits the wives of his predecessor in office and of his male dependants, although he usually allocates some of them to male members of the lineage.

(c) He arranges the marriages of all women of the lineage, except the first-born, receiving the major part of the gifts made by their husbands, and having first claim on their services. He also arranges the marriages of first-born daughters of females of the lineage. In the case of the *Fon* and the councillors this privilege is extended to grand-daughters and other descendants.

(d) He exercises *de facto* control over lineage land, allocating it to his dependants, although the *Fon* is the titular owner of all Nsaw land. The *fai's* control of land, in spite of the spread of Christianity, greater mobility of population, and opportunities for the attainment of a large measure of economic independence through the pursuit of new relatively lucrative occupations, is one of the main factors in his still very considerable authority over his dependants.[9]

Patriclans (Nsaw)

Nsaw patriclans are dispersed and the number of their component lineages varies widely from 3 to 22, and even to 24 in the case of Do clan. Some of the lineages are only three generations in depth, in so far as descent is traced back to the first man who was granted the title of *she* or *fai;* a parent lineage from which others have hived off may be 10 generations in depth. In some of the large patriclans there may be two or three *afai* who claim equality of status, though in matters of etiquette the seniority of one is recognized. In this case, each *fai* is the head of a lineage from which several other lineages have stemmed off, and so may be regarded as head of a sub-clan. Examples which may be cited are those of the Luun (or Mbitimbang), Do, Ka, and Djem clans. The Do clan originated at Ndjeng in Nsungli. They migrated from there to Kuyaar in Wiya where they split into two branches. One of these, Do-e-Run, went to Kingomen in Nsaw, to Kimbaw, and finally to Ketiwum. The other branch, Do-e-Ngven, left Kuyaar later; from there they went to Ketiwum, then to Kikai-Kengvenki, and back to Ketiwum. These two branches may be regarded as the sub-clans of Run and Ngven, each being headed by *afai* who are also *vibai* (councillors). In the Run branch there are 11 lineages in addition to several sub-lineages (*visheer*); in Ngven there are 13 main lineages. Other lineages have broken away and deny relationship with Do, and both *vibai* refused to enumerate them. It should be stressed, moreover, that even where relations remain close among the component lineages and sub-lineages of a clan, genealogical ties between them are rarely known. Social relations tend to be frequent and intimate among members of a sub-clan, though in the absence of geographical propinquity even these may weaken. In theory, the sub-clan head may demand a gift of firewood from the heads of the component lineages; in practice, he usually receives it only from the sub-lineages. In theory, he has a voice in the selection of the *afai* of the sub-clans to office; but more often this is limited to his presence at installation. From time to time lineages assemble for sacrifice; and, in the case of a major disaster or death of the clan head, *afai* and *ashe* would participate in a joint ritual. But it is the lineage rather than the clan which is the important political unit. The main Nsaw clans, including that of the *Fon*, number 22, but there are probably others in the conquered villages of Nkar, Djottin-Vitum, Mbinon, Lassin, Dom, Din, etc.[10]

[9] Kaberry, 1950, p. 312.
[10] Kaberry, 3, 1952, p. 13, and a written communication.

Relationship with Maternal Kin (*Nsaw*)

Although lineage membership, inheritance, and residence usually follow the paternal line, ties with maternal kin are close. There is much visiting among matri-kin, and joint participation in ceremonies connected with birth, marriage, death, and the various societies. The individual is believed to come under the influence of his maternal ancestors, and, in consultation with a diviner, sacrifices may be offered to them in the event of sickness or misfortune. When a man succeeds to the office of *fai* or *she*, he goes not only to the head of his patriclan, but also to the head of his mother's patrilineage, taking with him salt, fowls and firewood (the last a symbol of submission), so that the latter may make a sacrifice to invoke his ancestors' blessing. On occasion sacrifices are offered to the ancestors of the patri-lineage of the mother's mother or even the mother's mother's mother, the officiating priest in each case being the head of the lineage involved.

The fact, noted above, that first-born daughters of a patrilineage have their marriages arranged by the *afai* of their respective mothers' patrilineages constitutes a further tie with maternal kin. Finally, a man has rights of usufruct in land belonging to his mother's patrilineage, and receives assistance and hospitality from its members.

Rank influences the extent to which maternal ties are recognized. The term *kföö ye ku'un* (great group) is usually used for the father's patriclan, but may be used for the father's mother's clan or mother's patriclan where either is politically and socially more important. In the case of a man descended through his mother's mother from a *fon* or a *kibai* (councillor), her patrilineage may be referred to as *kföö ye ku'un;* but otherwise the mother's mother's patrilineage is spoken of as *ram* (literally, a runner from a plant) and kinship affiliation is unlikely to be recognized in the succeeding generation except in the case of a *fai* or *she*.[11]

The Royal Clan (*Nsaw*)

All those related to the *Fon*, firstly, by agnatic descent, and secondly, by cog-natic descent down to the sixth generation, are referred to as *wiri-e-Fon* and may be regarded as a limited kinship group. Often a son or paternal grandson of the *Fon* is granted the title of *fai* or *she*, and he may subsequently become the founder of a lineage or even a sub-clan within the *Fon*'s patriclan. In addition to those lineages which trace direct agnatic descent from a *fon*, the royal clan contains the sub-clans of three of the senior councillors (*vibai*)—Ndzendzef, Tankum, and Luun —whose ancestors came from other tribes but elected to become affiliated with the *Fon*'s clan, assuming the status of *wir duiy*.

Descendants of the *Fon* down to the fourth generation are generally referred to as *wonto* (children of the palace), exact generation level being indicated by pre-fixing to this the term for child: thus a great-grandchild would be described as *wanwanwanto*. At the fifth generation a descendant of the *Fon* is called *wir duiy*. The *Fon* has the right to take the first-born daughter of a *wir duiy* of the sixth generation as wife, and the first-born son as servant (*nshilaf*). A *kibai* has similar rights in the fifth generation removed from him.

Members of the royal clan and the clans of the *vibai*, like other Nsaw, retain close ties with maternal kin. A son of the *Fon* frequently goes to reside after marriage with his mother's father. A man related to the *Fon* or to a *kibai* through his mother is brought up in his father's compound and regards himself as a member of his father's patrilineage; but in times of hardship he may beg assistance from the *Fon* or the *kibai;* and, if he quarrels with his own *fai*, he may repudiate his patri-lineal connections and assert that he is a *wir duiy* or a *wan kibai*,[12] as the case may be.

11 Kaberry, op. cit., pp. 13–15.
12 Ibid.

Kinship: Other Patrilineal Tikar

Kaberry points out that in most other patrilineal Tikar groups the kinship system is similar to that of the Nsaw in so far as the lineage head allocates land and inherits the property of his male dependants, particularly livestock, money, and such trees as kola, raffia, mangoes, and oil-palm where these are cultivated. The lineage head is usually referred to by a term equivalent to the Lamnso term *talaa* (father of the compound): *telaa* (Wiya), *tufu* (Bamungo), *tifo* (Bamessing), etc. He is expected to assist his male dependants in procuring wives, and he arranges, with minor exceptions, the marriages of all women of the lineage, claiming a major share in the marriage payment. This arrangement does not, as it does among the Nsaw, exclude the first-born daughters. In Ndop and Bafut, the *Fon* has the right to take a first-born daughter of any family not closely related to his own as a wife, and he may also take a female twin. As in Nsaw, a woman is not consulted about the marriage of her daughter, but in Bamessi the consent of the mother's mother is important; she is treated with great respect, and may demand some assistance from her grand-daughter's husband. Here, as well as in Bamungo and Bangola, when his mother dies, the lineage head appoints either a sister or a daughter to act in her stead as the " great mother," and to perform minor sacrifices.[13] In all Tikar areas the lineage head is intermediary between his dependants and their lineal ancestors.

There is virtually no published information on Tikar kinship systems in sources other than Kaberry's book. Jeffreys[14] notes that in the Fungom patrilineal villages of We, Esu, and Nser, succession (presumably to headship of the lineage) passes collaterally, in order of age, to all brothers and half-brothers, until the generation is exhausted, then to the first son of the next generation, succession reverting to the senior branch of the lineage. In all other patrilineal groups in Fungom, he notes, succession passes where possible from father to son.

MATRILINEAL TRIBES (KOM AND FIVE FUNGOM VILLAGES)

Residence in the matrilineal tribes, today at least, does not appear to follow closely either patrilocal or matrilocal lines. A man may elect to reside, both before and after marriage, with his father, with an affine, or with a friend. Kaberry points out: " The strength of the tie between a man and his father, the considerable economic independence of a man after marriage, and his right to receive the major part of the marriage payment for his daughters—all these factors militate against the emergence of the matrilineage as a localised unit." Residence depends largely on personal relationships, availability of land, occupation, and, today, proximity to co-religionists, in the case of converts to Christianity or Islam.[15] It should be noted, however, that when a man inherits the property of his mother's brother he normally goes to reside in the latter's compound, and he may be joined by a younger brother.[16]

Village Sections

Jeffreys[17] describes the matrilineal[18] villages of Fungom as being divided into a number of " quarters " or " kindreds," each quarter being composed of a number of " extended families " which spring from the senior " extended family " of the quarter, whose head is the quarter head, and, in the case of the senior quarter of the village, the village headman as well. He presumably uses the term " extended family " rather than " lineage " owing to the varying patterns of residence.

---

[13] Kaberry, op. cit., pp. 15–16.
[14] MS.
[15] Kaberry, op. cit., p. 17.
[16] Kaberry, personal communication.
[17] MS.
[18] The patrilineal villages of Fungom appear to be divided in the same way. (Jeffreys, MS.)

C

Kaberry,[19] who visited Fungom village, states that it is divided into sections, usually referred to as " quarters " by interpreters. Each section is associated with a particular matrilineage (*sassende*, literally buttocks or rump of the house), and bears its name. The section head, *tshö* or *tshe*, is also the head or " first man " (*wundoma*) of the lineage. He is appointed by members of the lineage, but the *Fon* or village head ratifies the choice and shows him to the people. In Fungom the main sections are:

(a) *Atshaf* (that of the *Fon*, but with its own *tshö*).
(b) *Ameku* (said to be the equivalent of the Ekwü clan of the *Fon* of Kom).
(c) *Ake* (said to be linked with Ake in Kom).
(d) *Akulekang*.
(e) *Ekaiy*.
(f) *Mbulom*.
(g) *Ewa*.

Azang, Iwo, and *Neving* lineages have no lineage heads and the few remaining members are scattered. When necessary they attend sacrifices in Mme.[20]

Compounds[21]

In a section there are usually two or more compounds. For example, in Fungom Village there are four in Atshaf section and eight in Ameku. Each compound has its compound head (*kpe'apwi*, literally "father of the compound"). Compound heads of a section are, in the main, matrilineal kin—that is, mother's brother, brother, and sister's son, own and classificatory. Sometimes, howevei, a compound head is a son of the *tshö* or of another resident; or he may be an affine or a stranger who has fled from his own section or village in fear of witchcraft, or because he has been accused of being a witch. Exact genealogical links between matrikin of a section are not always known, but the link is assumed to be a close one and no intermarriage within such a group is permitted. A compound usually comprises three or four huts occupied by the compound head, his wives and children, and sometimes a married son. Marriage is, as a rule, patrilocal but sometimes a woman returns to her mother's compound to bear her child when so advised by a diviner. Occasionally a woman in old age returns to her brother's section. Where a stranger has, with the permission of the *tshö*, built a compound he may bequeath it (with the latter's consent) to his own sister's child. In general it may be said that in the Fungom villages, as also in Kom, the core of a section consists of male matrilineal kin together with their spouses and sometimes married sons. But the latter generally expect to inherit a compound from a mother's brother. Until that occurs many are content to remain with their fathers.

Succession and Inheritance

Succession and inheritance of property and wives follow the female line, passing, according to Jeffreys,[22] to the sister's son, mother's sister's daughter's son, or sister's daughter's son, in that order. According to Kaberry[23] character is an important qualification for succession and inheritance in Fungom, and any of those mentioned by Jeffreys are eligible. On the death of a lineage head or compound head, members of the *sassende* assemble for the rituals. After the burial this group comes to a decision on the succession, if the deceased has not indicated his successor, and on the division of the property. Widows select husbands from the members of the matrilineage. If there are no male children office may pass to a

[19] Kaberry, written communication.
[20] Kaberry when at Mme received a similar list of lineages resident in Mme and, in addition, those of Siibu, Iba, Tinelaa (also found in Kom), Tsha'a, Ikpwö, Angguu, Ise, and Bazhö.
[21] Kaberry, written communication.
[22] MS.
[23] Written communication.

man of another lineage of the same clan. Where there are male children who are too young to succeed, the oldest woman in the lineage looks after the sacrificial cup and, when sacrifice is to be performed, she summons a distant mother's brother, i.e., a senior man from another lineage, to carry out the rite. In Kom, according to Kaberry,[24] brothers by the same mother normally inherit before a sister's son.

The Lineage Head in Fungom[25]

The legatee, referred to as *zhiindɛ* (literally " one who eats the house," a common phrase in Bamenda), inherits plantain groves, raffia bush, and movable property such as livestock and ornaments. If he is lineage head he assumes control of the residential and farm land of the lineage, allocating unused land among his dependants and to strangers who request plots. The latter, if they came from other villages, should first approach the chief for permission to settle, but the actual assignment of plots is at the discretion of one of the lineage heads. The lineage head has no rights, in virtue of his status, over the property of members of the lineage. He has ritual and advisory functions.

Exogamy

Although in Fungom some members of the matrilineage are scattered, they return to the section or compound of the *tshö* for sacrifices and other rituals. When exact genealogical ties are not known, attendance at special sacrifices for the death of a man or a woman is the criterion of lineage (*sassendɛ*) membership. Such a lineal group is exogamous. Opinion as to whether marriage is permitted between lineages of the same clan (*utum*) varied. The consensus was that, where no genealogical link was known, and where participation in the first sacrifices at mourning did not occur, marriage might take place. The same ruling was given for Kom, where the term for lineage is " *sassendo* "[26] According to Jeffreys,[27] the rule of exogamy in the Fungom villages rarely obtains beyond the " extended family " (lineage?), with the notable exception of the Chap (Atshaf) family, which is the senior family in Fungom, Mme, Kuk, and Nyos, and whose members may not intermarry.

Marriage is forbidden between cross-cousins, but permitted between ortho-cousins if of different lineages (i.e., between a man and his father's brother's daughter).[28]

---

[24] Written communication.
[25] Ibid.
[26] Kaberry, written communication
[27] MS.
[28] Kaberry, ibid.

POLITICAL ORGANIZATION

NSAW

The following account of Nsaw political structure is derived from Kaberry's book, all information given being from that source unless otherwise stated.

The Fon-Nsaw

The *Fon* is overlord of all Nsaw territory. In the past he had the right to dispossess rebellious and criminal subjects, and to resume control of any area already allocated to a lineage head should he require it for personal or communal purposes. Although this was rarely done in practice, today these rights are evident, e.g., when land is leased to a Mission or to the Government. In general, the *Fon*'s overlordship of Nsaw land is a titular one, and its implications are political rather than economic. Residence in Nsaw is conditional on submission to the laws of the country.[1]

The *Fon* also has priestly functions and performs the major annual sacrifices to God and to the ancestors to ensure the fertility of all Nsaw land and Nsaw women.

The *Fon*'s palace at Kimbaw comprises his own inner courtyards, dwelling huts, kitchens, and stores; in front of this section lies a large courtyard (*takebu*), where he hears cases and discusses public affairs with his advisers. Separated from this by a small antechamber is a piazza (*mandengai*), flanked on one side by the quarters of the *Fon*'s wives, and on the other by the headquarters of the *ngwirong* society. Close male relatives of the *Fon* have their own society—*ŋgiri*—which is housed at the far end of the piazza. The management of the *Fon*'s palace, the guardianship of his wives, and the control of stores, are the responsibility of the *atanto* (literally "fathers of the palace"), of whom the seven most important have their compounds in the vicinity of the palace.[2]

The Wives of the Fon

In a count made by Kaberry in 1946, the *Fon* had at least 94 wives, including 15 girls who were being trained as wives. Among the adults, 23 were daughters of *nshilafsi*, 2 were daughters of *atanto* (who are also of *nshilaf* status), and 10 were grand-daughters of *wir duiy* (distant relatives of the *Fon*[3]). The remainder had been given voluntarily either by sub-chiefs or by men of *m'tar* status. (These ranks are described on p. 38 below.) The *Fon*'s wives are responsible for making his farms, in which they are directed by the *Yesum* and the *Yelaa*, the senior wife, who is not necessarily the first wife.

The Queen Mothers (Aya; sing. Ya)[4]

Upon the succession of a *fon*, the title of *Ya* is conferred upon his mother or if she is dead, upon a sister or daughter of a *fon*, usually the late *Fon*. As in the case of the *Fon* and other royal dignitaries, her mother must have been of *m'tar* status. She is given the name of the *Fon*'s mother, but this is used only by the *Fon*, and then only rarely. She may be referred to by the name of the compound where she resides. An alternative title for *Ya* is *Fengai* (literally, "for the family house," the hut where important family discussions take place). Thus the most senior *Ya*, *Ya-o-Faa*, is also known as *Fengai-wo-Faa*.

The *aya* of the previous reign retain their titles and seniority. In addition other *aya* may be created to act as representatives of the mothers of previous *afon*. The present *Ya-o-Faa* has been *Ya* during the reigns of four *afon*: Sembum, Mapiri Momfoi, and Sehm Atar (who succeeded in 1947). She acted as queen mother fo

---

[1] Kaberry, 1950, and 3, 1952, pp. 8–9.
[2] See below, p. **38**.
[3] See above, p. **32**.
[4] Kaberry, written communication, 1952.

the *Fon* Sembum, and also for Momfoi who was his full brother. Next in rank to her is the *Ya-o-Ki*, Ketiwum, and then the *Ya-o-Nsolaa*. There are other *aya*, and the present *Fon*, Sehm Atar, has appointed his own *Ya*. The selection is made on the basis of character and personality by the *Fon* and the most important *vibai*.

In addition to the queen mother, a *Tawong* (High Priest—"Father of the Country") and a *Yewong* (High Priestess—"Mother of the Country") are also elected when a *fon* succeeds, but they do not supersede those of the previous reign. They assist the *Fon* and *Ndzendzef* (senior councillor) in the major sacrifices, and follow the queen mothers in rank. They are elected by the *Fon, Yewong, Tawong*, and important *vibai*.

Queen mothers and high priestesses are given in marriage by the *Fon* to *afai*, but no marriage gifts are handed over to the *Fon* and the women are free to leave their husbands if they so desire. They may be given raffia stands and kola trees by the *Fon*, as well as servants (*nshilafsi*) to look after their farms. In addition, the women of the compound and the village where they reside give some assistance when necessary.

In titular rank and matters of etiquette they come next to the *Fon*, a status reflected in their seats in his *takebu*. The *Fon* sits upon a dais at the centre back of the courtyard; on his left, to the side, are the *aya* and *Yewong;* then the sub-chiefs, followed by the *vibai;* and finally, facing the *Fon*, but towards the right, are the *atanto* or palace officials. Although the *aya* and *Yewong* take part in council deliberations and judicial affairs, they rank politically below the more important *vibai* and the *Fai-o-Tawong*.

Succession to the Paramount Chieftainship of Nsaw

Only those sons or grandsons of a *fon* whose mothers are of *m'tar* status are eligible for the office of *Fon*. When a *fon* dies, the selection of the successor is made by the *Yewong, Tawong*, and the following *vibai:* Ndzendzef, Tankum, Yuwar, Ndzendzeftsen, and Luun. Some of the nobility, including the Ya-o-Nturkwi, also claimed that Tsinlaa and Run have a voice in the selection. But, while the final decision rests with these individuals, the opinions of the remaining important *vibai*, the *aya*, the *atanto*, and the heads of Nsaw clans are also sought. Once a decision has been reached, the inner group disbands and it is left to Ndzendzef to summon the *wanto* who has been chosen to the palace.[5]

The Other Afon (sing. Fon)

Nsaw Native Authority (and traditional Nsaw territory) is made up of Nsaw proper and a number of sub-chiefdoms which were conquered by or submitted to the Fon-Nsaw. Chiefs of these areas have retained the title of *Fon*, have their own *vibai* (councillors) and *atanto* (palace guardians), and their courts tend to be smaller replicas of that of the Fon-Nsaw. In the rank system for *afon* the Fon-Nsaw is paramount; next in precedence is the Fon-Mbiami who, according to tradition, is a descendant of a brother of an early Fon-Nsaw and was formerly the ruler of an independent chiefdom of Mbiami. After him come the Fon-Nkar, whose ancestor was conquered by a Fon-Nsaw, and then the Fon-Ndzerem (whose ancestor sought sanctuary with Nkar when his people were harassed by the Fulani at the beginning of the last century). Below these are the *afon* of the seven villages of Nsungli extraction—Dom, Din, Djottin-Vitum, Mbinon, Lassin, Nkor, and Nser.[6]

[5] Kaberry, written communication, 1952. Kaberry also notes that the relations between the *Fon* and Ndzendzef have, for the past 15 or 20 years, been marked by friction and that Ndzendzef has made extravagant claims to various prerogatives, such as having the sole right to elect the *Fon*—a claim which appears in Bridges's report. Kaberry investigated these claims thoroughly in the field, interviewing the *Fon*, aya, vibai, atanto, and *ngwirong*, sometimes individually and sometimes in groups, and is satisfied that Ndzendzef's claims are false. A confidential report was submitted to the Administration in 1946 and again in 1947. She hopes to publish a full account later.

[6] Kaberry, 3, 1952, p. 8.

The Councillors or Vibai (sing. Kibai)

There are 13 main *vibai* who act as councillors to the Fon-Nsaw. In the case of four (Fai-o-Ndzendzef, Fai-o-Tankum, Fai-o-Yuwar, and Fai-o-Luun), the office has been vested in their respective lineages ever since the settlement at Kovifem. A fifth councillorship (Fai-o-Tsinlaa) was created by the *Fon* who fled to Tauwvisa because of Fulani raids, while three more were established when Kimbaw was made the capital. The late *Fon* during his long reign (1910–47) appointed five others who are junior in rank.[7]

The most senior *kibai*, the Fai-o-Ndzendzef, is the descendant of a Tang (Nsungli) lineage head who elected to become affiliated with the clan of the Fon-Nsaw, i.e., to take the status of *wir duiy*.[8] He has his compound at Kimbaw. His successor is chosen, from among his agnates, by the Fon-Nsaw in consultation with the Ndzendzef lineage. He is the senior *kibai* of *Ye-ngwirong* (the inner circle of the *ngwirong* society), and the *Fon*'s principal adviser. As noted above he has a voice in the selection of the new *Fon*, the queen mothers, the members of *Ye-ngwirong*, and may in practice be consulted about the appointment of *vibai* and *atanto*.

Rank

There are three social categories among the Nsaw,[9] defined in terms of relationship to the *Fon* and his rights:

(a) The *wiri-e-Fon*,[10] including all agnates and other cognates of the *Fon* down to the sixth generation, together with lineages which have become affiliated to the *Fon*'s clan, e.g., that of the Fai-o-Ndzendzef (see p. 32).

(b) The *m'tar*, or descendants of men who became voluntary allies of the *Fon* many generations ago. Leaders of *m'tar* lineages have the right to retain leopard skins, after first presenting the animal to the *Fon*. Unlike *wiri-e-Fon* (of the sixth generation only) and *nshilafsi*, they are under no obligation to give daughters to the *Fon*, provided that the mothers of these girls are neither of *nshilaf* status nor related to the *Fon* at six generations' remove. They may, however, give one as a means of gaining prestige and favour.

(c) *Nshilaf* is a servant status and includes both men and women. The sons and daughters of a male *nshilaf* are all of this status. In the case of a female *nshilaf* married to a *m'tar* or *duiy* man, the first-born son and daughter only are of *nshilaf* status. In the old days, captives in war might also be recruited to this status. Finally, as noted above (p. 32), the first-born son and daughter of a *duiy* at six generations' remove from the *Fon* may be taken by the *Fon*. The man becomes a member of *ngwirong*, the woman may become a wife or be given in marriage by the *Fon* to a son or grandson. Among men of *nshilaf* status are the *atanto*, or palace guardians, whose office is vested in their respective lineages and of whom the seven most important are resident in Kimbaw (see p. 36).

The Ngwirong Association

The *ngwirong* association provides the attendants and messengers of the *Fon* and formerly acted as a police force, carrying out executions at the command of the *Fon* and his inner council of *vibai*, who are also members of *Ye-ngwirong* (literally, "Mother of Ngwirong"). The *vibai* concerned are Ndzendzef, Tankum

---

[7] Op. cit., p. 9.
[8] See above, p. 32.
[9] i.e., among the Nsaw proper, not including sub-chiefdoms.
[10] The term *wir duiy* (lit. "people of the *Fon*," i.e., of royal descent), although strictly applicable only to relatives five or more generations removed from the *Fon*, is often used as an alternative name for the royal "clan."

Luun, and Nkavikeng. The membership of *ngwirong*, banned to near kin of the *Fon*, is recruited from the first-born sons of men of *nshilaf* status, and also from the first-born sons of kin of the *Fon* at six generations' remove. These young men live in the *ngwirong* quarters by the palace. On marriage they leave and build their houses in Kimbaw or elsewhere; but they may be called upon for various duties, such as house-building, grass-cutting, and provision of firewood for the *Fon* throughout their lifetime.

The *Fon* selects from the young members of *ngwirong* his own personal attendants—*nshilafsi-se-fai*. In 1947 the *Fon* had two attendants, but sometimes there are three or more. The *nshilafsi* who live in the *ngwirong* quarters are known as *nshilafsi-se-ngwirong*. They remain there for about 10 years. From among their number two are elected to the position of *tshefon*, one from the *gham* section, one from the *baa* section (see *Mandjong*, p. 41 below). They are addressed as *she*, and when they appear in public their faces are covered with a hood of netting. They direct the work of the other *nshilafsi*. The most senior *tshefon* is called *Ta-ngwirong*.

At about the age of 20, a *nshilaf-ye-ngwirong* or a *nshilaf-fai* gives the *Fon* a fowl and five calabashes of wine, as well as providing about 10 calabashes for the other *nshilafsi* of the palace and *ngwirong*. The *atanto* formerly provided him with raffia poles with which to build a house, and he might be given a wife of *nshilaf* status by the *Fon*. He is thenceforth known as a *nshilaf-ye-ta*, but still performs tasks for the *Fon* when called upon. In 1938 it was estimated that there were over 200 *nshilafsi-se-ta* in Nsaw. At that time there were resident in *ngwirong* seven *nshilafsi* who were sons of *nshilafsi;* a *nshilaf* who was the first-born son of a daughter of Fai-o-Tsenkar; and the two *tshefon*, one of whom was *wan-nshilaf*, and the other the son of a daughter of Fai-o-Kimar. Nowadays only about four members will be recruited each year, but in the past the number was probably greater.

All *nshilafsi, atanto*, the *Fon*, and those *vibai* who are members of *Ye-ngwirong*, may attend the meetings of the society which are held on *ntangrin*,[11] a day in the eight-day Nsaw week.

Ye-ngwirong (Mother of Ngwirong)

Only a very few members of *ngwirong* are members of *Ye-ngwirong*, its inner circle: the *Fon* and certain of the *vibai* and *atanto*. At the time of Bridges's report, they numbered eight in all:

(*a*) The Fon-Nsaw.

(*b*) Three *vibai*: the Fai-o-Ndzendzef, Fai-o-Tankum, and Fai-o-Luun. Any *kibai* who is a member of *ngwirong* is automatically a member of *Ye-ngwirong*.[12] Membership is not hereditary, the selection being made by the *Fon* in consultation with Ndzendzef and the senior officials of *ngwirong*.[13]

(*c*) Four *atanto*, especially chosen for their wisdom. Two of these men are responsible for announcing the *Fon*'s orders, two for announcing *ngwirong* orders.[14]

Formerly, *Ye-ngwirong* took the initiative in legislation, in promulgating orders and precautions regarding epidemics and droughts, and in the settlement of disputes.[15] But there was also consultation with the senior *vibai* and the *aya*.[16] Bridges in 1934 noted that this body has not been accorded official recognition; it is powerless to enforce any orders and the *nshilafsi* have, mostly, run away. The

[11] Kaberry, written communication which incorporates notes made by the District Officer in 1938.

[12] Fai-o-Nkavikeng, who is now the fourth member, being a case in point. (Kaberry, written communication.)

[13] Kaberry, written communication.

[14] Although in another context Bridges notes that ordinary *atanto* have this task.

[15] Bridges, 1935.

[16] Kaberry, written communication.

only matters with which it now deals are in regard to the issuing of general advice and instructions. Meetings are still held once a week, to discuss remedies in periods of famine or epidemic.[17] Kaberry notes, however, that as its members comprise the two most senior *vibai,* while Luun is also of high rank, its lack of prominence is due not so much to non-recognition by the Government as to the friction which existed between Ndzendzef on the one hand, and the *Fon,* Tankum, and some of the *vibai* and *atanto* on the other.[18]

Sub-chiefdom Ngwirong Societies

The foregoing applies to Nsaw proper, but each sub-chiefdom,[19] including Mbiami, has its own society—membership, constitution, organization, and duties being very similar to those of the Nsaw *ngwirong.* Execution of criminals, however, could be carried out only by the Nsaw society, though cases were first tried in the sub-chiefdom.[20]

Legal Procedure[21]

All disputes and such matters as assaults and thefts were, and still are, tried first by the village head (*tantee*) and the lineage heads (*afai*) of the village concerned. The parties are questioned and, if necessary, statements of any eye-witness are heard. Such courts possess powers of arbitration but cannot enforce their orders. If parties do not agree to the verdict, the village head, with several *afai,* accompanies them to Kimbaw where the case is tried in the *takebu* by the *Fon* and councillors. Crimes of a serious nature traditionally went direct to the *Fon's* court, and *ngwirong* was then responsible for executing the penalties awarded.

In the *Fon's* court (*takebu*) the *tantee* concerned would explain the statements of all parties and eye-witnesses, and the decision arrived at by the village court. Should either of the parties not agree with this statement he might interrupt, and he would then be questioned on his counter statements. Then the *tantee, afai,* and parties would remain in the outer court while the *aya* and *vibai* discussed the matter. The *Fon* listened and made the final decision. According to Bridges, a very important case would be discussed by *Ye-ngwirong* in secret (i.e., by the *Fon,* three *vibai* and four *atanto*). The decision made by *Ye-ngwirong* was final; should either party disobey its ruling he would be reported by the other party (through his *fai*), and *nshilafsi* would be sent to flog the wrongdoer.

The *Fon* has never, according to Bridges, possessed powers of making laws; his orders would rather take the form of advice, his views always being broadcast by the *mandjong* society (see below) and through general meetings, as well as in the market place. According to Kaberry, the *Fon* and some of the *vibai* and *aya* claimed that the *Fon* could initiate legislation and make the final decision, although he would give full weight to the advice of his council. Any man might make his complaint to the *Fon,* through one of the *nshilafsi,* who would report it to one of the *atanto* and ask him to present the case to the *Fon.* But if either party were dissatisfied with the *Fon's* ruling, he could report the matter for trial by the *Fon*-in-Council.[22]

Punishments[23]

The most usual punishment awarded by the court was a flogging, carried out by *ngwirong.* Imprisonment was never resorted to except in the case of a *nshilaf*

[17] Bridges, 1935.
[18] Kaberry, written communication.
[19] " Sub-chiefdom " refers to village areas of conquered or allied *afon,* and not to sections of Nsaw proper. See above, pp. 23–4.
[20] Bridges, 1935.
[21] Kaberry, written communication, 1952; Bridges, 1935.
[22] Kaberry, written communication.
[23] Bridges, 1935.

or *tanto* who disobeyed *ngwirong* orders, and then for a maximum of three weeks. The killing of another man, even in self-defence, was punishable by hanging, as also was adultery with a wife of the *Fon*. But murderers—and all wrongdoers, except possibly thieves—were never convicted by the court unless the definite evidence of eye-witnesses, or of " equally certain facts " was produced.

The Mandjong Association[24]

Formerly the *Fon* had a military organization called *mandjong*, which was divided into two sections—*gham* and *baa*. Most of the villages to the north and north-east of Kimbaw belonged to *gham*, and those to the south and south-west to *baa*. Each village had its own club-house (*laf mandjong*) under a *Ta-mandjong* (Father of the Mandjong). Adult males automatically became members and met regularly for wine-drinking and hunting, and gave military service when called upon. Kimbaw itself was divided into two sections, *gham* and *baa*, each having its own club-house near the palace, and its own *Ta-mandjong*, and supreme commander, *nfoomi*.[25] The association no longer has any military function but exists for the purposes of hunting, recreation, and, until recently, the collection of taxes.

The sub-chiefdoms have their own *mandjong* associations, which are ultimately under the authority of the leading houses at Kimbaw.[26]

POLITICAL ORGANIZATION—OTHER TIKAR AREAS

The political organization of all Tikar chiefdoms, with the exception of some of the Fungom villages, is basically the same, although smaller in scale than that of the Nsaw.[27] But detailed information is not available from other areas. The following remarks are from Jeffreys's notes, and from Kaberry's notes from administrative reports.[28]

Kom

The *Fon* of Kom, like the Fon-Nsaw, built up a centralized chiefdom, although his seven sub-chiefs—of Nchang, Ake, Majang, Mejung, Basaw, Ajung, and Besanoku—had a fair amount of independence.[29] According to Jeffreys,[30] the *Fon*, having conquered these villages, established his rule and secured tribal solidarity by marriage alliances. Conquered villages were required to send girls annually to the *Fon;* they might become his wives, but more usually were married to court officials. Daughters of such marriages would become wives of village heads, or heads of lineages (*tshesi*).

The royal clan is known as Ekwü and the *Fon* is selected from a lineage referred to as Wanangebo, namely " children of Gebo " who is alleged to have been the sister of the first *Fon* of Kom. According to a genealogy collected by Kaberry there have been at least 10 chiefs, the office passing in some cases to younger brothers, in others to sisters' sons. The queen mother, *Nafon*, is usually a sister of the *Fon* and is treated with great respect. She is present at some of the important sacrifices but exercises no political or judicial functions. Ideally she should reside at Laokom, but in fact she does not always do so.

Laokom, the capital of Kom, is the residence of the *Fon*. In addition to the Ekwü clan, three other clans are represented in Laokom: Atchaf, Tinelaa, and Egan. The heads (*tshesi*) of Atchaf and Tinelaa are councillors and are said to " hold the

[24] Kaberry, 3, 1952, p. 9.
[25] Bridges, 1935, notes that each *mandjong* house in Nsaw has two *Ta-mandjong*, of whom the senior is called the *nfawme* (*nfoomi*) and the junior, *ngwang*.
[26] Bridges, 1935.
[27] Kaberry, 3, 1952, p. 8.
[28] Only Bridges's notes on Nsaw have been available for full consultation for this Survey.
[29] Evans, 1927.
[30] 1951, p. 242.

chief.'' They have important ritual duties at the installation of a new *Fon* and at the annual ceremonies for guinea-corn.

The palace of the *Fon* at Laokom had, in 1927, 252 houses of which six were his own apartments.[31]   According to a 1948 estimate, his wives numbered about 100, each of whom had her own house.[32]

The association corresponding to the Nsaw *ngwirong* is called *nkwifon*. It differs from the Nsaw association in that sons of the *Fon* join it.[33]   It carries out decrees and orders of the *Fon* and formerly executed criminals. Its members dance at the funerals of the *Fon* and other important men.[34]   According to Evans, its council consisted of the Fon and five " big men." Its messengers or *nikan* live in the *Fon*'s palace, under their head, the *Bobe-nikan*, and do not marry until they are middle-aged.

Both Jeffreys's and Evans's notes suggest that the functions of the *nkwifon* were executive rather than judicial, and that the *Fon* personally exercised more judiciary powers than the Fon-Nsaw. According to Evans, cases were tried at the *Etwi* or *Etwisa*—a circle of stones in Laokom—by the *Fon*, " elders " (*tshɛsi*), and adult sons of the *Fon*. Sub-chiefs settle minor disputes in their respective areas.[35]

The military organization of the *Fon* of Kom was called *manjon*.[36]

Bum

According to Jeffreys,[37] Bum has a council called *Tala*,[38] with 19 members. Ten of these men form the more important council called *Tshe*, the governing body of the country. *Tshe* is presumably equivalent to *Achi* or *Ache* in the official reports. Pollock[39] describes the judiciary authority of the country as being vested in the council composed of the *Achi*, with the chief of Bum as its head. *Achi* hold courts and try cases in their own villages, but appeal may be made to the chief, who hears cases in the presence of the senior *Achi* council, consisting of five men. Posts in the council are hereditary, but succession must be approved by the chief. Its senior member is the headman of Fonfuka. The *Achi* council is the chief's advisory board; it acts as a kind of jury, the chief making no decision without its full consent; it instructs *nkwifon* to carry out its orders.

Pollock describes the *nkwifon* society as having been introduced to Bum from Babungo in the Ndop area about one and a half centuries ago. Its headquarters, *ngumba*, are in the chief's compound. According to Bridges,[40] its inner circle is made up of nine men, whose positions are hereditary. *Nkwifon*, he writes, was responsible for making peace and war, for allocating land to strangers, for taking precautions in matters of hygiene, for punishing delinquents and for supervising road-work, the making of paths, etc.[41]   Its power has waned, being largely superseded by European government and native courts. *Ndatut*, a religious association with some secular functions, which would appear to overlap with those of *nkwifon*, has remained comparatively strong.[42]

In other areas chiefdoms are much smaller, being little more than large villages or groups of villages and hamlets. The information available is too scrappy and incomplete to be anything but misleading if reproduced.

[31] Evans, 1927.
[32] Jeffreys, 1951, p. 246.
[33] Evans, 1927. Kaberry's informants said that grandsons of the *Fon* might join *nkwifon*, but there was disagreement about whether his sons were eligible.
[34] Jeffreys, 1950–51, p. 96.
[35] Evans, 1927.
[36] Ibid.
[37] MS.
[38] Probably the word for lineage head. See above, p. 33.
[39] 1927.
[40] Notes on Bum.
[41] Ibid. The relationship between the *Achi* council and *nkwifon* is not very clear.
[42] Bridges, op. cit.

LAND TENURE[43]

The *Fon* is the titular owner of all Nsaw territory but, as has been noted, this has political rather than economic significance. He also has certain areas of land reserved for himself—farm-lands, hunting-grounds, areas for cutting thatching grass, etc. In addition, certain tracts near the villages of Bamgam and Waasi are vested in the *Fon*, although they are in effect common land, open to cultivation by anyone unable to obtain sufficient land by other means.

Apart from these areas, Nsaw land is divided, subject to the authority of the *Fon*, among lineage heads or *afai*, some of whom—the sub-chiefs, the more important *vibai* and the village heads—control large tracts. Usually a *fai*'s land does not form one continuous tract. Sometimes a *fai* moved to another village where he acquired new land while retaining his right to land in the ancestral settlement. Or his dependants may have increased and he had to find more land for them. Or again, a single tract of land may not include the different types of soil and elevation necessary for the variety of crops which the Nsaw grow.

Land in Nsaw cannot be pledged or sold, although it has sometimes been transferred from one *fai* to another. This usually involved the transfer of the right and obligation to perform sacrifices to the local god of the earth (*nyooiy*). There is a close tie between the land, the local god, and the people who live on and cultivate the land.

The *fai* makes the original allocation of plots among members of his lineage, his sisters' children, and among more distant relatives, affines, friends, or strangers who ask him for land. In granting land to non-members of the lineage, however, he must consider his dependants' interests first. In practice, plots tend to remain with the individual to whom they were first allocated, and with his descendants, provided they are lineal relatives. The *fai* has the responsibility of caring for kola and raffia plantations, which are really lineage property, though vested in him. He reaps the major profit from the sale of the produce, but he is expected to help his dependants in time of hardship.

De facto control of land by the *fai* is not contingent on cultivation. But this does not apply to the individual's right of usufruct in a particular plot of land allocated to him or her by a lineage head. Such rights of usufruct depend on continuous cultivation, allowing for periods of fallow, which are decided by the individual. Normally an individual expects to retain the usufruct of plots received from the heads of the lineages of both parents. Men and women have almost similar rights in this respect, although a woman usually obtains sufficient land for her needs from the *fai* of her husband or her father; and it is only when she has a large family and is living near her mother's *fai* that she is likely to make use of her ties with him.

Other Areas

The system of land tenure in most[44] other Tikar areas appears to be very similar to that of Nsaw. Where centralized political systems exist, as in Bum, Kom, and Nsaw, the *Fon* has titular claim to all land in his territory. Where the village is the largest autonomous unit, the village head exercises a similar claim in regard to village lands. But in both cases titular ownership is of secondary importance compared with the *de facto* control exercised by the heads of kinship groups within any one village. In Kom, and in the Fungom villages where descent is matrilineal, the system is reversed in that the individual has a prior claim on the land of his or her own matrilineage, and a subsidiary claim on the land of the matrilineage of his or her father.

[43] Based on Kaberry, 1950, and 3, 1952, chap. 3.
[44] Nsungli, Mbem, Bamessi, Bamungo, Bafut, Kom, and the villages of Bentsan, Mashi, Munkap, Fang, Fungom, Mme, and Zhoaw in Fungom N.A. were the other Tikar areas visited by Kaberry. There is no information on the system in French Territory.

THE LIFE CYCLE

The following information is drawn from communications from Kaberry and articles and manuscripts by Jeffreys, Sieber, and Schmidt; in most cases it refers to specific groups of Tikar.

BIRTH

Pregnant women normally continue to work on the farms until the eve of delivery. The child is usually born in the woman's own hut, but sometimes she may return to her mother's compound for the birth. A neighbour generally assists unless the birth is a difficult one, in which case a professional midwife may be called in.[1] Women rest for a period after the birth; among the Mbem-Mbaw, Sieber[2] gives eight days as the rest period, while among the Nsaw[3] it is three weeks or more.

NAME-GIVING

Among the Mbem and Mbaw, the name is given on the day of birth by the father, and is preferably the name of the grandfather, or of the eldest of the lineage.[4] A Nsungli woman usually chooses her daughter's name.[5] Twins receive special names, and are welcomed as a gift from God.[6]

The name given in childhood is kept until adulthood is reached. On the birth of their first child parents receive new names—"father of Nyeke," etc., and their old names are no longer used. Young boys and girls also have ceremonial names.[7]

INFANCY

A child is suckled until it is two years old, or sometimes longer, although solid food is given in addition from about six months.[8] After three months Nsaw women rarely carry their babies to the farm unless they are unable to find nursemaids. A child's hair is shaved off by its mother as soon as it can sit up.[9]

CHILDHOOD AND ADOLESCENCE

After the early years a girl's education is the responsibility of her mother, a boy's that of his father. Among the Nsungli, according to Sieber,[10] boys enter a " secret society " (of which he gives no details) and are circumcised at the same time, in groups of six or seven. From the age of five or six years boys are expected to assist in collecting wood and similar household tasks.[11] Later they are taught to hunt. When a youth spears his first game, he takes the animal to his mother's father; the next he takes to his own father, and the third to his mother's mother's father.[12]

A girl goes to help in the fields from an early age. From five or six years she grinds corn, washes dishes, etc., and cares for younger children.[13] Later on she is initiated into one of the women's societies.[14]

[1] Sieber, 1938 (Nsungli), and 1935 (Mbem-Mbaw).
[2] Kaberry, written communication.
[3] Kaberry, 3, 1952, p. 80.
[4] Sieber, 1935.
[5] Sieber, 1938.
[6] Jeffreys, 1950–51 (Kom, et al.).
[7] Sieber, 1935.
[8] Kaberry, 3, 1952.
[9] Sieber, 1938.
[10] 1938.
[11] Sieber, 1935.
[12] Kaberry, op. cit.
[13] Sieber, 1935.
[14] See Kaberry, op. cit.

MARRIAGE

In Nsaw, a man may not marry into his own patrilineage, nor into those of his mother, mother's mother, or mother's mother's mother.[15]

In the matrilineal groups (the five Fungom villages and Kom) marriage between cross-cousins is forbidden, but is permitted between ortho-cousins if of different lineages (i.e., between a man and his father's brother's daughter).

Marriage payment is customary in all Bamenda Tikar groups, except among the Nsaw, where the wife's kinsfolk receive a series of gifts and services throughout her lifetime and after her death if she has borne children. The cash value of the articles handed over varies from £5 or £6 in Bamessi to £10 or £15 in most other areas.[16] Usually it is reckoned in goats, shovels, cloth, or drums of oil. In addition, subsidiary gifts are made to female relatives and junior kinsmen of the bride, and the husband may also be expected to help them in house-building and harvesting, etc. Today, in such areas as Ndop and Bafut, marriage payment is frequently made almost entirely in cash. Wealthy traders or regular wage-earners may be expected to make higher payments.[17]

In the matrilineal areas the largest portion of the marriage payment is given to the father of the girl, who may or may not pass it on to his mother's brother or his own brother if either of these has helped him in obtaining a wife. Sometimes he retains it to obtain a wife for himself or for a younger brother. In Fungom a second portion, "payment of the firewood," is retained by the father of the girl for household and personal expenses, while in both Fungom and Kom another portion is given to the mother of the bride, who retains some of the goods and distributes the rest to her own mother's brother, if he is alive, to her brothers, mother, and female siblings. In the case of a woman who is the child of an unmarried mother, the mother's father takes the main payment, and the rest goes to the mother and her matrikin.[18]

Bridges gives the following information about the contracting of marriage in Nsaw: a man who wishes to marry asks the girl's fai for his consent; this gained, he must bring about five shillingsworth of mimbo in a week's time to the fai, bringing with him his relatives or friends or perhaps his mother. Friends and parents of the bride-to-be are summoned and the betrothal is announced. The day when the first marriage payment is to be made, and the marriage festivity is to take place, are decided by the fai. Girls usually marry at the age of about 16 or 17. On the marriage day the man gives a feast. After the ceremony he returns home, to be followed about a week later by his bride, who is handed over by her mother and her immediate female relatives, and is washed and rubbed with camwood for a few days before going to the farm.

Kaberry notes[19] that a woman who is given away in marriage with the consent of her fai is called a wiiy-o-noone (a woman who enters the house), or a wiiy-o-foone (a woman who is given). Her children belong to her husband's lineage, and when he dies she is expected to marry a member of his lineage who has been selected by her husband's fai; or at least to remain in the compound unless she is very old. If a woman contracts her first marriage without the consent of her fai, and efforts to secure her return have failed, her children will belong to her father's lineage, and should return there after the age of about six years. The fai of her own lineage then has the right to arrange the marriages of her daughters. Similarly the child of an unmarried woman of the lineage belongs to its mother's patrilineage. According to Bridges, it is believed that if the annual payments are not made, the children of the marriage will die, and for this reason payments are continued even after the death of the woman; this is confirmed by Kaberry. A man usually attempts to

[15] See Kaberry, op. cit.
[16] Schmidt, 1951, p. 19.
[17] Kaberry, op. cit., p. 24; Sieber, 1935, pp. 269–70.
[18] Kaberry, written communication.
[19] 3, 1952, p. 12.

collect the goods for his first instalment, although his father may assist. Sieber's notes suggest that among the Mbem-Mbaw group the parents of the man are asked to assist and negotiate the marriage.[20]

Schmidt[21] notes that among the Bamessing people young men often go to the coast to earn money for the payment for their first wife. According to a list of tax-paying males which she quotes, 473 men in the village had between them 843 wives: 262 had one wife, 152 had 2–3 wives, 34 had 4–5 wives, 18 had 6–7 wives, 6 had 7–12 wives, and the chief had 17.

Sieber noted that in the Mbem-Mbaw villages where he stayed up to 50% of the men had no second wife, partly because of lack of money, partly because of the scarcity of marriageable women.

Very little information is available concerning grounds for and frequency of divorce. Sieber notes that in Mbem-Mbaw a woman who commits adultery may be beaten by her husband if she does not confess it to him; if she does confess the lover may be brought before the chief and required to pay a fine. If she runs away with her lover, the husband may claim the return of the marriage payment.[22]

DEATH

According to Schmidt,[23] the Bamessing do not recognize natural causes of death; accusations of witchcraft may be made, or death may be attributed to the spirits. A widow goes to live on her farm, but does no work for three weeks after her husband's death; a child of the deceased mourns for one week. Most of her information concerns ceremonies held at the death of a chief.

Sieber notes[24] that all relatives collect in the hut of the dying, including if possible those from outside the village. The body is washed; formerly it was rubbed with camwood, but nowadays it is wrapped in a white cloth. The grave is dug behind, or sometimes under, the hut of the deceased, the body being protected from contact with the earth by sticks and mats. A commoner is buried lying down, a chief or other important person in a sitting position.[25] Men face east, women west, the heads of both sexes facing north. Relatives sacrifice a white cock on the grave. If the deceased was the head of a family or a village elder, the widow places on the grave an empty calabash and a pipe, which must be filled annually with palm-wine and tobacco. No money or possessions are buried with the dead.

[20] Sieber, 1935.
[21] Schmidt, 1938–39.
[22] Sieber, op. cit.
[23] 1943.
[24] Sieber, 1935.
[25] 1943.

RELIGION AND MAGIC

Belief and Ritual

According to Kaberry,[1] opinions differ as to whether there is one god (*nyooiy*) or many. Some said that there were many, but that one, unnamed like the rest, was supreme. He created the first human beings and is associated with the earth and its fertility. Prayers and sacrifices are offered to him both at the annual agricultural rituals of all the Nsaw, and by individual *afai*. According to Bridges,[2] he may send plagues if the religious ceremonies are not carried out.

The duty of supervising the general welfare of the people and of supplicating God on their behalf is entrusted to the Fon-Nsaw, the *Tawong* (High Priest), the *Yewong* (High Priestess), and Fai-o-Ndzendzef (the senior *kibai*); rites are performed at the *Lawong* (House of the Country) in Kimbaw and Kovifem, where the *afon* of Nsaw are buried. The Kimbaw ritual takes place before new crops are planted, the Kovifem ritual during the dry season before the finger-millet crop is harvested.[3] Kaberry writes: " Once a year, at the end of December when the *Fon* has given permission to his people to harvest their finger-millet, he makes the journey along the route which once linked Kovifem with the royal raffia plantations at Mba', south of Kimbaw. Minor rituals are carried out at altars along the path. . . . At Kovifem the *Fon*, with the *Yewong*, *Tawong*, and Ndzendzef, performs the major sacrifice to his ancestors and to *nyooiy* to ensure the fertility of all Nsaw land and Nsaw women."[4]

Each sub-chiefdom has similar ritual centres or " houses " called *Ewong*. There are stone altars, where offerings are made to God, in the *Lawong*, the *Ewong*, and in the compounds of many *afai*.[5]

The ancestors are regarded as intermediaries between God and their living relatives. The *fai* acts as priest for members of his lineage, and, as has been noted, *afai* of the same clan assemble for joint rituals in times of hardship. An individual may also have sacrifices made to the ancestors of his mother's patrilineage, or mother's mother's patrilineage, who are believed to have power over their descendants.[6]

Usually, annual ceremonies performed for the whole community—whether tribe or village—are carried out by men, with the assistance of the *aya* in some cases; but specific rituals are carried out by women, although they tend to be subsidiary and limited to the needs of a smaller group. Nsaw, Nsungli, Bamessi, Bum, Ndop, Kom, and Fungom all have women's societies, whose leaders invoke the blessing of God and the ancestors and brew magical herbs to endow the women with health and ensure an abundance of crops.[7] " The association between the fertility of women as childbearers, their agricultural role, and the fertility of the land, would seem to be implicit in much of the ritual. . . . On occasion an individual woman working on her farm will ask for the blessing of her female ancestors on the crops, and pour a libation of water or palm-wine if available on the ground."[8]

Diviners[9]

In Nsaw the office of *ngam* man, or diviner, is not inherited but depends on the individual's gift for the task. Diviners are consulted, when children are born,

[1] 3, 1952, p. 33.
[2] 1935.
[3] Communication from Kaberry.
[4] Kaberry, 3, 1952, p. 33.
[5] Bridges, op. cit.
[6] Kaberry, op. cit., p. 14.
[7] Ibid., pp. 97–101.
[8] Ibid., p. 151.
[9] Bridges, op. cit.

regarding the precautions that must be taken to ensure their safety. They are obliged, if they foresee famine or troubles, to inform their village head, who passes on the information to the *Fon*. The name *ngam* in Nsaw is that of a black spider used in the divination procedure.

Medicine-men[10]

Ngashi (*ngashiib*) or medicine-men have various duties: they make protective charms, dispense remedies for physical ailments and practise protective magic against witches. Some specialize in the care of children. How they learn and qualify for their craft Bridges does not state.

Charms (Nsaw) include one called *menkan*, consisting of a piece of dark wood cut from a special tree (possibly ebony).[11] Before planting, the chief wife of the *fai* obtains from each woman of the group a few grains of corn, which are treated with *menkan* by the *fai* before being shared out among all the women. All crops may then be sown, provided the *Lawong* society has held its annual meeting.[12]

Christianity and Islam

According to Bridges, in 1933 over 80% of the population of Nsaw were pagan. Kaberry notes that Islam has been introduced through the Hausa and Fulani.

Nsei (Bamessing in Ndop N.A.)

According to Schmidt, the supreme deity in Bamessing is called *Mbonga*, and is never worshipped, his name being mentioned only at important events. " Three spirits are worshipped by the whole village; the supreme one causes the birth of twins, and from his fountain the young daughters of the royal family fetch water for the annual rejuvenation of the chief."[13]

Schmidt describes[14] a 12-part annual vegetation or fertility ceremony called *Nsiä* which takes place during the dry season, at a time decided by the chief. All 13 of the village sections participate in the final ceremony. She notes that the rituals symbolize death, reconciliation, and rebirth—of what is not very clear. The following is an almost direct translation of her own synopses of the rituals:

(1) The God who gives food has died, and is mourned for by the Nsei as they would mourn a dead chief. Masked dancing takes place.

(2) Each farmer gives one hen; some of these are offered to deceased chiefs and mothers of chiefs, the rest retained by the chief for feasts during the *Nsiä*.

(3) Priests sleep in grass huts on the grave of the deceased chieftains.[15] Next day the *Nsiä* is dedicated to all gods and dead chiefs; the ceremony means death and rebirth.

(4) Virgin girls of the chief's family fetch consecrated water for the chief to drink; the drinking renews his magical powers.

(5) Women clear paths leading to " the places where the gods live." The priests make offerings at these places, which are repeated after one week has passed.

(6) The chief with his councillors and members of the secret society[16] meet in the society's drinking house. Palm-wine is brought in from each part of

[10] Bridges, op. cit.
[11] Kaberry, written communication.
[12] Bridges, op. cit.
[13] Schmidt, 1951, p. 15.
[14] 1942.
[15] Sieber, 1935, mentions a similar ceremony among the eastern Tikar groups, but gives no details.
[16] Schmidt writes: " All men can belong to the secret society by paying a small fee " But apparently chiefs' sons are excluded.

the village, and mixed with special ceremony. The rite symbolizes the new union of the chief with his people.

(7) The secret society sends men and boys dressed in leaves to bring gifts into the village. In the afternoon a dance takes place, members of the secret society and their sons taking part. The dance is repeated in front of the farm of the chief's mother. The rite symbolizes the effort to win back fertility.

(8) A rite similar to (6) is carried out, the main participants this time being members of the chief's family, who are excluded from membership of the secret society.

(9) The chief's relatives (but not the chief or his wives) make offerings on the chief's farm, and dance in the market place. They receive presents from commoners.

(10) The chief begins with a solo dance; general festivities follow, which may include guests from outside the village. The men perform a spear dance. General dancing continues for a week, symbolizing joy at the return of fertility.

(11) The day after the commencement of planting the fields an offering is made on the spot where an ancestral chief is thought to have disappeared into the earth. Masked dancers (who are " death dancers ") swear loyalty to the chief. The ceremony usually performed for childless women then takes place.

Schmidt does not describe the 12th ceremony; possibly the 11th as described here is two ceremonies; possibly the 12th is the general dancing in all the sub-villages referred to above.

D

BIBLIOGRAPHY

Ankermann, B.
" Bericht über eine ethnographische Forschungsreise ins Grasland von Kamerun."
Zeit. f. Ethnol., XLII, 1910, pp. 288–310.

Annual Reports on the Administration of the Cameroons for the Years 1946–51
Colonial Office, London: H.M.S.O.

Barth, H.
Travels in Central Africa. London, 1857.

Belleau, H.
Du Cameroun au Hoggar. Paris: Alsatia, 1945.

*Bridges, W. M.
Notes on the Bum Area, 1933 (Unpublished).
Notes on the Banso District, 1934 (Unpublished).

Bruens, A.
" The Structure of Nkom and its Relations to Bantu and Sudanic." *Anthropos,*
XXXVII/XL, 4–6, 1942–45, pp. 826–66.

Burton, R. F.
Abeokuta and the Cameroon Mountains. London: Tinsley, 1863.

*Cantle, I. L.
Notes on the Area between the Katsina River and Wukari and Gashaka
Boundaries, 1930 (Unpublished).

*Carpenter, F. W.
Notes on Mbaw, Mbem, and Mfumte Areas, Hitherto Jointly Known as the Kaka-
Ntem Area, 1933 (Unpublished).
Notes on the Nsungli Area, 1934 (Unpublished).

Cozens, A. B.
" Bamenda Wedding " (Mbem). *Nigerian Field,* XIV, 4, Oct., 1949, pp. 162–7.

*Drummond-Hay, J. C.
Notes on the Clans of the Bandop Area, 1925 (Unpublished).

Dugast, I.
" Essai sur le peuplement du Cameroun." *Et. Cam.,* I, 21/2, 1948, pp. 19–33.
Inventaire Ethnique du Sud-Cameroun. Mém. I.F.A.N. (Centre du Cameroun)
Série: Populations, No. 1, 1949.

*Evans, G. V.
Notes on the Kom (Bikom) Clan, 1927 (Unpublished).

*Gorges, E. H. F.
Notes on the Kaka-Ntem Area, 1932 (Unpublished).

Greenberg, J. H.
" Studies in African Linguistic Classification: 1. The Niger-Congo Family." *South*
Western Journal of Anthropology, V, 2, 1949, pp. 5–7.

Guernier, E.
" Cameroun-Togo." *Encyclo. de l'Afr. Française,* Paris, 1951.

*Hawkesworth, E. G.
Notes on the Banso District, 1922 (Unpublished).
Notes on the Nsungli Clans, 1924 (Unpublished).
Notes on the Bafut Area, 1926 (Unpublished).

*Hook, R. J.
Notes on the Associated Village Groups Occupying the Bafut Native Administration
Area, 1926 (Unpublished).

*Hunt, W. E.
   Notes on the Bali Clan, 1925 (Unpublished).

Hutter, F.
   " Zeremonien beim Schliessen von Blutfreundschaft bei den Graslandstämmen im
      Kamerun-Hinterland." *Mitt. Deutsch. Schutzgebieten*, V, 1892, pp. 176–8.
   Wanderungen und Forschungen im Nord-Hinterland von Kamerun. Berlin, 1902.

Jeffreys, M. D. W.
   1. " Some (West) African Tribal Names." *J. Roy. Afr. Soc.*, XLI, Jan., 1942,
      pp. 47–9.
   2. " African Suicides in the Bamenda Division, British Cameroons." *Transac. Roy.
      Soc. S. Africa*, XXX, 2, 1944, pp. 135–41.
   3. " Salep." *Farm and Forest*, VI, 3, 1945.
   4. " The Death of a Dialect." *Afr. St.*, IV, 1, 1945, pp. 37–40.
   5. " Nsangu's Head." *Afr. St.*, V, 1, 1946, pp. 57–62.
   6. " Serpents = Kings." *Nigerian Field*, XII, 1, 1947, pp. 35–41.
   7. " Notes on Twins, Bamenda." *Afr. St.*, VI, 4, 1947, pp. 189–95.
   8. " Stone-age Smiths (Fungom)." *Arch. f. Völkerkunde* (Wien), III, 1948, pp. 1–23.
   9. " Some Notes on the Bikom." *East. Anthrop.*, IV, 2, 1950–51.
   10. " Some Notes on the Fon of Bikom." *Afr. Affairs*, L, 200, 1951, pp. 241–9.
   11. " Notes on Nsaw History and Social Categories." *Africa*, XXII, 1, 1952, pp. 71–2.
   12. " Some Notes on the Bikom Blacksmiths." *Man*, LII, 75, April, 1952, pp. 49–51.
   13. Tribal Notes from Bamenda (Unpublished).

*Johnson, V. K.
   Notes on the Fungom Area, 1936 (Unpublished).

Kaberry, P. M.
   1. " Land Tenure among the Nsaw of the British Cameroons." *Africa*, XX, 4, 1950,
      pp. 307–23.
   2. " Notes on Nsaw History and Social Categories." *Africa*, XXII, 1, 1952, pp. 72–5.
   3. *Women of the Grassfields.* Colonial Research Publication No. 14. London :
      H.M.S.O., 1952.

*Kay, F. W.
   Notes on the Ndu, Mbwat, and Tang N.A. Areas, Formerly Known as the Nsungli
      Tribe, 1936 (Unpublished).

Kunike, H.
   " Narbentätovierung eines Banso-Mädchens." *Der Erdball*, II, 11, 1928, p. 243.

Mathews, A. B.
   " The Kisra Legend." *Afr. St.*, IX, 3, 1950, pp. 144–7.

Meek, C. K.
   The Northern Tribes of Nigeria. London : Oxford University Press, 1925, 2 vols.

Meyer, E.
   " Kreditringe in Kamerun." *Kol. Rundschau*, XXXI, 1940, pp. 113–21.
   " Stand und Aufgaben der Sprachforschung in Kamerun." *Z. Eing. Spr.*, XXXII,
      4, 1942, pp. 241–85.

Migeod, F. W. H.
   Through the British Cameroons. London : Heath Cranton, 1925.

Nchami, V. C.
   " Land of Polygamists " (Bikom). *W. Afr. Rev.*, XXI, 279, Dec., 1950, pp. 1,477–9.

*Newton, R.
   Notes on the Mbem and Mfumte N.A. Area, 1936 (Unpublished).

Olivier, G., *et al.*
   " Documents anthropométriques pour servir à l'étude des principales populations du
      Sud-Cameroun." *Bull. Soc. Et. Cam.*, 15–16, 1946.

Pfeffer, G.
   Die Weisse Mah. Berlin, 1929.

*Pollock, J. H. H.
    Notes on the Bum Area, 1927 (Unpublished).

Schmidt, A.
    1. " Der Markt in Nsei." *Kol. Rundschau,* XXXI, 1940, pp. 122–42.
    2. " Arbeit und Beruf im Leben der Eingeborenen von Nsei." *Kol. Rundschau,* XXXI, 1940, pp. 225–65.
    3. " Das Kornfest Nsiä: Darstellung und Psychologie des Vegetationskultus im Dorf Nsei im Grasland von Kamerun." *Arch. Afr. Anthrop.,* N.F., XXVIII, 34, 1942, pp. 89–125.
    4. " Totengebräuche in Nsei im Grasland von Kamerun." *Beiträge zur Kulturgeschichte und Linguistik* (Wien), 5, 1943, pp. 125–63.
    5. " Feld Forschungen über das Leben der Frau im Grasland von Kamerun, 1938–39." *Arch. f. Völkerkunde,* 4, 1949, pp. 165–85.
    6. " Some Notes on the Influence of Religion on Economics in a Tikar Sub-tribe." *Afr. St.,* X, 1, 1951, pp. 13–26.
    7. Unpublished MSS.

Sieber, D. and J.
    " Das Leben des Kindes im Nsungli-Stamm." *Africa,* XI, 2, 1938, pp. 208–20.

Sieber, J.
    " Aus dem sozialen Leben der Nord-Tikar." *Zeit. f. Ethnog.,* LXXVII, 5/6, 1935, pp. 269–78.

*Smith, J. S.
    Notes on the Clans of the Fungom Native Court Area, 1929 (Unpublished).

Talbot, P. Amaury
    The Peoples of Southern Nigeria. London: Oxford University Press, 1926, Vol. IV.

Thorbecke, F.
    " Die Tikar." *Deutsche Kolonialzeitung,* XXXI, 18, 1914, pp. 296–7.
    Im Hochland von Mittel-Kamerun. Hamburg, 1919, 3 vols.

Westermann, D., and Bryan, M. A.
    Languages of West Africa. London: Oxford University Press for International African Institute, 1952.

Zintgraff, E.
    Nord-Kamerun. Berlin, 1895.

* Notes taken by Dr. Phyllis Kaberry on the Assessment and Intelligence Reports which she has kindly made available to the International African Institute and the author of this Survey.

II. THE BAMUM OF THE FRENCH CAMEROONS

LOCATION AND DISTRIBUTION

NOMENCLATURE

The peoples here termed Bamum are referred to variously in the literature as Môm, Banun, or Bamoum; they call themselves *Shupaman*. There is similar variation in the spelling of village names depending on whether the English, French, or German version is given. There are three suggested derivations of the name Bamum:[1]

(1) In his *History*, King Njoya writes that Nchare, the first king of the Bamum, called his people *Pa-mom* because he set out from his natal chiefdom at Rifum on the day known as *Fmtmom*.[2] Martin states that this derivation is unlikely to be the correct one, since, according to tradition, it was not Nchare but Manju, the third king, who gave the Bamum the names of the week.

(2) The name Môm may have come from the verb *yi mommə*, which means to dissemble, or conceal, *Pa-mom* therefore meaning " those who dissemble."

(3) Another suggested derivation of the name Môm is from *Nji-mom*, a village where Nchare first settled before going on to Fumban, and over whose people he proclaimed himself king.

LOCATION

The territory of the Bamum, who number approximately 79,850,[3] is situated 10° 30′ to 11° 10′ east and 5° to 6° north; it has an area of roughly 2,812 sq. miles. To the north it borders on the British Cameroons and the chiefdom of Banso or Nsaw; to the west and south-west across the Nun River lies Bamileke country; the Mbam and Mape rivers form its eastern boundary beyond which stretches the territory of the French Cameroons Tikar. To the south lies Banen country.

ETHNIC GROUPING AND TRIBAL MIXTURE

The Bamum population is composed of two different ethnic groups. There are those people of Sudanic origin who, some 250 years ago, broke away from Tikar, settled at Rifum and moved southwards; secondly there are Bamileke people who were found living in present-day Bamum country and who were conquered by the invaders. According to Olivier, the assimilation of these Bamileke people is not yet complete and there are physical differences distinguishing these two elements of the population.[4] They all speak a common language—the invaders having adopted that of the autochthones—and are united in a centralized political system. About 1,660[5] Tikar live to the north of the Mvi River, and these have for a considerable period come under the authority and jurisdiction of the Bamum king. Other peoples living in Bamum territory include Hausa, settled largely in Fumban, the

---

[1] Martin, 1951.

[2] King Njoya wrote a book describing the history and customs of his people, which has been translated by Pasteur Martin.

[3] These are 1951 figures and have been supplied by the Director of Centrifan (Centre local de l'Institut Français d'Afrique Noire), Douala.

[4] Olivier. *Bulletin de la Société d'Etudes Camerounaises*, Sept.–Dec., 1946, numéros 15–16, p. 30.

[5] Figures for 1951 supplied by the Director of Centrifan, Douala.

capital; Bamileke,[6] both in Fumban and on the rich lands around Fumbot; and Fulani herdsmen living in the Mbapit Mountains.

A large number of Bamum (17,000) is settled in Fumban, the capital of the country where the king or sultan has his palace. All social and cultural investigations made among the Bamum have been centred upon this large section of the population, probably because the great majority of the descendants of the conquerors live within the capital. Martin writes that if any of these descendants live elsewhere in the country, as, for instance, on the coffee plantations to the west of Fumban, they all come back to the capital at some time during the year to spend a few days or even months.[7] Unlike the Bamileke, very few Bamum are found outside their own territory.

DEMOGRAPHY[8]

Population figures from 1944 show a steady increase. The figures for 1944 were as follows:

Sub-division	Male	Female	Total
Fumban	28,900	27,400	56,300
Fumbot	9,600	9,100	18,700
Totals for Bamum region ..	38,500	36,500	75,000

By 1951 population figures for Fumban Sub-division had risen to 57,750, and those for Fumbot Sub-division to 22,100. Fumban town itself had 17,000 inhabitants and Fumbot town 7,511. The latest figures are as follows:

Sub-division	Population
Fumban	60,791
Fumbot	22,045
Total for Region ..	82,836

POPULATION DENSITY

The following figures are available for 1951:

Sub-division	Approx. Area (sq. miles)	Population	Approx. Density
Fumban	1,875	57,750	30·8
Fumbot	937·5	22,100	23·5
Totals for Region.. ..	2,812·5	79,850	28·4

In the same year the density of Fumban town, which has an area of roughly 3.5 sq. miles, was 4,857. The density of the total Bamum region today is given as 11.13 per sq. kilometre, i.e., c. 29 per sq. mile.

[6] This does not, of course, refer to the descendants of the conquered Bamileke population It refers to immigrant Bamileke coming from the right bank of the Nun. See " Migration " Section for Bamileke, pp. 90-4.
[7] Martin, op. cit., p. 12. In the existing literature, the term Bamum is often synonymous with Fumban and its inhabitants.
[8] All figures supplied by the Director of Centrifan, Douala.

TRADITIONS OF ORIGIN AND HISTORY

BEFORE THE INVASION[9]

Before the Bamum occupied the territory in which they live today, it was inhabited by Tikar and Bamileke. The Tikar occupied the area to the north and south-east of the Mvi River; 22 of their villages were established between the Mvi and the Mape, and four others were in the Mvi Valley, between the Mvi and Nchi Rivers.

To the south of the Mvi there were a number of Bamileke chiefdoms. When the territory was invaded, most of the Tikar remained where they were; two of their villages were abandoned and the inhabitants crossed the Mbam River. After attempting to resist the invaders, some of the Bamileke left the territory, either crossing the Nun River or moving in the direction of Bali or Nsaw country into what is now the British Cameroons. The remainder were conquered and came under the rule of the Bamum king.

AFTER THE INVASION

The establishment of the Bamum kingdom and the major events in its history are described by Idrissou Mborou Njoya.[10] Nchare, the founder of the ruling dynasty, was the son of a Tikar chief living at Mbouakou, known to the Bamum as Rifum. He emigrated with his followers, crossing the Mape and Mvi Rivers. Jeffreys states that the natives regard famine, population pressure, and internecine struggles for the kingship as the causes of this migration which took place over 250 years ago.[11] Nchare settled first at Dji-Mom (Nji-Mom), a village to the north-east of Fumban, and rallied round him many of the inhabitants of the country, including 18 chiefs who accepted his authority. He proclaimed himself king and the royal residence was established at Mfom-Ben, the site of present-day Fumban. Nine of his descendants and successors to the throne did not seek to enlarge the territory ruled by the first king, Nchare. Then King Mbouo Mbouo, or Mbuembue,[12] son of King Konatou, declared that he would fix the boundaries of his territory at the Mbam and Nun Rivers. A long series of wars followed, resulting in the conquest of this territory, and 48 chiefs were forced to submit to Mbuembue's authority. It was during his reign, at the beginning of the 19th century, that Fumban was attacked and severely damaged by the Fulani;[13] the king fled and did not return till the Fulani had gone. One of Mbuembue's councillors, Njifenkoundou, suggested that deep trenches should be dug round the town for defence, but this was considered a cowardly proposal and he was put to death. Forifoun, the Tikar king of Bankim, however, sent word to Mbuembue that the suggestion was a sound one, and that the Fulani would always conquer Fumban unless trenches were built.[14] Consequently ditches and fortifications around Fumban were ready for the next Fulani attack, in which the Bamum defeated them.

The reigns of the next four kings were marked by conflicts and rivalry within the royal household.[15] Then followed the reign of Nsangu. He continued to wage wars and was killed fighting against the Nsaw about 1888. Jeffreys gives various accounts of this war including the events which led to the death of Nsangu and the final recovery of his skull.[16]

Nsangu was succeeded by his son Njoya, then a child, his mother acting as regent until he was old enough to rule. In his *History* Njoya states that in

[9] Dugast, 1949, pp. 126–7.
[10] Idrissou Mborou Njoya, 1935, p. 81.
[11] Jeffreys, 3, 1946, p. 57.
[12] Despois (1945) gives 1757–1814 as the dates of his reign.
[13] Dubié, 1949–50.
[14] Ibid.
[15] Dugast, op. cit., p. 126.
[16] Jeffreys, op. cit., pp. 57–62.

1920 he had been king for 25 years; thus, on his reckoning, he must have come to the throne in 1895.[17]

On his accession, Njoya dismissed from his position and from the capital a certain Bentkom, who had been a councillor during the period of his mother's regency.[18] Bentkom rallied his own supporters around him, including two of Njoya's brothers, with the intention of killing the king and acquiring the throne for himself. Only Fumban and two villages supported Njoya, and the stronger position of Bentkom led Njoya to seek the aid of the *Lamido* of Banyo, promising him generous gifts in return for his help. The *Lamido* sent cavalry troops and achieved a brilliant victory over Bentkom, who was later burnt alive on the orders of Njoya. The Fulani soldiers remained in Fumban for a month, collecting the promised gifts, which included 15,000 prisoners, 8 young girls, 170 loads of salt, and 300 pots of palm-oil. Njoya retrieved some of these by attacking the Fulani on their return journey, informing the *Lamido* that the raid was the work of rebel Bamum who would be put to death.

Njoya was deposed by the French in 1923[19] and died in 1933. He was the 16th Bamum king since they became independent of their Tikar parent stock. The present king or sultan, Hadj Seidou Njmoluh, is one of Njoya's sons.

MODERN DEVELOPMENTS

The Administration

For administrative purposes the French at first grouped Bamileke and Bamum territory together into a single Region, the Nun Region, which comprised the Sub-divisions of Dschang, Fumban, Bafang, Bafoussam, and Bangangte. Later Bamum country itself was given the status of a Region, and it now comprises the two Sub-divisions of Fumban and Fumbot, each with its Sub-divisional head. Fumban, the capital of the country, is the headquarters of the Region where the Regional Head is established.

Two roads run through Bamum country, linking it with Bamileke country and these are being extended to form a single road, now under construction, to Banyo.

Islam and Christian Missionary Activities

A fairly detailed description of the processes whereby Islam spread throughout Bamum country is given by Dubié.[20] He traces the beginnings of its popularity among the Bamum to the success of the *Lamido* of Banyo's troops in routing Bentkom's army. When Njoya asked what magic he used, the *Lamido* informed him that his strength lay in his Mohammedan faith and prayer. Njoya had been impressed with the communal prayer of the Fulani soldiers during their stay in Fumban, and he and certain members of his family and other titled men in the town proceeded to practise this same form of prayer. Since their visit, moreover, he had taken to wearing flowing robes and turban and had become interested in horses, exchanging prisoners for them at Banyo. The presence of Hausa traders who were beginning to settle in Fumban was another factor promoting an interest in and adherence to the Mohammedan religion, establishing as they did regular contact between Bamum country and Kano, Yola, and Adamawa through their economic activities.

The Germans reached Fumban in 1902 and the first Protestant missionaries in 1906. Njoya was impressed by their teaching and commanded members of his family and others to give up Moslem prayers. The small mosque which had been built was destroyed by Njoya and he erected a chapel in its place. He sent several of his children to the Mission school. Since he would not agree to give up all but one of his wives, Njoya was never baptized but continued for a time to support

---

[17] Jeffreys, op. cit., p. 62.   Jeffreys, however, considers this date too recent.
[18] Dubié, op. cit., pp. 5–6.
[19] Ibid., p. 31.
[20] Dubié, op. cit., *passim*.

and help the missionaries. Later, however, he again fell under the influence of Islam, for considerable numbers of Hausa began to arrive in Fumban, forming a colony of about 2,000; and, furthermore, the German missionaries were forced to leave Fumban in 1915. Njoya consequently declared himself a Mohammedan and forbade the practice of Christianity. Those who remained Christians were persecuted. Njoya now began to call himself sultan, destroyed the chapel and built another mosque. However, in order to reinforce his position as chief, which he feared might dwindle in importance in the face of the activities of the Administration, Christian Missions (the French Protestants had arrived in 1917), and Islam, he devised a new religion of which he was to be the leader. He expounded its doctrine in his book, *Nouot Nkwete (Endeavours and Achievements)*, and claimed that it amalgamated the best in the Bible and the Koran. But Njoya failed in his attempts to gain adherents for his new religion and finally abandoned it himself, being converted to Islam in 1918. His son, Koutou Aboubakan, was the first Bamum to become an Iman in 1937. Realizing, however, that Catholic and Protestant Missions were firmly established in his country, Njoya maintained friendly relations with them and came to approve of freedom of faith for his subjects. Today Islam is spreading rapidly to all the outlying areas of Bamum country and mosques have been built everywhere.

Dubié tabulates the position of the Christian Missions and Islam as follows:

	Number of Churches, Chapels and Mosques	Number of Adherents	Teachers	Number of Pupils
Protestants	64	11,300	21	903
Catholics	48	4,000	18	592
Mohammedans ..	44	Between 20,000 and 30,000	62	716

LANGUAGE

Greenberg places the Bamum language in the Bantu sub-group of his central branch of the Niger-Congo family of languages.[1] Dugast, on the other hand, claims that the Bamum are a Semi-Bantu-speaking people, and that they learnt their language from the autochthones whom they conquered on coming into the area.[2]

Westermann and Bryan treat the Bamum, with the Bamileke, as an isolated language group, considering the inclusion of these languages into a wider classification to be premature since linguistic knowledge of the area is inadequate.[3] Bamum (own name: *Shupamam*) is spoken throughout the administrative area of Fumban, and it is also used as a lingua franca in the southern part of Ndop Tribal Area in the British Cameroons.

Westermann and Bryan list the following characteristics of the Bamum language:

(1) There are noun classes. Plurals are formed by: (*a*) change of prefix; (*b*) change of tone; (*c*) reduplication. Some nouns do not distinguish between singular and plural.

(2) There appears to be no concord. The demonstrative distinguishes number, not class.

(3) The word order in the simple sentence is subject—verb—object.

THE WRITTEN LANGUAGE OF THE BAMUM

In 1907, the missionary Göhring reported the existence of a script which was the invention of the Bamum king or sultan, Njoya;[4] it was later reported on by Delafosse in 1922 and by Labouret in 1935.[5]

In 1936 Dr. Jeffreys, who was then carrying out administrative duties at Bamenda in the British Cameroons, discovered that Musa, a son of Njoya, was living there in voluntary exile, and had in his possession a copy of one of his father's books. Jeffreys made a thorough investigation of the script, analysing the changes and developments which took place before the appearance of its final form. In 1947 Jeffreys sent the results of his researches to Madame Dugast, who was able to consult Njoya's scribes and also many hundreds of documents at Fumban. Their joint investigations resulted in the publication of *L'Ecriture des Bamum*, the most authoritative work on the subject.[6]

Göhring describes how, in the reign of Njoya's father, Nsangu, Hausa merchants brought into Fumban certain very old books in Arabic script. Nsangu bought seven of these. It is possible, therefore, that even at an early age Njoya was shown and took an interest in his father's books. He was later to see both German and English scripts. He himself describes the invention of his own script and alphabet in his book *The History of the Laws and Customs of the Bamum;* from Jeffreys's translation of this we learn that Njoya had a dream in which he was told to make the mark of a man's hand on a plank of wood, then to wash it and drink the water. Later, Njoya told his courtiers to mark out many signs and bring them to him; this they did, and after consultation with two Mohammedan Mallams, his first alphabet was ready.[7]

[1] Greenberg, 1949.
[2] Dugast, 1949, p. 127.
[3] Westermann and Bryan, 1952, pp. 130, 131–2.
[4] 1, 1907.
[5] See Bibliography, pp. 84, 85.
[6] Dugast and Jeffreys, 1950.
[7] Jeffreys, 1952, p. 429.

The work of Dugast and Jeffreys shows that Njoya's dream came to him between 1895 to 1896. Altogether, Njoya devised seven alphabets; his first one contained roughly 510 signs, his fourth 205, and his last 83, 10 of which were numerals. Bamum is a tone language, and Dugast discovered that Njoya introduced tonal indications when the meaning of a homologue had to be made clear. After he had invented his script Njoya opened a school at Fumban, where he taught a large number of his people. Scribes were installed in the courts and cases were recorded.

Njoya commanded some of his scribes to interview the old people and record the histories, laws, and customs of the Bamum and surrounding peoples. When this was completed he invented another script, the royal script, in which the history, all but the last 27 chapters, was recopied.[8] It was this second, incomplete, copy which Jeffreys found in Musa's possession. A replica of this book is now housed in the Pitt-Rivers Museum, Oxford.

Njoya ordered one of his courtiers to prepare a printing press; but when, after seven years' work, this man was ready to begin the printing, casting the type by the *cire-perdue* method, Njoya destroyed the type in anger. The book which Njoya wrote expounding his own religion has already been referred to. Dugast and Jeffreys have established that this book was written between 1916 and 1917. In 1922 Njoya brought out a second edition of this treatise on religion; with the help of two Hausa Mallams, Isofu and Meriga, he added to it a large number of texts and Mohammedan prayers. In yet another book which Njoya wrote, he described the medicines and medical treatment employed among the Bamum. As well as writing his books, Njoya also drew a map of his territory with the help of 20 specially chosen men. The work was begun in 1912 and finished in 1920. Nji Mama, who was Njoya's principal assistant in the work, and his brother were then given the responsibility of drawing and annotating the map. The map is reproduced in *L'Ecriture des Bamum*.[9]

---

[8] Dugast, 1950, pp. 231–60.
[9] See also Struck, 1908, pp. 206–9.

PHYSICAL ENVIRONMENT

The Bamum plateau land is very similar to Bamileke country in that it is mountainous and transitional between the southern forest zone and the true savanna zone to the north. It does, however, display more characteristics of the latter zone and its mountains do not reach the height of those in Bamileke country.

To the south, the plateau is 2,296 ft. high, rising in the north to 3,937 ft. and sinking to 1,968 ft. to the east. Several large mountain ranges rise up from the plateau reaching a height of 8,202 ft., and include those of the Mbam, Nkogam, and Mbapit, which succeed each other in a north to south direction. The country is watered by three principal affluents of the Mbam, all of which run a parallel course—the Mvi, the Nchi, which passes through Fumban, and the Nja. Only the southern triangle of the country, between the Nun and Mbam Rivers, is watered by affluents of the Nun. Dugast divides the country into four geographical zones as follows:[1]

(1) In the west, extending to the centre of the country, volcanic mountain ranges slope down to the Nun River whose waters have decomposed the rocks, giving rise to rich black soil and red clays. This particularly is the area where European coffee plantations are found. In its most northerly course, the Nun River spreads out into a swampy marsh-like region.

(2) The Fumban plateau is situated to the east of these mountains. This is rather flat, savanna-like country and the soil is poor. Here are found wide bare stretches of territory sometimes relieved by groves and gallery forests of raffia-palms near rivers and at the foot of the mountains.

(3) To the south, the plateau slopes down following an uneven rocky course towards a low flat plain through which flow several affluents of the Mbam. The valleys are covered with shrubs and bushes which become more dense as the forest zone is approached.

(4) There is finally the Mbam Valley, a true forest area, 12½ miles wide, where a large variety of trees grow in abundance.

Soils are not uniformly good throughout Bamum country; the black or grey soil around Fumbot, where there is a great deal of coffee-growing, is particularly rich in lime and potash. The high valleys in the mountains sometimes have these fertile lands, but for the most part the soils on the slopes of the mountains are not thick and are very stony.

Climate and Rainfall

There is little variation in temperature throughout the year. Despois gives the maximum annual mean temperature for Fumbot as 81.6° F., and the minimum annual mean as 57.4° F.[2] February is the month when the maximum annual mean is at its highest; in Fumbot it then reaches 86.4° F. In January the minimum annual mean is at its lowest, 51.3° F.[3]

The annual rainfall at Fumbot is 65.7 ins., but there is great variation over the year. From early November to February a dry dusty wind blows almost continuously and there is very little rain, the dryest months being December and January. The rainy season begins in March, when there are heavy intermittent showers. These gradually become more regular until September when the rains

[1] Dugast, 1949, p. 124.
[2] Despois, 1945.
[3] Ibid., p. 599.

are at their heaviest; during this month as much as 1.2 ins. of rain may fall in a day. The rains cease abruptly in October. As in Bamileke country, therefore, there are two cultivation periods, one from March to July and another from August to December.

MAIN FEATURES OF ECONOMY

AGRICULTURE

The economy of the Bamum has many features in common with that of the Bamileke. Despois reports that cultivated areas are not so large to the east of the Nun River, and are not usually fenced round.[4]

Bamum state that on their arrival in the country they were acquainted only with the cultivation of the two varieties of millet and manioc; at a later stage they learnt about maize-growing, and this took the place of millet, which grew poorly in the area. Crops are inter-sown on the same cultivation plot, as among the Bamileke. Manioc and the sweet potato are the chief foods after maize.

Groundnut production has recently increased. There are many oil-palms in the gallery forest stretching along the Mbam Valley, and banana trees grow round compounds. Coffee is a recent introduction; plantations are grouped round Baigom to the east of the Nun on good rich soils. An area of 26,250 acres, to the south-west of Fumban and in the valley of the Nun, has been granted to 30 or more French colonists for the cultivation of coffee.[5] At Mantum, the sultan owns vast cocoa plantations. The Bamum seldom hunt, and then only in the dry season at the time when the grassland is burnt. Animal flesh is often smoked and then stored for a considerable time.[6]

Most of the cattle in the country are kept by European planters, who use the dung for fertilizing their plantations. There are also Fulani cattle-keepers on the Mbapit Mountains. King Njoya is reported to have possessed 4,000 oxen.[7] There are a few horses and most people possess a certain number of chickens and goats.

There is some fishing, and fish are often smoked and stored.

The Bamum are not traders to the extent that the Bamileke are. Some are engaged in the sale of kola nuts, which was formerly the monopoly of the sultan,[8] but for the most part trading is in the hands of the Hausa and increasingly in the hands of the Bamileke. Formerly the court absorbed a great part of the farm produce and livestock. Thirty years ago the Bamum had to provide it with about 4,000 goats, 2,000 calabashes of oil, and 1,000 baskets of maize each year; moreover they had to work without payment on the sultan's lands.[9] Rein-Wuhrmann states that taxation on farm produce varied according to the amount of land a man possessed and the number of workers at his disposal. If the harvest was a bad one, he could request a reduction in the taxes for which he was liable, and this was usually granted.[10]

A man's farm-land may surround his compound, or lie some considerable distance away from it.[11]

DIVISION OF LABOUR

According to Dugast, both men and women farm the land,[12] although Rein-Wuhrmann leads one to believe that the women do most of the work.[13] Both sexes join in hut-building but the crafts are usually the work of the men, some being specialists; the women are the potters.

---

[4] Despois, 1945, p. 628.
[5] Ibid., p. 629.
[6] Rein-Wuhrmann, 1917, p. 22.
[7] Dugast and Jeffreys, 1950, p. viii.
[8] Despois, op. cit.
[9] Ibid.
[10] Rein-Wuhrmann, op. cit., p. 90.
[11] Hutter, 1907, pp. 26–32.
[12] Dugast, 1949, p. 127.
[13] Rein-Wuhrmann, op. cit., p. 24.

MARKETS

These are held frequently in all areas; very large markets are held in Fumban and Fumbot twice weekly.[14]   Agricultural produce, palm-oil, and livestock are brought for sale as well as the craftsmen's goods.   The Hausa have their own place in these more important markets selling their goods which include leather and iron products.   There were always slave dealers in the markets even up to the time of the 1914–18 war.   Formerly goods were largely bartered for cowrie shells, but European currency has now been introduced.   Lieutenant Hirtler, who made an expedition into the country early in the century, states that the markets were held in Fumban every day in different wards and that from time to time, apart from the ordinary market, a special one was held in which ivory and horses were exchanged for food produce and other goods.[15]

The *ta ngu*[16] was responsible for the maintenance of order in the markets held in the capital, and any brawls or disturbances brought to the notice of the ward head were reported to him.

CRAFTS

House Construction[17]

The most common type of house found in Bamum country is very similar to the Bamileke house, with square mud walls and a thatched roof.   It is in the roof construction that the main difference lies, for the framework is much lighter and simpler in the Bamum house, and it is four-sided; the characteristic tall summit of the Bamileke roof is also lacking.   When the walls are erected they are held in place by large stones and are finally covered with clay.   Nowadays it is more usual to find walls built of a coarse brick.   The ceiling may project beyond the walls for as much as 29 ins. and it is sometimes supported by wooden columns.   The roof, consisting of four separate sides, is made of a framework of rattan sinews and raffia mid-ribs to which are attached bundles of dried grass.

Houses are frequently decorated with frescoes, and the doors may be embellished with geometrical designs.   Exterior walls are often smeared all over with red, yellow, grey, or white clays.

There are other, though rarer, types of hut noted by Binet: one of these is hemispherical in shape, made of branches and straw, and used as a temporary dwelling by those who fish in the Nun River.   Binet also observed an oval-shaped house which may formerly have been more common in Bamum country.[18]   Finally, Binet briefly reports the existence of circular houses with conical roofs.

House Furniture

The typical house consists of a single room and a granary, this being situated between the ceiling and roof.   There are rarely separately constructed granaries.

Near the door is usually found a construction of bamboo shelves on which cooking utensils are placed; it also serves as a screen against the wind when the door is opened.   In the centre of the room is the oval-shaped pottery hearth, seven to eight inches high.   Its sides are decorated with geometric patterns.   On one end of the hearth are five raised stones which serve to support the cooking pots over the fire; embers are kept on the other end at night.   The wall opposite the door may be taken up with a kind of hanging cupboard, which is about three to four feet above the ground; three bamboo planks form a set of shelves which are partly enclosed by a framework of raffia mid-ribs.   Beneath this there is a strip of carefully beaten earth shaped to receive convex-bottomed pots.   Against another wall is

[14] Hutter, op. cit., pp. 44–7.
[15] Dugast and Jeffreys, 1950, p. 16.
[16] See Section entitled " The Capital " under Political Organization, p. 66.
[17] Binet, 1950, p. 189.
[18] Ibid., p. 193.

placed a bed; this is constructed of raffia mid-ribs placed side by side and fixed into a framework by means of wooden pegs. It is raised up on four wooden legs which may be sculpted with figures regarded as classical in Bamum country—two-headed serpents, spiders, or perhaps geometrical designs.

Stools, baskets, flat grinding-stones, and a ladder for reaching the granary complete the general list of furniture and domestic utensils. Sometimes an important rich man may build for his favourite wife a more elaborate house, containing a wider variety of furniture and possessing perhaps two rooms. Men's houses, more frequently than women's, may have two or three rooms.

Canoe-building[19]

Canoes known to the Bamum as *pah* are used on gently flowing rivers and lakes. They are constructed of raffia-palm mid-ribs, rattan-cane, and small pieces of timber. A long stick is used to propel the canoe.

Dancing-masks

These may be carved in wood, made of terra cotta, or even of bronze, by the *cire-perdue* process, which was known to the Bamum before their first contact with the Germans in 1899. The mask is often placed above the face on the head, and the face is concealed by means of raffia attached to the base of the mask. Lecoq has noted a development in the execution of the mask faces over the past 60 years; from being idealized and figurative they have become gradually more life-like and realistic.[20] In decorative designs, on the other hand, he notes the opposite development; thus a realistic portrayal of an animal such as the toad has gradually become highly symbolized.

Carving and Sculpture

Stools, door-posts, and wooden boxes may be elaborately carved with human and animal figures depicting realistic scenes. The Bamum are also very skilled in carving statues and statuettes, which may be highly stylized or even caricatures.[21]

The craftsman's instruments are few: a matchet to cut the wood which is to be worked, a knife to chip and shape, and a nail with which the details of the particular carving are initially marked out.

Embroidery

This is also men's work. Men's trousers, as well as strips and squares of material, are embroidered, and great skill is shown in the selection and arrangement of the colours used in a pattern; typical motifs are circles, semi-circles, squares, and diamond shapes.

Stencil-plate and Batik work show the use of the same motifs, but here several may be combined to form a single pattern. The stencil-plate craftsman places his diamond-shaped, triangular, or rectangular pieces of leather on to the material and draws their contours with a stick soaked in a blue dye. He can execute what designs he pleases by adding more blue dye; such designs are made up spontaneously by the craftsman.

Bead-working

Beads are used to decorate calabashes, masks, and sometimes sculptures. The sultan's throne is partially ornamented in this way. The object to be decorated is first covered with a piece of material through which two holes are pierced; the beads are strung on to a cotton thread which is then passed through the two holes until the desired design is completed.

[19] Arouna Njoya, 1945.
[20] Lecoq, 1951, pp. 175–81.
[21] Truitard, 1934, pp. 2–7.

Leather-working

Cushions and footwear are the most usual objects made. Tanned sheepskins are dyed yellow, red, green, beige, or black, and the work may be decorated with patterns applied by the stencil-plate technique.

The Two-headed Snake Design

Jeffreys throws light on the origin of this design or motif.[22] According to Bamum tradition, the notion of the two-headed snake goes back to the time of King Mbuembue; his power and might were held in such regard that he was likened to a snake with two heads, so difficult was it to escape from him or to overcome him. From that time the snake motif was probably used only on objects royally possessed, and a belief grew up that a strong bond existed between king and snake. Jeffreys quotes a passage from the Sultan Njoya's *History* of the Bamum, in which he gives permission to all his people to use the snake motif in the carvings on their beds and in the designs of their head-coverings. He also gave permission for the use of the tarantula and chameleon motifs.

Other crafts are: cotton-weaving, basket-making, bronze-working, which includes the making of spears, pins, small bells, pipes, bracelets, and necklaces; forging, and pottery, the last being the women's work.

These crafts flourished and developed particularly during the reign of Njoya, who encouraged and patronized his craftsmen. At Fumban the French have formed an association of craftsmen of all kinds, who work in special huts in the road known as the " craftsmen's road." There is now also a museum of native art in Fumban.

[22] 1945, p. 7.

LOCAL AND KIN GROUPING

The inadequacy of the material at present available is most apparent when attempting to describe the social and political organization.[1] No comprehensive study of Bamum kinship has yet been published and since this aspect of native life was ignored or only briefly mentioned by early explorers and missionaries, there is very little information at our disposal. The following account is based mainly on brief statements made in the writings of Binet, Rein-Wuhrmann, Dugast, and Hutter.

The Bamum trace descent patrilineally and practise patrilocal marriage. It appears that, as among the Tikar, the localized exogamous patrilineage is the basis of the social organization.

LOCAL ORGANIZATION

The Household

A married woman has her own hut which she shares with her small children; married women's houses are built in two straight lines on either side and in front of the house of the household head. Binet reports that since the introduction of Mohammedanism, this plan has remained the same except in certain cases where women's houses are placed behind those of the household head—a practice which is thought to be related to the custom of the claustration of women.[2]

When a son marries he builds a hut for himself and his bride, but the literature does not make it clear whether it is within his father's compound or near it. There may be no fixed rule for this.

The head of the household eats his meals alone; if children or slaves are present, they eat from their own bowls. Women eat in their own huts.[3]

The Compound

There are no available statistics showing sizes of compounds, but it appears that there is considerable variation. Binet writes that sons and brothers of the compound head build their huts within a small radius around his.[4] It also seems that there may be a series of smaller compounds built near each other, the males and unmarried female members of which are all related agnatically and come under the authority of the head of the large compound who acts as the lineage head.

Compounds are usually surrounded by banana plantations and gardens, but the main farming land may be a considerable distance away.

The Village

A series of patrilineal groups living in compounds, as described above, make up a village under the authority of a village head. He is responsible for the maintenance of order within the village and for carrying out the commands of the king. Villages are dispersed and vary considerably in size, which may account for the apparent contradictions in the literature. Thus Dugast writes that " the Bamum live in large villages,"[5] whereas Hutter states that, apart from the thickly populated centres, settlements are few and small.[6]

---

[1] The Ethnological Institute of Paris has undertaken to publish a comprehensive work by Dr. Koch on the Bamum, which should be of great value in remedying this deficiency
[2] Binet, 1950.
[3] Rein-Wuhrmann, 1917, pp. 23–7.
[4] Binet, op. cit., p. 189.
[5] Dugast, 1949, p. 119.
[6] Hutter, 1907, pp. 1–6. It may be also that they have taken a different type of unit to mean a village.

E

Dellenbach states that formerly a mighty warrior might receive a village as a reward for his services.[7]

The Clan

There is almost no information on the clan structure of the Bamum. Martin makes the single statement that each clan has its own secret society (*yu nju*) whose importance varies with that of the clan; it appears that all male clan members have the right to belong to the clan *yu nju*, but not all invariably do so.[8]

POLITICAL ORGANIZATION

It will be remembered that the Bamum kingdom was created by a group who broke away from Tikar and who, on entering the territory about 200 years ago, conquered the independent chiefdoms and villages. Today most of the descendants of the ruling group live in the capital, Fumban; the majority of those living outside it are the descendants of the conquered population.

THE CAPITAL, THE ADMINISTRATIVE CENTRE

The first king of the Bamum, Nchare, established the royal residence on the site of present-day Fumban, then called Mfomben (Fomben: *fom* = ruin, *mben* = the Mben, the name of the local inhabitants).[9] Today it has an area of about three square miles and a population of about 17,000. In 1905 there were 500 Hausa settled in the capital,[10] and a number of Bamileke traders. The town has often been called the " show-piece " of the Cameroons, with its craftsmen's road, museum, and palace. The palace, built by Njoya and recently reconstructed, has numerous courtyards, rooms, and passageways.[11] The fortifications built round Fumban can still be seen. They were constructed about 100 years ago[12] in order to defend the capital against Fulani attacks. The first of these attacks was made during the reign of the fifth Bamum king, Ngu the First, and two more successful attacks were made during Mbuembue's reign.[13] The outer defences consist of deep holes hidden by grass; behind these extends a deep ditch which is overlooked by a wall, about seven feet high, surrounding the town.

Most of the following information on the administration of Fumban comes from Labouret[14] and Martin.[15] The town is divided into eight wards, named as follows: Mfeuyouom, Mfeunntin (Mfintan),[16] Manka, Njise (Njisse), Zinnka, Zinntut, Kounnga (Nkunga), Mamben. Each ward has its own head who comes within the category of officials known as *mfoyomə*.[17] Other *mfoyomə* and their duties are discussed below (p. 67). The deputy of the ward head is known as the *ngbatnyifoyomə*. Martin writes that the ward head is chosen by the people over whom his authority extends and that he remains in office for three years. The king has the right to depose him at any time. It is to the *mfoyomə* that the king makes initial allocations of land, and it is part of his duty to distribute it fairly among his people. Formerly the ward head had the responsibility of sounding the alarm by ringing a special bell when he was warned of a threatened attack upon the town. He also reports army recalcitrants

[7] Dellenbach, 1931.
[8] Martin, 1951, p. 30.
[9] Dugast, op. cit., p. 126.
[10] Hutter, 1907, p. 6.
[11] Described in detail by Labouret, 2, 1935, pp. 121–6.
[12] Labouret, 1, 1935, p. 111.
[13] Martin, op. cit. Also personal communication.
[14] Labouret, op. cit., *passim*.
[15] Martin, op. cit.
[16] The alternative spellings in brackets appear in Jeffreys, 4, 1947.
[17] Labouret's spelling is *mfoouom*. Madame Dugast states that under the modern Administration these functionaries no longer exist. (Personal communication, 1953.)

or disturbances within his ward. He does not, however, have to punish offenders, since the maintenance of law and order within Fumban is the duty of the man holding the title of *ta ngu*. (Martin states that this is an abbreviation of *tita ngu*.) All offenders are reported to him. The *ta ngu* is at the head of a body of men known as the *mwtngu* (" husband of the country ") who execute royal commands. The *ta ngu* is responsible for the proclamation of the decisions on important affairs made by the king and his advisers. When doing this he is accompanied by several members of the *mwtngu;* he walks in a wide circle around the market place uttering loud cries and holding in his hand an ox or buffalo horn decorated with beads and cowries. The people gather together and squat down in the market place watching respectfully. The *ta ngu* fills his horn with palm-wine, drinks a little, and then passes it to the members of the *mwtngu*. When the horn has described a complete circle he makes the proclamation and finishes by telling his audience that they must abide by these decisions or be punished by the *mwtngu*. The *ta ngu* is greatly feared and is the only man who is not obliged to uncover his head before the king. Martin writes that the *mwtngu*, who were formerly of slave origin, are also feared.

In the walls surrounding the town are eight doors, one for each ward; formerly a guard of 15 men, armed with swords, was placed at each door. They were recruited from the young men of the ward who took it in turns to form the guard, keeping watch by night and day on all those who entered or left the town, questioning the people on their movements and searching through any packages they were carrying. It was their duty to see that all those who were leaving the town had the king's authority to do so.

ADMINISTRATION OF THE BAMUM KINGDOM

Binet analyses the processes whereby the autonomous chiefdoms conquered by the invading group were united into a centralized political system.[18] This could not have been accomplished by superior military force alone; successful assimilation of the conquered population depended to a certain extent on their co-operation and their willingness to acknowledge one king as their leader. Binet stresses that the notion of the sacredness of the king was partly responsible for the gradual voluntary acceptance of his authority. Magico-religious regalia, symbols of chieftainship, were often taken from the conquered chiefs to the capital, thereby contributing to their loss of chiefly power and transferring it to the king. Those conquered chiefs who persistently resisted the king's authority were deposed, but those who immediately accepted his rule became vassal chiefs with the title of *mfontuo*[19] or *mfontue* instead of *fon* or chief. Whenever there was open revolt the offenders were killed and their wives and children distributed among the king's warriors. In order to prevent such risings, the king often forced whole groups of people to move from their ancestral land to a different part of the country where they would be among strangers. Binet writes that a number of old men still recall that in their youth they were forced to move several times in this way, as their fathers had been before them. It was through such means as these that a number of chiefdoms which had formerly been autonomous were linked together in common allegiance to the supreme ruler of a single political unit.

In order to maintain this centralized political organization a number of officials with specific administrative duties were stationed throughout the kingdom.

The category of officials known as the *mfoyomɔ* have already been mentioned in connection with the office of ward head. Other *mfoyomɔ* were placed in charge of groups of villages throughout the kingdom and their position and duties were much the same as those of a ward head; thus, the people over whom the authority of these *mfoyomɔ* extended elected him and he remained in office for three years. He also, like a ward head, received the initial allocation of land from the king and distributed it among his people. He had furthermore the general responsibility

[18] Binet, 1952, pp. 399–415.
[19] This is the spelling given by Idrissou Mborou Njoya, 1935, p. 81.

E2

of transmitting any orders issued by the king to the people under his control. Binet writes that the villages in each administrative group were not necessarily adjacent, this being a precaution taken by the king against any individual official acquiring too much local power.

Other officials, holding the hereditary title of *kom,* were sent out by the king to different regions of his kingdom to act as intelligence officers responsible for sending back reports and information to the capital.[20] This hereditary title was created by Nchare and conferred upon seven of his close companions.[21] Dugast and Jeffreys refer to the *pa kom* as the seven hereditary councillors who have the right to sit on stone seats in the king's presence when in council.[22] The *kom* gathered together in the capital at the request of the king and also for the harvest festival. Rein-Wuhrmann states that during the harvest festival the *kom* gave the king a report of all the activities which had taken place in the area under their supervision and the king made a reply.[23]

The *kom* made their reports not only to the king but also to three officials known as the *titamfon.* These two sets of officials, *kom* and *titamfon,* formed the body of the king's advisers on all important issues. According to Rein-Wuhrmann important decisions made by the king had to be approved by the *titamfon* before they could be acted upon.[24] Jeffreys lists their titles and duties as follows:[25]

(1) *Njifonfon.* He holds the hands of the king-designate when installing him and is also the court intermediary between the king and all the Bamum vassal chiefs.

(2) *Ŋga minyi tutuet.* The intermediary between the king and the group known as the *Ŋget Ŋgu,* or " friends of the country."

(3) *Ŋgu kpwita.* He shaves the king every Friday. Each king appoints his own *titamfon;* thus Njoya gave the title of *Ŋgu kpwita* as a reward to one Ndam Banso who was reported to have recovered Nsangu's head from the Nsaw.

Titamfon receive many presents from the king. They play an important part in selecting the king's successor (see below, p. 70).

TITLE-HOLDERS

The Nji

The title of *nji* is held by sons and daughters of the king, the *kom,* and twins.[26] It is a title of nobility, and does not necessarily carry specific duties with it. It is hereditary, subject to the king's approval. *Nji* title-holders are divided into four categories according to the degree of contact and personal association existing between them and the king.[27]

The *nji* play an important part in the ceremonies which take place on the occasion of a king's burial and coronation. In Njoya's account of these ceremonies he mentions the following *nji* title-holders:[28] *njifonfon, njimonchara* (the first *njimonchara* was Nchare's principal attendant; it was he who brought back Nchare's head to Fumban), *njitampuɔ, njimoŋaŋka, njimonfira, njiamfu, njiamsum,* and *njikumjua.* Jeffreys writes that the original *njikumjua* was a brother of Nchare

---

[20] Martin, 1951.
[21] According to tradition, when Nchare and these seven companions arrived in Bamum country they each sat on a stone and Nchare thereupon swore to observe certain laws and customs (Binet, op. cit.). Hence arose the privilege mentioned by Dugast and Jeffreys.
[22] 1950.
[23] 1917, p. 22.
[24] Ibid., p. 37.
[25] Jeffreys, 1950, pp. 38–45.
[26] Martin, personal communication, 1953.
[27] Martin, 1951, p. 16.
[28] Martin briefly mentions one of these categories, the *ya-njii.* (Personal communication, 1953.)

and that there was a dispute between the two for the kingship.[29] To settle the matter a race was arranged and Nchare was the winner. Later Nchare tried to borrow certain garments from this brother who refused to lend them; Nchare therefore returned to Rifum to collect what he had left behind and was slain there. His death was then attributed to the miserliness of his brother. There is always a mock race and scenes of mock rivalry between the *njikumjua* and the king-designate during the coronation ceremony.

From the account given by Labouret of the palace buildings and their inhabitants, other court officials can be briefly listed as follows:[30]

The Chunnchut

These may be the paternal and maternal relatives of the king, but may also include husbands of princesses. It would appear then that many of them must be *nji* title-holders. *Chunnchut* are arranged in a hierarchy and their duty is to form the king's bodyguard. Within the palace there is a building known as " the house of a hundred men," or *nda kut mouin*, where live those *chunnchut* of lower rank who have not yet proved their worth. Of superior rank are those who live in " the house of forty men " or *nda kouanngam moui*, also within the precincts of the palace. There are also the " great " *chunnchut* who belong to the *mbansye* society (see below, p. 74). The other societies to which *chunnchut* belong are the *keumouet*, the *kpouefon*, and the *meutimbye*, but it is not explicitly stated whether membership of these is determined by the particular rank attained within the hierarchy. There is no further information about this hierarchical structure.

Other Palace Officials

Ta kam. The official in charge of a group of young men housed in a palace building called the *pa nda ta kam.* They have the duty of calling the people together and of arresting wrongdoers.

Ta meunya. The official at the head of about 100 attendants who are housed in a palace building called the *nda mfo meunya.* They are among the most courageous young men, who formerly carried out perilous missions.

Nschotou. The official who guarded the great warrior drums.

Ta ndam. The official in charge of the prepared food.

Ta ngouet. The official in charge of the palm-oil. He had the right to fine those who sold poor quality oil.

The Queen Mother (Na)

Great respect is due to the queen mother even from the king himself. She holds the hereditary title of *na*. Martin writes that there are two such titles, *na mandu* and *na ndam*, which are given to queen mothers and princesses. The two titles can be held by the same person.[31]

Lieutenant Hirtler, in the account of his expedition into Bamum country in 1903, remarks on the king's attitude of submission towards his mother, who seemed to be held in as much esteem as the king himself.[32] In the king's absence it was she who took over his duties as judge and she had the authority to mete out punishments.[33] She could act as regent if her son were too young to succeed when his father died.

[29] Jeffreys, loc. cit.
[30] Labouret, 2, 1935.
[31] Martin, loc. cit.
[32] Dugast and Jeffreys, 1950.
[33] Rein-Wuhrmann, op. cit., p. 54.

The King or Sultan (Fon)

At the head of the hierarchy of titled officials stands the *Fon*, or sultan as he is now called. His position as the supreme ruler and judge of the Bamum kingdom is conferred upon him by hereditary right; he is the descendant in the male line of the first ruler and founder of the kingdom. During his lifetime the *Fon* designates the future king from among his sons and seniority by birth may be disregarded. The " absolute power " of the king is frequently stressed in the literature. Although the *titamfon* are in a position to veto his commands, it appears that they did not always exercise this prerogative effectively enough to prevent his rule from being despotic. An obituary notice for the Sultan Njoya severely criticized him for his tyranny, and claimed that his people rejoiced when he was deposed by the French Administration.[34]

In the past the *Fon* was the leader of his warriors in battle and he was revered by the people for his courageous exploits. In Chapter 20 of Njoya's *History*, he quotes Nsangu as saying " A king's great work is to make war and administer justice." The bravery of Nsangu in the hand-to-hand battle with the Nsaw is stressed by Njoya. The notion of the king as a mighty warrior is explicit in the coronation ceremonies when he is exhorted with the words " Cease not to be a proud and haughty warrior."[35] He is identified with the leopard, the lion, and the elephant and is often addressed by these names; all leopards in his territory must be delivered up to him. That he is also equated with the python is known only to a small number of officials.[36]

The sacredness of the *Fon* has already been mentioned; he is not only the political but also the ritual and ceremonial head of his people. He sacrifices to his ancestors, the former rulers of the country, to ensure its prosperity, and decides when the annual harvest rites are to take place. During these rites he alone is able to touch and use the sacred stick, brought into the country by Nchare, which is in his charge.[37] He is also the head of all the secret societies.[38]

The *Fon* is regarded as the embodiment of the mystical power and majesty of all former kings, and the continuance of these qualities in him is ensured at his coronation in a series of rituals which include the holding of the head or skull of the deceased king.[39] The following account is taken from Jeffreys's translation of Chapter 29 of Njoya's *History*.[40]

Before the burial of a *fon* the king-designate raises and lowers his father's head, whereupon the seven councillors (the *kom*) acclaim him as the man to take the dead king's place. After the burial, the king-designate is taken and placed on the special stone of the country (*wongu*); *njimonchara* expounds to him the laws of the Bamum which were brought from Rifum, and also the rules which bind the councillors, the heads of the *mungu*[41] society, and administrative officials in common allegiance to the king. After this, the king administers the oath of allegiance to those present. When it is daylight, the king goes to bathe in the Nchi River, where " medicines " and special regalia have been taken previously. He is accompanied by the three *titamfon, njimonchara*, and his senior slave. *Njimonchara* rubs the " medicine " between his hands and then scoops up water, pouring it over the king; only the king is allowed to bathe in this particular part of the river. *Njimonchara* addresses the king, asking the supreme god *Yorubaŋ* to bless him, and to make his spear mighty. The medicine is then rubbed over the king's body and the remainder is thrown into the water together with a sheep's head, a pot of palm-oil, camwood powder, and salt. The double-mouthed iron gong is sounded

34 " Mort de l'ancien Sultan Njoya," *Togo-Cameroun*, Oct., 1933, pp. 162–3.
35 Jeffreys, 1950, p. 41.
36 Jeffreys, 5, 1947.
37 Rein-Wurhmann, 1917, chap. III.
38 Ibid., p. 81.
39 Jeffreys, 3, 1946, p. 59.
40 Jeffreys, 1950.
41 See p. 74.

and the people rush to cheer the king; they bathe lower down the river in the common watering-place. Finally the king returns to the palace, while the people cry " Nchare has returned, a warrior, the land is happy again." Then follow scenes of mock rivalry between the king and *njikumjua,* with the king securing victory over his rival.

Before the king may cohabit with his wives, palm-wine is poured into a trough belonging to the royal consorts and a special fruit called *garlegh* is added to it. As they drink this they promise not to alter the laws that govern royal consorts. Hereafter the king's first-born son takes the name of that foreign king whose complimentary gift first reaches the Bamum king. The Rifum king sends two councillors who bring water from the spot where the ancient Rifum kings washed; the Bamum king immediately washes himself in it. The Rifum king also sends three of his consorts to instruct the new Bamum king in the ancient traditions. One has the title of " Mother of Nchare," another " Mother of Fumban," and another " Mother of Nso." The people of Rifum give the king a gown, a matchet, a spear, and a sheep, and the three consorts receive presents in return.

It is interesting to note that the historial connection with Rifum is given such prominent recognition in the Bamum coronation ceremony, and that the links with their original home are still so strong after some 250 years.

THE POSITION OF THE KING TODAY, AND NEWLY CREATED OFFICIALS

Today the sultan, Seidu Njimolu, may frequently be consulted on matters relating to the social, political, and economic development of the country, but his is now only an honorary title, and he has no decisive voice in these affairs. He receives about 80,000 francs per year from the Administration, 20,000 of which are specifically for the maintenance of the palace.

In 1923, when King Njoya was deposed after causing the Administration a great deal of trouble, the French set up 17 " regional " or " superior " chiefs, many of whom were *nji* title-holders. It was thought that by conferring some measure of political authority and responsibility upon such regional chiefs the influence of the king would be considerably diminished. A certain number of villages are placed under the control of the regional chief, and it is his responsibility to transmit to these villages the orders of the Administration and to supervise the paying of taxes. Regional chiefs also settle disputes brought to them by the heads of their villages. They receive an annual salary of 24,000 to 30,000 francs.

The creation of these official posts has not been an entirely satisfactory measure; many of the regional chiefs have abused their authority, thinking that they have been endowed with the power formerly enjoyed by the king. Moreover as a result of this, many of them no longer show any respect for the king, and the relationship between them is often one of open antagonism.[42] The regional chiefs are now attempting to make their positions hereditary.

LEGAL PROCEDURE

Rein-Wuhrmann states that the king was the ultimate authority in all legal disputes and the supreme judge.[43]

The maintenance of order within Fumban was the special task allotted to the man holding the title of *ta ngu*.[44] All squabbles, brawls, and misdemeanours were brought to his notice and it was his duty to deal with these, bringing offenders before the courts. He announced to the people the rules and laws formulated by the king and his advisers, and threatened that unless they complied with these, the *mwtngu* would punish them (see above, p. 67).[45] Both *ta ngu* and *mwtngu* were greatly feared. Labouret mentions the existence of a police force whose head was known

[42] Martin, personal communication, 1953.
[43] Rein-Wuhrmann, 1917, p. 45.
[44] Labouret, 1, 1935, p. 111.
[45] Martin, 1951.

as the *ta mouinngou*.[46] (It is possible that *mouinngou* may be an alternative spelling for *mwtngu*, but these may be two distinct bodies; this is not made clear in the literature.) The deputy head of the police force was known as the *ta fon*, the first sub-chief was the *ta meunan*, and the second sub-chief was the *ta mbouin*. The *ta mouinngou* and the *ta meunan* are the respective heads of the *mouinngou* and *meunan* societies.[47] All these officials had their quarters in the palace, where was also the prison (*nda mbouta fon*).

Three kinds of court are mentioned by Labouret:[48]

(a) *Mamba sa*. A man comes to this court when he wishes to lodge a complaint. He is heard by an official known as the *ga pa sa*.

(b) *First Court of Enquiry*. The judges of this court make the preliminary investigation in cases of delict and bring the accused before the king.

(c) *Nda ga tinnsa*. Here judgments are pronounced. The earth spider oracle was often used to establish innocence or guilt.[49] There was also the trial by *le*, when the accused was led out into the full sunlight and made to drink a mixture consisting of water and the crushed bark of the *le* tree. If he vomited he was innocent, but if he fell unconscious his guilt was established and he was set upon and killed.[50]

Punishments

Rein-Wuhrmann makes the general statement that punishments were hard and included exile, enslavement, and whipping.[51] She also describes how a convicted murderer might be publicly executed after his clothes had been torn from him and insults hurled at him from the jeering crowd. His body was thrown into the bush. Any of his wives or kinsfolk who showed the customary signs of mourning might also be executed. According to the law, the compound of the murderer should be destroyed, and his wives and children sold into slavery by the king, to whom passed all the dead man's goods.[52]

Any of the king's wives who had displeased him were shut up in a special room in the palace known as the *nda njom byefon*.[53] For grave offences the king would have his wives executed; the clothes of these deceased wives were placed in the sacred house of the *mouinngou* society.[54]

There was another room in the palace where those who had left the capital without first seeking the permission of the king were kept locked up for some time on their return.

INHERITANCE AND SUCCESSION

Inheritance and succession follow the patrilineal line; the heir takes the dead man's name, inherits his wives and all his goods and enjoys the same rights as did his predecessor. Martin states that a woman may sometimes be chosen as the heir.[55] A man selects his heir before his death, and his name is kept a secret among certain of his friends until the time comes for him to succeed.[56] The king selects his successor in this way, and tells only the *titamfon* which of his sons is to be the new king. The heir need not necessarily be the eldest. When the king is at the point

---

[46] Labouret, op. cit., p. 121.
[47] The personnel of these two societies would appear to be the members of the different sections into which the police force was divided. See section on Societies, pp. 73–4.
[48] Labouret, op. cit., pp. 121–2, and p. 126.
[49] See Section entitled " The Diviner," p. 81.
[50] Martin, op. cit., p. 28.
[51] Rein-Wuhrmann, loc. cit.
[52] Rein-Wuhrmann, 1931, p. 8.
[53] Labouret, op. cit.
[54] Ibid.
[55] Martin, personal communication, 1953.
[56] Rein-Wuhrmann, 1917, p. 75.

of death, the *titamfon* call the king-designate to the death-bed, where he receives his father's last wishes. If the king dies without having chosen his heir, it is for the *titamfon* and the *kom* to make the selection from among the king's sons.[57]

The mother of an heir has a higher status once her son has come into his inheritance. Her co-wives treat her with great respect and address her as " mother-in-law."[58] If her son is still a child at the time of his predecessor's death, then she looks after the inheritance for him, and is called *na nga njii* (" mother of the one who eats ").[57] She directs the activities of her son's wives and slaves.

LAND TENURE

There is almost no published information on the Bamum system of land tenure. It has been briefly outlined by Martin as follows.[59]

The king is the titular owner of the land. He allocates sections of land to the *mfoyoma*, arranging with them where the boundaries of the sections shall lie. Each *mfoyoma* distributes plots to the members of those compounds lying within the area under his control. According to Rein-Wuhrmann tracts of cultivated land usually surround the compound.[60] The king has the right to take back and redistribute at any time land thus allocated, but he does so only in extreme cases, if, for example, a man commits a serious offence and so forfeits his rights to the land. Furthermore, sons of kings must, according to traditional practice, live within the capital, and they establish themselves there by taking for their own use land which had originally been allocated to someone else. A man thus deprived of his land must give up immediately his usufructuary right to it, since he must leave it without harvesting any crops. Martin writes that this practice explains why fruit-trees are rarely grown in Fumban. After three generations the descendants of the brothers of the king must leave the capital; they are told " *ywn ŋom suərə* " (" your sun is setting ") or " *ywn ya* " (" your time is over "). Thus, Njikam and Njimuluəm, descendants of King Nsangu's brothers, can no longer live in Fumban.

The king's titular ownership of the whole of Bamum territory has political as well as economic significance, in that he is entitled to receive annually a share of the produce harvested from all parts of the country. Martin writes that he redistributes a large part of this in such a way that there will be no shortage of a particular item of food in any region.

Finally Martin draws attention to a special category of land users who are referred to as *nufa'*.[61] A *nufa'* is one who is cultivating a tract of land outside Fumban and who returns there for only a certain period of time during the year. The land of a *nufa'* may not have been allocated to him originally, but custom permits him to cultivate it if he found it unused; in such a case he has only a usufructuary right, and can make no other claim to the land.

Martin writes that nowadays, with the increase in the number of coffee plantations, and the growing awareness of the cash value of land, the concept of private ownership of land is becoming more familiar.

Land is inherited according to the principles outlined above (p. 72).

THE SECRET ASSOCIATIONS[62]

Martin speaks of the secret associations or societies as being the pillar upon which the social organization rested,[63] but it is impossible to understand the full significance of this statement since no comprehensive investigation of them has been made. They are referred to as the *pa nju* (sing.: *yu nju; yu:* that which is real,

---

[57] Martin, personal communication, 1953.
[58] Rein-Wuhrmann, op. cit., p. 76.
[59] Martin, personal communication.
[60] Rein-Wuhrmann, op. cit., p. 19.
[61] Martin, personal communication, 1953. See also Martin, 1951, pp. 12–18.
[62] Dubié states that all the activities of the traditional secret societies have now stopped; MS. 1949–50.
[63] Martin, op. cit., p. 29.

that which exists; *nju:* that which is mysterious, supernatural). *Yu nju* is also the name of the musical instruments (usually buffalo horns, bamboo flutes and drums) used by members of a *yu nju*. Martin states that each clan has its *yu nju* whose importance varies with that of the clan. Initiation is painful, and initiates are bound not to tell non-members what they see at meetings, and to keep secret the decisions made by the *yu nju*.[64] On the death of a member, his *yu nju* will take part in the mortuary lamentations, but on such an occasion they must not be seen by women or by any male non-member.

Most of the information about the societies is taken from Labouret; he describes in detail the plan of the palace at Fumban, and many societies appear to have their lodges or meeting-houses within the precincts of the palace.[65] He mentions the following societies:

Mbansye or Mbanshie: the society to which the higher ranking *chunnchut* (members of the royal family) belong. *Mbanshie* also refers to part of the royal regalia, a double-mouthed iron gong, on which only a king may gaze.

Mouinngou:[66] its sacred house is known as the *nda mfo mouinngou.* Its president (*ta mouinngu*) is the head of the police (see p. 71); he guards the drums and other paraphernalia belonging to the society. It seems likely that its members form a section of the police force, and that they have police duties, but this is not made clear in the literature.

Meunan: its president is the first sub-chief of the police force, known as the *ta meunan.* It seems likely therefore that the members of this society also form a section of the police force.

Ngeurri or Ngirri: this is composed of the sons of the king. On each side of the entrance to their meeting-house are several rooms usually occupied by young princes under 15 years of age. The relatives of the sultan who lived away from the capital could stay here when they visited Fumban. The store-room in which were kept the musical instruments and other paraphernalia belonging to the society was known as the *ma ngeuri.*

Other associations are: *nikeup, ntere, channtou, meusi, mfeukegni, mfomu, nsye,* and *mbalou* (described by Labouret as a dancing society); *keumouet, kpouefon,* and *meutimbye* are *chunnchut* societies (see p. 69).

Some of these societies are greatly feared, since they are believed to perform evil deeds.[67]

There is no information on the internal organization of a society; whether, for example, members are arranged in a hierarchy; nor are we told whether membership is in all cases hereditary, or whether payment of entrance fees may form the sole condition of entry.

SLAVERY

From accounts given by Rein-Wuhrmann of life within Fumban, it appears that every rich man had a number of slaves and that the king had several hundred.[68] The queen mother and the daughters of the king also had their own slaves. Hutter writes that many of the slaves were the descendants of the original population who were subjugated.[69] There were also those whom the king had sold into slavery as a punishment for some offence; wives and children of a murderer might, according to Rein-Wuhrmann, be sold as slaves.[70] Prisoners of war became the king's slaves.

A slave had no rights, and a master was free to ill-treat him, give him away as

[64] Martin, op. cit., p. 30.
[65] Labouret, 2, 1935, pp. 121, 122, and 126.
[66] See also Jeffreys, 1950, p. 40. Here the *muŋgu society* is mentioned; *muŋgu* may be an alternative spelling for *mouinngou.*
[67] Rein-Wuhrmann, 1917, p. 81.
[68] Rein-Wuhrmann, op. cit., and 1931.
[69] Hutter, 1907, pp. 2–6.
[70] Rein-Wuhrmann, 1931, p. 8.

a present, or to resell him.[71] He could do likewise with his slaves' offspring, except in the case of twins who were adopted in the usual way by the king.[72] However, slaves were often well treated by their masters and given many wives. It appears that slaves were arranged in a hierarchy and senior slaves had slaves of a lower rank to labour for them.[73] In his description of the coronation ceremony, Njoya mentions that the senior slave of the *njimonchara* accompanied his master during the ceremony of the ablutions in the Nchi River.[74] The status of slaves therefore was not necessarily low. In Chapter 15 of Njoya's *History*, of which Jeffreys gives an account, it is stated that a slave by the name of Ŋguwo usurped the Bamum throne in Nsangu's lifetime and, to stabilize his position, began to kill off the males of the ruling family.[75] This gives a good indication of the influence and power which a slave might obtain.

WARFARE

The Bamum esteem themselves as mighty warriors and in their traditions there are numerous accounts of wars and skirmishes with neighbouring tribes. Nchare is particularly remembered for his skill and bravery in war, and all Bamum kings are exhorted during the coronation ceremony to follow his example. Thus, when the king is washing in the special washing-place, the *njifonfon* exclaims, " this water is the water of our land wherein previous kings washed before you were born. They made a law that no descendant of a foreigner should wash himself here or lead people to hold him in awe as king of the Bamum. . . . This law was made because many foreign kings were the enemies of Nchare. Because he carried a conquering war spear they would be delighted to see the kingship pass from such warriors. Cease not to be a proud and haughty warrior. On these qualities depends the increase of your domains. *Yorubaŋ* stands behind you when you fight in a good cause."[76]

There were many bitter conflicts with the Nsaw. Njoya gives an account of some of these, describing how his father Nsangu was slain in a battle with the Nsaw after he and his heralds had shown extreme bravery, using matchets in hand-to-hand fighting.[77] There were also fierce internal struggles; Njoya writes that in a battle against one of his rivals, a certain Bentkom, more than 3,000 Bamum were killed. In order to overcome this rival Njoya sought the aid of the *Lamido* of Banyo, and gave him many presents in return for his services. (See above, p. 56.)

Bamileke, Banen, and Fulani have all, at some period in their history, waged war with the Bamum.

The great war drums are housed in a special room in the palace known as the *le*, and here also were placed skulls of the enemy. In times of peace these drums would sound if the king was about to hold audience, or if he was preparing to go out.

War was followed by singing and dancing; the dance of victory could only be performed by those who had killed one of the enemy.[78] Warriors who had not killed merely accompanied the dancing and singing. These victory dances took place in the capital, were attended by the king, and might last from one to two months. When the festivities ended the king rewarded the warriors; to those who had brought a lower jaw of one of the enemy he gave a wife, and to those who had brought an enemy's skull he gave 15–20,000 cowries.[79] Twice yearly warriors were called together to the capital when the special calabashes of *kakua* were assembled and special ceremonies performed to ensure success in future battles.[80]

---

[71] Rein-Wuhrmann, 1917, p. 67.
[72] Ibid., p. 72. See also sections on Life Cycle (Birth), p. 77.
[73] Rein-Wuhrmann, op. cit., p. 22.
[74] Jeffreys, 1950.
[75] Jeffreys, 3, 1946. Nsangu escaped and made a successful insurrection.
[76] Jeffreys, 1950, p. 41.
[77] Jeffreys, 3, 1946, p. 58.
[78] Dellenbach, 1931.
[79] Dellenbach, op. cit.
[80] For further details of these ceremonies see Section entitled " War Magic," p. 82.

It is interesting to note that ties with the Rifum parent stock were acknowledged in the Bamum war procedure. Thus Njoya writes that when the Bamum made war they sent a captive and the head of the first enemy slain to Rifum and the Rifum king sent back a woman for the Bamum king.[81]

There is no information available on how warriors were recruited or mobilized when required. From the literature it can be inferred that their tactics and strategy on the field of battle were highly organized.[82]

[81] Jeffreys, 1950, p. 42.
[82] See Jeffreys, 3, 1946, and Martin, 1951, p. 11.

MAIN CULTURAL FEATURES

MENTAL AND PHYSICAL CHARACTERISTICS

Olivier notes two distinct physical types among the Bamum population; the first is represented by the descendants of the original conquerors of the country who are termed " pure Bamum " and the second by the conquered population, the Bamileke, who remained in the area.[1] Olivier selects three physical features which show most clearly the distinction between the two types.

(1) The average height of the " pure Bamum " is greater than that of the conquered population; Olivier gives the following figures (male): " pure Bamum " 177.1 cm.; conquered population 169.6 cm.

(2) " Pure Bamum " are brachycephalic, whereas the conquered population is usually mesocephalic. Cranial deformation which resulted in the extreme elongation of the skull was forbidden in 1910 by Njoya.

(3) The long, convex-shaped nose is characteristic of the " pure Bamum."

Olivier points out that, owing to the intermingling of the two populations over a number of years, there is a considerable range of variations between the two types.

Egerton reports that the Bamum women are cicatrized on the upper part of the chest and abdomen.[2]

The Bamum are generally described as being robust, with an " open, frank character " and able to adjust themselves to new situations.[3]

DRESS

In Fumban particularly, where a considerable portion of the population is Mohammedan, the most immediately striking difference from the Bamileke lies in the clothing worn by men and women. According to Despois, rich garments worn at court were imported from the Sudan.[4] Men may wear the very full trousers and embroidered tunics, and on their heads a small cap, but often they may be seen wearing the simple loincloth. Martin states that they weave most of their clothing themselves.[5] The majority of the women wear brightly coloured cotton robes and ornament themselves with necklaces and bracelets; women at court decorate their hair with bright beads. Dubié states that outside Fumban and the larger centres, robes are not so elaborate or so full, but that only rarely is the simple loincloth worn.[6]

THE LIFE CYCLE

We have very little information about the ceremonies and rituals associated with the major events in the life cycle.

BIRTH

As among the Bamileke, the toad is the symbol of a woman's fertility and it is never harmed or killed.[7] Rein-Wuhrmann reports that having many children (especially twins) gives prestige to the mother; a supernatural power is thought to bestow favour upon twins and they are named and adopted by the king.[8] Labouret reports that twins were always the guardians of the burial ground of

---

[1] Olivier, 1948.
[2] Egerton, *African Majesty,* 1938, p. 249.
[3] Lawless, Oct., 1936, Jan., 1937.
[4] Despois, 1945.
[5] Martin, 1951, p. 12.
[6] Op. cit., p. 27.
[7] Rein-Wuhrmann, 1917, p. 29.
[8] Ibid., p. 72.

kings,[9] and they also play a part in a king's coronation ceremony.[10]   All boys are circumcised.   Young girls help their mothers with the agricultural work.   Fathers were able to give their daughters in payment of debts in former times; Rein-Wuhrmann also states that a father had to present two of his daughters to the king as tribute; these the king either kept as wives for himself, or gave to his servants.[11]

MARRIAGE

A girl was usually betrothed at the age of five or six; she then went to live in the compound of her future husband, and took up the rights and duties of a married woman at the age of 12.[12]   When Rein-Wuhrmann was writing in 1917 the bride-wealth was about 95 marks (£5).[13]

A man was able to give his slaves' daughters in marriage, but the bridewealth he received was not so great as that for a free man's daughter; moreover the girl could not appeal to her previous master if she were cruelly treated.[14]   Rein-Wuhr-mann states that the king gives his daughters in marriage to the members of the " aristocracy ";[15] the bridegroom must give presents to the royal family.   The marriage festivities last for many days.

A man who has married the daughter of a free Bamum cannot sell her into slavery or give her away as a present; if she is unfaithful she is sent back to her father.   Rein-Wuhrmann does not state if this returning of an unfaithful wife con-stitutes a legal divorce, nor what happens to the children in such a case.[16]   Baumann and Westermann refer briefly to the sexual liberty of princesses.[17]

If a wife dies without giving birth to any children, then her father must provide another wife in her place, but he will receive no further bridewealth.[18]

DEATH

Illness and death are attributed to malevolent forces.   The earth spider and the medicine man are consulted to discover their causes more specifically.[19]   The chameleon is thought to be the messenger of death and whenever possible a man will kill it, thinking that he has thereby escaped an untimely end.[20]

On the death of their husband, a man's wives immediately begin to mourn for him, taking off their fine clothes, necklaces, and bracelets, and smearing their bodies with white clay.   Rein-Wuhrmann describes how widows, after thus smearing their bodies, re-enter their compound leaning on large sticks which signifies that they are " robbed of their support."[21]   During the night following the death of a man, men and boys, friends of the deceased, beat on a drum and sing away any evil spirits who may not be satisfied with one death alone.[22]

Burial of a King

Njoya gives the following account of how dead kings were buried.[23]   On the death of a king, a large circular pit is dug.   The body is clad in an *mfwot* cloth;

[9] Labouret, 1, 1935, p. 122.
[10] Jeffreys, 1950, pp. 38–45.
[11] Rein-Wuhrmann, op. cit., p. 66.
[12] Rein-Wuhrmann, 1931, p. 22.
[13] Rein-Wuhrmann, 1917, p. 60.
[14] Ibid., p. 66.
[15] By " aristocracy " Rein-Wuhrmann presumably means a descendant of the original conquering people, who will probably hold an important official post.   Egerton also states that one of Njoya's daughters was married to the Bangangte chief in Bamileke country. (*African Majesty*, 1938, p. 106.)
[16] Rein-Wuhrmann, op. cit., pp. 63–4.
[17] Baumann and Westermann, 1948, p. 332.
[18] Rein-Wuhrmann, op. cit., pp. 63–4.
[19] Rein-Wuhrmann, 1931, p. 5.
[20] Rein-Wuhrmann, 1917, p. 29.
[21] Rein-Wuhrmann, 1931, p. 5.
[22] Ibid.
[23] Jeffreys, 1950.

pieces of leopard-skin are tied round his ankles and just below his knees. Beads and ivory bracelets are placed round his neck and arms, and a bead cap on his head. He is then put into a chair decorated with the carved figure of a man and with beads. In his right hand is placed a bag with a drinking horn, and in his left a sheathed matchet. The *ŋgwen* oracle is placed in front of him, the *moma* behind him, the *mbansye* to his left and the *ŋgirri* to his right.[24] A calabash of palm-wine is also placed in front of him. Earth is packed around him, leaving his cap uncovered; the hollow end of an elephant's tusk is placed on the king's head,[25] and a large stone is put near the tusk. The rest of the earth is now replaced, leaving half of the tusk and stone above ground. The stone is rubbed with palm-oil and on the top are placed leaves of the *mbupwot* and red feathers from the *turaco*. An iron manacle is put near the elephant's tusk, which is draped with leopard skin; the head of a sheep is put between the stone and the tusk, and the grave is encircled with small iron gongs. There are 13 people who may attend the king's burial and who know how to bury a king; Njoya lists them as follows: two *titamfon* and the *njifonfon, njimonchara, njitampuɔ, njimoyaŋka, njimonfira, njiamfu*; also the first two slaves whom the king had before he was crowned, and three twins, renowned for wisdom.

When a king dies he is placed upon a bed in the *mfum* (*mfom*) house, where the *ŋgwen* oracle speaks;[26] thence he is carried to the graveside, where *njifonfon* calls upon the seven councillors to see that he is dead. After the king-designate has lowered and raised his father's head, these seven councillors acknowledge him as their king. The *njiamfu* and *njimonchara* enter the grave with the king's body. The *njiamfu* receives the horn the dead king last used for drinking palm-wine, and also his bag, calabash, and pipe, because he is a descendant of a king. The *njiansum* stands on the left of the palace doorway and the *njikumjua* on the right, and they ask for some of their brother's goods because they have just looked upon his hand.[27] Each is then given a slave. After three years have elapsed it is time to make the *paaŋgu;* this is a bag or sacred bundle containing the hair of the king's head (obtained before he was buried), the bones of his hand and fingers, and any teeth available. These are mixed up and placed in a small bag decorated with beads, which is henceforth known as the *paaŋgu.* The bones are obtained by digging a hole on the right-hand side of the body; the hole is filled with cloth before the earth is put back and the place made level.

Today, according to Njoya, when a burial takes place and all the rites have been performed, the grave must be cemented over. An iron fence or a shelter may also be built around the grave of a king. On the tomb of Njoya himself there is a small brick monument with an epitaph in French and Arabic.[28]

[24] Jeffreys gives the following note (op. cit., p. 43): " The *ŋgirri* is a secret society composed of the sons of the king, part of whose insignia is a large pot. In it is placed a long bamboo decorated with beads. Down this tube is blown a blast of air which makes a deep booming note. *Mbansye* is another secret society but here it refers to a double-mouthed iron gong, part of the royal regalia. Only the chief may gaze upon *Mbansye* "
[25] Jeffreys was informed of this; it is not in Njoya's account.
[26] Njoya states that the *ŋgwen* oracle is heard because it came with the Bamum kings from their home in Rifum. No further information about the oracle is given (Jeffreys, op. cit., p. 40). Labouret reports that the king's cemetery is also referred to as *mfom*, and that the *mfom* house was built within it (2, 1935, p. 122).
[27] The hand of the dead king is sacred. Jeffreys (op. cit., p. 44) writes: " The hand of the dead king as a ' sacra ' of the Jukun tribe is mentioned by Dr. C. K. Meek " [in *A Sudanese Kingdom*, 1931].
[28] Dubié, MS. 1949-50.

RELIGION AND MAGIC

THE SUPREME GOD

The Supreme Being, the creator of all things, is known as *Njinyi*, or *Nnui* (" he who is everywhere, he who sees and hears everything "). It is this god who, through the medium of the toad, announces the birth of a child; thus if the animal enters the hut, it is the object of great honour and it is anointed with palm-oil. The Bamum believe that this god can be deceived; for example, if many of a woman's children have been stillborn, or if they have died in early childhood, she decides that the next child which she bears will not be named, and God will therefore think that the child is a thing, not a human being, and will not harm it.[1]

In the first script invented by Njoya the Bamum word for God appears as *Nnui;* in the later royal script, however, this is replaced by the word *Yorubaŋ*. Jeffreys gives the following information which may explain the appearance of this word: the word *Yaruba,* for God, occurs among the Tangale, a tribe in Northern Nigeria, some of whom are found in the extreme south-west of Bornu Province and others in the independent pagan division of the Province, under the Chief of Bashamma. They worship a god (*Yaruba*) who is the personification of all the souls of the dead. In the course of their migrations the Bamum may have picked up the name of this deity and retained it as a royal or court form of address for God.[2]

Yorubaŋ is invoked during the coronation ceremony (see p. 70); the *njifonfon* beseeches him to bless the king, to grant him many children, to make his war-spear mighty and his work strong. *Yorubaŋ* is also requested to give the king good advice and to increase his wealth.[3]

EVIL SPIRITS

Martin states that belief in spirits is more important to the Bamum in their day-to-day lives than is the belief in the Supreme God.[4] The Bamum designate the power of evil by the term *nga-mbüket;* this power of evil is served by the elements, thunder, tornado, fire, rivers, lakes, and also by the leopard. Sometimes *nga-mbüket* will take into his service human beings, who will then harm their fellows, often unconsciously and involuntarily.

All the elements and people in the service of the power of evil are classed under the generic term of *pa-rwm* (sing. *nzwm*). The evil spirit which possesses them is the *rwm*, which is believed to live in the stomachs of women, and to be transmitted by women; the children of a female *nzwm* are all known as *pa-rwm*. *Pa-rwm* are thought to be the authors of nearly all illnesses and misfortunes.[5] When a death occurs in a family someone is frequently accused of being *nzwm* and of having caused the death. The trial by *le*[6] may then be used to establish innocence or guilt (see p. 72).

The Bamum distinguish two kinds of *pa-rwm:*

(a) Those which are unable to inflict injury until they are given the means; for example, if someone has broken a customary law or is involved in a quarrel he would be open to attack from a *nzwm*.

(b) Those which bring misfortune because they are jealous and envious of a man's prosperity. If a strong and healthy man were suddenly to die, his

---

[1] Martin, 1951, p. 27.
[2] Jeffreys, op. cit., p. 44, f.n. 16.
[3] Ibid., p. 41.
[4] Martin, loc. cit.
[5] Ibid., p. 28.
[6] See " Legal Procedure," p. 72.

death would be attributed to a jealous *nzwm*. This kind is thought to be far more dangerous.

For protection against *pa-rwm*, the Bamum have two kinds of weapon:

(a) *Kwshuop*, which usually consists of an antelope horn containing different sorts of crushed bark and pieces of wood. It is placed in a hidden corner of the house or at the head of the owner's bed. The owner must observe all kinds of taboos in order to make the *kwshuop* efficacious.

(b) *Fu* or medicine, which is thought to be both curative and preventive. It may be a liquid or a paste, with which one covers part of the body, or may consist of a number of amulets worn on the neck and arms. These amulets are referred to as *nshuop*.

THE DIVINER (*Mfɔn ngamə*)

Magical power is given to the *fu* by the diviner, the *mfɔn ngamə*.[7] He is also consulted when the *nshuop* are thought to have become powerless. For his divination he uses the earth spider (*ngamə*). There is a small spider-hole near his house which is protected by a small roof or more often by pieces of calabash. After clearing the ground around the hole in the presence of those who are seeking his advice, the diviner unties his bundle of leaves all of which have saw-like edges, each one being slightly different. There is one series of leaves for men and another for women. He places the leaves which he has selected on top of the hole; when the spider comes out the leaves are disturbed, whereupon the diviner addresses the spider, revealing to it the purpose of the consultation. The diviner then examines the leaves and gives his verdict.

ANCESTOR WORSHIP

The spirits of the dead are revered and worshipped by their living descendants. Offerings of palm-wine are made to them, but there is no information as to how many times or upon what occasions such offerings are made.[8] Rein-Wuhrmann reports that the king always goes barefooted when he visits the burial ground of his ancestors.[9] Jeffreys states that " the cult of the skull forms an important part of Bamum culture,"[10] but this may refer to kings' skulls only. Concerning these, Jeffreys writes that the skull of the deceased king must be present at the installation of the new king, for it is a vital step in the coronation ritual for him " to hold the head or skull of the deceased king in order to ensure the continuity of power and majesty in the new king."[11] It was for this reason that there was so much rejoicing when Njoya recovered the head of his father, Nsangu, which had been cut off during battle with the Nsaw and had fallen into the hands of the enemy.

ANNUAL FESTIVALS

Rein-Wuhrmann gives a very brief account of two of these.[12] At the end of March, after the sowing has been done, there are celebrations to mark the beginning of the rains. These take place in the open square in front of the palace at Fumban. Here the men dance; the women are the spectators. The main dancers wear masks; occasionally the king too appears in a mask and dances.

[7] Martin, 1951, p. 29.
[8] In the German account of its recovery (Jeffreys, 3, 1946, p. 61).
[9] Rein-Wuhrmann, 1917, p. 31.
[10] Jeffreys, op. cit., p. 57.
[11] Jeffreys, op. cit., p. 59. In Njoya's account of the coronation ceremony the skull of the dead king is not severed from the body when the new king raises and lowers it, and Njoya states that it is not the usual practice to sever it (Jeffreys, 1950). Njoya thus contradicts a German account quoted in Jeffreys, 3, 1946, which states that the skull was severed from the body and placed in a special house. The Bamum did of course possess skulls of their kings who had been decapitated by the enemy in times of war, etc.
[12] Rein-Wuhrmann, op. cit., pp. 89–90.

F

The biggest festival takes place at harvest time, either in July or August; it is for the king to announce exactly when it will be held, and by that time all the taxes from the harvest must be paid. Labouret reports that gifts of palm-oil are made to the king during the festival and placed in the special oil-house (*nda nkouet*) in the palace.[13]   All the *kom* gather at the capital during the festival and give a report of the important happenings in their territories during the past year.[14]

SACRED SNAKES

Jeffreys made an investigation of the Bamum lore on sacred snakes.[15]   He discovered that the king's identification with the python was known only to an inner circle, those who offered the important national sacrifices.

Jeffreys also reports the traditional belief among the Bamum that the python keeps a shining fire at its dwelling place and this light guides it back to its nest at night.   It is believed that the piece of wood which the python uses as a pillow is full of good luck, and that anyone who gets hold of it will have wishes fulfilled.   A Bamum, Mfopu, informed Jeffreys that the Bamum have now been told that the python's shining fire is of value to the white man and that if he finds such a fire he should throw a black cloth over it and run away, lest the snake should see and kill him.   Later, when the snake has given up the search for the fire, he should return and collect the fire in safety.

Jeffreys considers that the snake-king complex has been diffused from Egypt; linked with the snake cult of Egypt were other cults, such as those of the sun and vulture, and in fact the vulture and snake both appear in the Bamum account of the rescue of King Nte.[16]

WAR MAGIC

Dellenbach gives the following account of trophy calabashes used by the Bamum in war magic.[17]   The calabashes are enclosed in a network of rattan fibres and covered with a reddish-brown plaster; human mandibles are suspended from the rattan fibres.   According to Dellenbach it was an old Bamum custom for a warrior to show to the sultan the ear of the enemy he had killed in battle, but since the ear decomposed, it became customary to show him the lower jaw instead.   When two warriors killed the same man together, one of them took the jaw and the other the skull.   These two warriors would exchange their swords on the battlefield as a sign that they had assisted each other.   When the warriors returned to their respective villages, the magician[18] took possession of the jaws and bound them to the trophy calabash known as the *kakua*.   On certain *kakua* were hung sheep's skulls; this meant that the sultan and one of the warriors in the village had jointly killed one of the enemy.   The sultan also had his own *kakua,* on which he hung the jaws of the enemies killed by his own servants.   When the village *kakua* was sufficiently covered with jaws, each warrior had the right to possess a trophy calabash himself; this calabash was smaller than the *kakua,* and was known as *toungou*. On it were hung not only jaws but charms which were supposed to preserve the warrior from the vengeance of the dead man.

Twice yearly the sultan gathered together his warriors and the *kakua* were brought from each village.   These reunions were the occasion of great festivities; the *kakua* were placed in two long rows and sheep's blood was scattered over the jaws attached to them.   This was thought to blind the enemy during the next combat.   Palm-wine was drunk at this reunion only by those warriors who had killed one of the enemy.

[13] Labouret, 1, 1935, p. 122.
[14] See Section " Administration of the Bamum Kingdom," pp. 67–8.
[15] Jeffreys, 5, 1947.
[16] Jeffreys, 1945.
[17] Dellenbach, 1931.
[18] Dellenbach uses the word " sorcier " but " sorcerer " is kept here to refer to one who possesses bad medicines and uses them illicitly.

Dellenbach quotes a letter from Josette Debarge in which the following information is given.[19] When a warrior slaughters one of the enemy, there is always the danger that his ghost may seek vengeance. Therefore, on returning to his village, the warrior goes to the magician or medicine man who prepares him a medicine to protect him against the spirit of the dead man. This medicine consists of the blood of a cock, meat, and various herbs; all these ingredients are cooked together. The warrior drinks some of this and is given the calabash containing the rest of the medicine. This calabash is carefully guarded, and women and children are not allowed to touch it. Whenever the warrior feels ill, he pours palm-wine into it and drinks from it. He may place his victim's jaw on this calabash. If he places it in front of his house, it is thought that thieves will be prevented from entering.

Labouret reports that before soldiers went into battle, they assembled in one of the courts of the palace and were given medicines to make them brave and invulnerable.[20]

[19] Dellenbach, op. cit., p. 99.
[20] Labouret, loc. cit.

BIBLIOGRAPHY

Ankermann, B.
  " Bericht über eine ethnographische Forschungsreise ins Grasland von Kamerun."
    Zeit. f. Ethnol., XLII, 1910.
    (Information on the Bali also given here, pp. 288–310.)

Aufrey, R.
  " Naissance d'une écriture." (Cameroun.) *L'Anthropologie*, XLVI, 1936.

Baumann, H., and Westermann, D. [trans. L. Homburger]
    Les Peuples et les Civilisations de l'Afrique. Paris: Payot, 1948, pp. 331–6,
    339, 454.

Binet, J.
  " L'habitation dans la Subdivision de Foumbot." *Et. Cam.*, III, 31–2, 1950, pp.
    189–99.
  " Le commandement chez les Bamoum." *Le Monde Non-Chrétien*, 24, Dec., 1952,
    pp. 399–415.

Bouchaud, J.
    Histoire et Géographie du Cameroun sous Mandat Français. Douala: La Procure
    du Vicariat Apostolique, 1944.

Carton, C.
  " Etude démographique comparée des Bamiléké et Bamoum." *Ann. Medic. et
    Pharm. Colon.*, XXII, 1934, pp. 350–63.

Crawford, O. G. S.
  " The Writing of Njoya." *Antiquity*, IX, Dec., 1936, pp. 435–42.

Delafosse, M.
  " Naissance et évolution d'un système d'écriture de création contemporaine." *Revue
    d'Ethnographie et de Traditions Populaires*, III année, 1er trim., No. 9, 1922,
    pp. 11–36.

Dellenbach, M.
  " Une calebasse-trophée utilisée dans la magie guerrière chez les Bamoums."
    L'Ethnographie, No. 23–4, 1931.

de Pedrals, H.
  " Contribution à l'établissement d'un inventaire ethnique du Cameroun." *Bull. Soc.
    Et. Cam.*, 15–16, 1946, pp. 30–1.

Despois, J.
  " Des montagnards en pays tropical Bamiléké et Bamoum." *Revue de Géographie
    Alpine*, 4, 1945, pp. 595–635.

Deutsches Kolonialblatt, 1907, pp. 258–9. " Der Kopf des Bamum-Herrschers."

Dubié, Paul
  " Christianisme, Islam et Animisme chez les Bamoums (Cameroun)," 1949–50
    (Unpublished).

Dugast, I.
    Inventaire Ethnique du Sud-Cameroun. *Mém. I.F.A.N.*, Série: Populations, No. 1,
    1949, pp. 123–8.
  " La langue secrète du Sultan Njoya." *Et. Cam.*, III, 31–2, 1950, pp. 231–60.

Dugast, I., and Jeffreys, M. D. W.
  " L'écriture des Bamoum, sa naissance, son évolution, sa valeur phonetique, son
    utilisation." *Mém. I.F.A.N.*, Série: Populations, No. 4, 1950.

Ernst [Missionaire]
  " Account of a Journey into Bamum Country." *Der Evangelische Heidenbote*, mars,
    1904.

Gohring, M.
   1. " Der König von Bamum und seine Schrift." *Der Evangelische Heidenbote*, LXXX,
       année no. 6, juin, 1907, pp. 41–2.
   2. " Die Bamumschrift [avec le fac-simile en double page de l'alphabet]." *Der
       Evangelische Heidenbote*, année no. 11, nov., 1907, pp. 83–6.

Greenberg, J. H.
   " Studies in African Linguistic Classification." *South-Western Journal of Anthro-
      pology*, IV, V. VI, 1949.

Hirtler [Leutn.]
   " Bericht über eine Expedition nach Bamum." *Deutsches Kolonialblatt*, 1903, pp.
      491–3.
   " Bericht über eine Erkundungsexpedition von Bamum nach Jabassi." *Deutsches
      Kolonialblatt*, 1904, p. 597.

Hutter [Hauptm.]
   Globus, XCI, 1, Jan., 1907, pp. 1–6; 2, Jan., 1907, pp. 26–32; 3, Jan., 1907,
      pp. 44–7.

Jeffreys, M. D. W.
   1. " Snake Stones." *J. Roy. Afr. Soc.*, XLI, 165, 1942, pp. 250–3.
   2. " Le serpent à deux têtes Bamum." *Bull. Soc. Et. Cam.*, 9, 1945, pp. 7–12.
   3. " Nsangu's Head." *Afr. St.*, V, 1, 1946, pp. 57–62.
   4. " The Capture of Fumban." *Afr. St.*, VI, 1, 1947, pp. 35–40.
   5. " Serpents = Kings." *Nigerian Field*, XII, 1, 1947, pp. 35–41.
   6. " Notes on Twins, Bamenda." *Afr. St.*, VI, 4, 1947, pp. 189–95.
   7. " The Bamum Coronation Ceremony as Described by King Njoya." *Africa*, XX,
      1, 1950, pp. 38–45.
   8. " The Alphabet of Njoya." *West African Review*, XXIII, 296, 1952, pp. 428–30,
      433.

Koelle, S. W.
   Polyglotta Africana. London : Church Missionary House, 1854.

Labouret, H.
   1. " En pays Bamoum; la ville de Foumban." *Togo-Cameroun*, avril-juillet, 1935,
      pp. 111–20.
   2. " L'ancien Palais Royal de Foumban." *Togo-Cameroun*, avril-juillet, 1935, pp.
      121–6.
   3. " L'écriture Bamoum." *Togo-Cameroun*, avril-juillet, 1935, pp. 127–33.

Lawless [Adm. Adjoint]
   Togo-Cameroun, oct., 1936–jan., 1937.

Lecoq, R.
   " Quelques aspects de l'art Bamoum." In Diop, A. *L'Art Nègre*. *Présence
      Africaine*, 10–11, 1951, pp. 175–80.

Martin, H.
   " Le pays Bamoum et le Sultan Njoya." *Et. Cam.*, sept.-déc., 1951, pp. 5–40.
   " Note relative à l'organisation politique au pays Bamoum," 1953 (Unpublished).

Njoya, Arouna
   " Fabrication des pirogues du Monoun." *Notes Africaines*, avril, 1945, pp. 7–8.

Njoya, Idrissou Mborou
   " Le Sultanat du pays Bamoum et son origine." *Bull. Soc. Et. Cam.*, 1, 1935,
      pp. 81–5.
   Histoire et Coutumes des Bamum (Translated by Henri Martin). *Mém. I.F.A.N.*,
      Série : Populations, No. 5, 1952.

Oldenburg, R.
   " Bamum, ein Negerreich im innern Kameruns." *Atlantis*, 3, 1930, pp. 160–5.

Olivier, G.
   " Contributions à l'étude anthropologique des Bamoum." *Bull. et. Mém. Soc.
      d'Anthrop.*, Paris, IX, 1948, pp. 138–42, 151–62.

Ramsay [Hauptm.]
" Uber seine neueste Reise im Gebiet der Nordwestkamerun Gesellschaft." *Deutsches Kolonialblatt*, 1902, p. 607.

Rein-Wuhrmann, A.
1. *Vier Jahre im Grasland von Kamerun.* 1917.
2. *Mein Bamumvolk im Grasland von Kamerun.* Stuttgart u. Basel: Evang. Missionsverlag, 1925.
3. *Liebes und Liedes aus Kamerun* (Erlebnisse im Missionsdienst). Stuttgart u. Basel: Evang. Missionsverlag, 1931.
4. *Two Women of the Cameroons* (Translated by M. Bryan). 1931.
5. *Fumban, die Stadt auf dem Schutte.* Basel, 1948.

Struck, B.
" König Ndschoya von Bamum als Topograph." *Globus*, XIV, 206, 1908.

Thorbecke, F.
Im Hochland von Mittel-Kamerun. Hamburg, 1914.

Togo-Cameroun, oct., 1933. " Mort de l'ancien Sultan Njoya."

Truitard, S.
" L'art chez les Bamoums." *Arts du Cameroun à l'Exposition d'Art Colonial de Naples*, 1934, pp. 2–7.

van Gennep, A.
" Une nouvelle écriture nègre; sa portée théorétique." *Rev. Et. Ethnog. et Sociol.*, VIII, 1908, pp. 129–39.

" Une nouvelle écriture nègre." *Religions, Mœurs et Légendes*, 2ème série, Paris, 1909.

von Boxberger, L.
" Beiträge zur Landeskunde von Bamum." *Erdball*, 1, 1926.
" Das Opfer. Eine Erinnerung an meine Residentenzeit in Bamum." *Atlantis*, 2, 1930, pp. 357–61.

Ward, I.
" The Phonetic Structure of Bamum." *Bull. S.O.A.S.*, IX, 1938, pp. 423–38.

Westermann, D., and Bryan, M. A.
Languages of West Africa. London: Oxford University Press for International African Institute, 1952.

III. THE BAMILEKE OF THE FRENCH CAMEROONS

LOCATION AND DISTRIBUTION

NOMENCLATURE

There is general agreement among the ethnographers and linguists of this region that the term " Bamileke " is incorrectly applied to the peoples who are to be described here. The people designated by this name do not refer to themselves as Bamileke, nor do the Bamum, their neighbours to the north, who, according to Despois, call them Batongtou, " people of the mountains."[1] Stoll states that the name is a European corruption of the native word current in Dschang, *mbaliku* (*mba*—the first ones, *liku*—a hole in the ground). The Dschang people refer to their chief as *efoo liku Tsan* (" chief of the Dschang hole "), which relates to the belief that their first ancestors emerged from the earth.[2] Other informants attribute its invention to the Bali peoples in the British zone of the Cameroons; these call the inhabitants of Dschang, Lekeu, which means valley or ravine. The Bantu plural form *ba* was prefixed at the time of the European occupation, giving Balekeu, which afterwards developed into Bamilekeu—" the people of the valleys."[3] Bouchaud maintains that the name Bamileke properly belongs to a small group of some 4,000 people situated on the Franco-British frontier to the west of Dschang.[4] The name, however, does not appear anywhere in Tessmann's linguistic and ethnic map.

Bamileke, then, is the current official term under which are grouped together a number of chiefdoms " having the same origin and enjoying a common culture."[5] As there are only minor variations in the culture and social organization from one chiefdom to another, it seems useful to keep the term to refer to this congeries of peoples who distinguish among themselves by reference to the chief to whom they owe allegiance.

LOCATION

The area within which the Bamileke peoples live is situated between 10° to 10° 30′ east and 4° 45′ to 5° 45′ north, and occupies 2,162.5 sq. miles of high plateau land.[6]

To the north and north-west of Bamileke country rise the Bambuto Mountains, reaching a height of 8,858 ft.; these mark the beginning of the British zone of the Cameroons. To the east, beyond the Nun River, lies Bamum country, while the territories of the Mbo and Baneka peoples border on the western side of the region. To the south and south-east the plateau land slopes away to the more low-lying areas inhabited by the Mbang, Bandem, and Banen.

There is considerable intermingling of populations on some of the boundaries of the country. Buisson has drawn a map showing such a mingling of Bamileke with the Mbo to the west and south-west, and with the Bamum to the east.[7] There is a similar mingling of Bamileke and Bandem around the Makombe River region.[8] Large numbers of Bamileke can be found scattered throughout French Cameroons territory; details of migratory movements are given in a separate section.

[1] Despois, 1945.
[2] Dugast, 1949, pp. 113–22.
[3] Delarozière, 1949, pp. 8–68.
[4] Bouchaud, 1944, p. 42.
[5] Labouret, 1935.
[6] Dugast, op. cit., p. 113.
[7] Buisson, 1, 1931, pp. 83–7.
[8] Dugast, op. cit., p. 112.

DEMOGRAPHY

The Bamileke population is distributed in about 90 chiefdoms, which vary considerably in size. Listed in administrative sub-divisions, they are as follows: [9]

Sub-division. DSCHANG. (Area : 860·6 sq. miles)

Chiefdom	Population	Chiefdom	Population
Bafou	19,667	Fossong-Wentcheng	1,294
Bansoa	13,665	Fossong-Ellelem	369
Bamendou	11,376	Fotetsa	762
Foto	12,040	Batcham[10]	13,941
Baleveng	7,201	Babadjou	8,967
Balessing	6,702	Bagam	5,754
Foreke Dschang	5,606	Bamessing	4,908
Fongo-Tongo	5,708	Babete	3,868
Baloum	3,674	Bamenkombo	4,231
Fontsa-Touala	3,835	Bamendjinda	3,259
Santchou	2,830	Bamendjo	3,494
Fongdonera	2,632	Bamougoug	2,603
Fomopea	2,432	Bafounda	2,339
Fongondeng	1,929	Bamendjing	1,600
Fotomena	1,662	Bamesso	1,381
Fokoue	1,462	Bati	1,319
Fombap	1,323	Bamenyam	1,586

Sub-division. BAFANG. (Area : 490 sq. miles approx.)

Chiefdom	Population
Bana	6,013
Banka	5,920
Fotouni	4,762
Babouantou	4,490
Bandoumgia	4,434
Bafang-Centre	4,068
Fonjomekwet	2,678
Babontcha-Ngaleu	2,492
Bakondji	2,351
Bafang	2,288
Ba(n)kassa	1,626
Babone	1,720
Fontsinga	1,422
Babontcha-Fongam	1,148
Fondjanti	902
Komako	943
Batcha	1,050
Bandoumkassa	1,003
Banfeko	1,094
Bandoumka	794
Fombele	701
Fonti	780
Fomessa	594
Bankambe	695
Baboate	1,028
Fondanti	922

Sub-division. BAFOUSSAM. (Area : 463 sq. miles approx.)

Chiefdom	Population
Banjoun	27,257
Baham	13,144
Bangou	8,404
Baya(n)gam	8,255
Bamougoum	13,838
Bamendjou	11,152
Bafoussam	7,681
Baleng	11,196
Batoufam	4,949
Bameka	7,172
Batie	7,602
Bahouan	3,821
Bangam	2,287
Bandenkop	3,158
Bandrefam	1,239
Bapi	1,148
Bandeng	458

[9] The following lists reproduce those sent from the Director of Centrifan, Douala.

[10] Chiefdoms listed from (and including) Batcham appear now to have been grouped in a new sub-division, the *Dembouda Sub-division*, which includes all those chiefdoms formerly in the northern half of the Dschang Sub-division. This is a very recent administrative measure, and in this Survey references to the Dschang Sub-division do not take account of the new situation.

Sub-division. BANGANGTE. (Area : 481 sq. miles approx.)

Chiefdom				*Population*	*Chiefdom*				*Population*
Bangangte ..	..	..	..	11,158	Bazou ..	..	..	..	8–9,000
Bangoua ..	..	..	..	7,065	Bakong ..	..	..	..	1,694
Bagang-Fokam	..	..	..	1,332	Bahouok ..	..	..	..	712
Batchingou..	....	..	..	2,901	Bangoulap ..	..	..	..	4,863
Bamana ..	..	..	..	6,771	Bandounga	..	..	..	6,337
Balengou ..	..	..	..	5,124	Baguou ..	..	..	..	481
					Maha Bossinga Bachui	..		..	542

Egerton gives the following figures from a census of the Bangangte Sub-division which was completed during his visit in 1937: [11]

Men subject to tax payment	..	..	2,187
Women subject to tax payment		..	4,229
Boys below the age of 10	..	..	3,431
Girls below the age of 10	..	..	2,883
Old men above taxable age	..	..	118
Old women above taxable age	..	..	217
Total ..	..	..	13,065

The total population figures for the Bamileke have shown a steady increase for many years.

From 1933 to 1949 the figures rose from 320,000 to 417,070. The figures for the four sub-divisions in 1949 were as follows :

Sub-division	Population	Approx. density	
		per sq. km.	per sq. mile
Dschang	154,215	70	179
Bafang	61,632	49·1	126
Bafoussam ..	133,267	87·2	223
Bangangte ..	67,956	29·5	75·5
Total.. ..	417,070	58·9	171·7

The 1951 approximate total population figures show a further increase: [12]

Sub-division	Population
Dschang	174,305
Bafang	75,149
Bafoussam ..	143,205
Bangangte ..	62,622
Total	455,281

The 1951 figures for births were as follows: [12]

Sub-division			Boys	Girls	Total
Dschang ..	..	..	4,058	2,940	6,998
Bafang ..	..	..	1,906	1,618	3,524
Bafoussam	..	..	4,178	3,520	7,698
Bangangte..	..	..	1,895	1,688	3,583
Total ..	..	..	12,037	9,766	21,803

[11] Egerton, 1938, p. 74.
[12] Figures received from the Director of Centrifan, Douala.

Delarozière gives the following table showing density of population for the years 1946–47, within the Bafoussam Sub-division:[13]

Chiefdom	Population	Approx. area in sq. kms.	Approx. area in sq. miles	Approx. density per sq. km.	Approx. density per sq. mile
Bandjoun	27,257	80	31·2	340·7	872·0
Baham	13,144	70	27·3	187·7	480·5
Bangou	8,404	45	17·5	186·7	477·9
Baya(n)gam	8,255	25	9·8	330·2	845·3
Bamougoum	13,838	40	15·6	345·9	885·5
Bamendjou	11,252	70	27·3	160·7	411·3
Bafoussam	7,681	150	58·5	51·2	131·1
Baleng	9,480	300	117·0	31·6	80·9
Batoufam	4,359	30	11·6	145·3	371·9
Bameka	6,480	20	7·8	324·0	829·4
Batie	7,602	80	31·2	95·0	243·2
Bahouan	3,468	20	7·8	173·4	443·9
Bangam	2,159	18	7·0	119·9	306·9
Bandenkop	3,163	20	7·8	158·1	404·7
Bandrefam	1,270	15	5·8	84·6	216·6
Bapi	1,092	10	3·9	109·2	279·5
Bandeng	440	15	5·8	29·3	75·0
Settlement on left bank of Nun River[14]	2,358	180	70·3	13·1	33·5
Total	131,702	1,188	463·2	110·8	264·3

There are 275 Europeans in Bamileke country; the Administration accounts for 84 of these; 80 are engaged in missionary work and the remainder are engaged in commercial and similar enterprises.

MIGRATIONS

Bamileke are found in many areas of the Cameroons, either developing fertile lands hitherto unexploited or settling down as traders in the large commercial centres. Dugast considers that there are three main population movements directed outside Bamileke territory:

(1) *South-westerly Movement to Mungo Region*

There are large groups of Bamileke settled in the Mbanga area as well as in the urban centres of Mbanga itself and Nkongsamba. Early in the century Bamileke loaned their services to the indigenous agriculturists in this region, working mostly on the prosperous cocoa farms. As a result of the economic crisis of 1928–32 the owners of the farms were forced to make payments to their Bamileke labourers in the form of portions of the plantations; this handing over of the plantations became the current practice so that many of the Bamileke are now in charge of their own farms.

Farther to the south another group of Bamileke settled among the Pongo, Abo, and Bakoko peoples. They are for the most part found near Nkapa, cultivating abandoned land.

To the north of this group, in the administrative sub-division of Nkongsamba, Bamileke settled in the Dibombe Valley and in the commercial centre of Nkongsamba itself. In 1936 there were over 6,000 of them here as against 21,000 autochthones. Figures obtained by Dugast at Douala show that the number of Bamileke who migrate to the south-west is increasing: in 1933 Bamileke living at Douala numbered 1,432 and in 1945 this had risen to 4,167. During these years there was an added impetus to move into the region since the rapid expansion of agricultural enterprises

[13] Delarozière, 1950.
[14] See " Emigration to Bamum country," p. 91.

created a strong demand for labourers. The majority of the immigrants were men who left their wives and children behind, being joined by them later when they had become well established in the area.

Dugast gives the following figures obtained in 1947, which show the numbers of Bamileke immigrants as compared with the autochthonous populations:

					Autochthones	*Bamileke*	
Bakaka	..	..	..	..	5,473	690	
Baneka	..	..	..	..	2,874	4,747	(including Nkongsamba town)
Manehas	..	..	..	..	2,127	5,182	
Bongkeng	..	..	..	..	1,690	6,165	
Balong	..	..	..	..	2,406	3,700	
Abo	..	..	..	..	10,232	843	
Douala (town and surrounding villages)					22,927	10,598	out of a total population of 59,899

In terms of administrative sub-divisions:

Nkongsamba	..	..	..	..	10,727	Bamileke out of a total population of 33,542
Mbanga	..	..	..	..	11,538	Bamileke out of a total population of 21,876

(2) *Emigration towards Ndikinimeki*

Through the northern part of Banen country runs the road connecting Yaounde to Nkongsamba so that conditions for trading are particularly good in the area.

There are Bamileke in the administrative post of Ndikinimeki itself, on the extreme north of Nyokon territory, and on the border of Banen country near the Makenene River, an affluent of the Nun.

(*a*) *In the Administrative Post.* All the shops in this centre are managed by their Bamileke owners; some are already rich, possessing their own lorries, and often have shops elsewhere, particularly at Bangangte. There are besides a number of Bamileke itinerant merchants, travelling between the market at Tonga to the north-west of Ndikinimeki and the market of Nitoukou to the south.

(*b*) *Northern Nyokon Territory.* To the extreme north of Nyokon country flows the Nde River which forms the natural boundary separating it from Bamileke country. This area was formerly very sparsely populated but now much larger numbers of Bamileke are found here, between the right bank of the Nde River and the right bank of the Nun. Whereas before there was but one small Bamileke village, Batoum, there are now two large ones, and in four years the population figures have nearly doubled, the inhabitants in 1949 numbering more than 1,200.

(*c*) *Borders of Banen Country.* Several miles from Batoum towards Ndikinimeki live a number of Bamum, grouped around their own chief. They are separated from the Banen by the Makenene River. In 1940 five or six Bamileke arrived here from Bafang and obtained permission from the Bamum chief to settle on some of the village land. They began to grow rice and maize in considerable quantities and prepared cocoa plantations. By 1946 their numbers had grown to 250; their cocoa plantations are now yielding large crops and the Administration has opened a weekly market for them. In 1947 the numbers of Bamileke agriculturists and traders together reached 1,969.

(3) *Emigration to Bamum Country*

Early attempts by the Administration to direct Bamileke from the Bafoussam Sub-division to the left bank of the Nun did not meet with great success. However, in recent years there has been a voluntary immigration of Bamileke into the area as a result of the economic development of the Fumbot zone. In 1949 there were 763 individuals, coming from the chiefdoms of Bamougoum, Bameka, Baham, and Bandjoun, settled in four villages on the left bank of the Nun to the north of the Bafoussam-Fumban road. There were also 306 individuals settled in the Fumban Sub-division.

The emigrants rarely completely break the bonds linking them to their original territory and there is a tendency to group themselves together according to the chiefdom from which they came. They are all Bafoussam men who control the passage of the kola along the route which starts at Bafoussam and runs across the Cameroons to the markets of Garoua and Maroua. Similarly immigrants in all areas tend to develop the same characteristics of political and social organization found within Bamileke country.

Internal Migrations

In addition to these external migrations there are also those which occur within the Bamileke territory, involving movements from one chiefdom to another. Delarozière's data, collected for the year 1946–47 for the Bafoussam Sub-division, show that 552 people of this Sub-division emigrated to the Dschang Sub-division, 250 to the Bangangte Sub-division, and 279 to the Bafang Sub-division.[15]

[15] Delarozière, op. cit.

TRADITIONS OF ORIGIN AND HISTORY

The controversial ethnic classifications of Bamileke peoples is an index of the lack of any certain knowledge of their history prior to European occupation.[1] Delarozière attempts an outline of the history of the peoples found in the present-day Bafoussam Sub-division, but he states that with so little information available it can only be a very provisional one.[2]

Evidence suggests that the Bamileke peoples came from the region of the upper Mbam which is today occupied by the Tikar. Pressure from the invading Fulani in the 17th century led to a series of migrations southwards, undertaken at different times by separate sections of the population. Many remained where they were under the domination of conquering peoples.

The migrants travelled across the area now occupied by the Bamum, and remained there long enough to found villages; Bamileke claim that they founded such villages in Bamum country as Nkoupit (Bapi), Folepon (Baleng), and Kounden (Bandeng). Large numbers of Bamileke remained in Bamum country and inter-married with the Bamum. The natural frontier of the River Nun and the high plateau rising beyond it were temporary checks on their movement southwards; they might well have remained where they were but for the advance of the Bamum who were themselves being forced southwards by the Fulani.

OCCUPATION OF THE PLATEAU

In his exposition of the early migratory movements of peoples in the present-day Bafoussam Sub-division, Delarozière distinguishes five different stages of settlement on the plateau. He states that the Baleng were probably the first group to cross the Nun at the beginning of the 18th century and went immediately to the most mountainous region where they are still settled today. They were followed by the Bandeng and the Bapi who were forced to circle round them before penetrating farther on to the plateau. The Bafoussam took the same route, and settled to the south of the Baleng, slowly progressing to their present position.

The groups of Bandjoun, Bankassa, and Balengou were later founded by peoples from Baleng.

Second Group. Another section of the population arrived on the plateau to the west of the Baleng. These were to found such chiefdoms as Bagam, Bamendou, and Bansoa. Travelling farther south, men from these groups founded yet other groups; thus Baham and Bangou were founded by men from Bamendou, and the Bazou group was similarly founded by Bangou men.

Third Group. The Bati crossed the Nun at the Bangang-Fondji ford and settled in this region. They were later driven out by the Bandjoun, and after long wanderings through the chiefdoms of Bafoussam, Baleng, Bamenkombo, Bafounda, and Batcham, finally established themselves in their present position.

Fourth Group. Delarozière admits that the origin of the Bafamgwa (or Bandrefam) group is unknown; he suggests that its founders also came from the left bank of the Nun. The neighbouring groups of Bangwa and Batoufam were founded by peoples of this group.

Fifth Group. This group consists of peoples whose founders are traditionally stated to have come from the south; the Bamougoum coming from Bandoumgia, Bangam coming from Fondjomekwet, and Bandenkop from Fotouni.

Nothing is known of the peoples whom the Bamileke found on the plateau at the time of their arrival. Delarozière suggests that it was a small very scattered

---

[1] See Delarozière, 1949, p. 11. Also de Pedrals, 1946, p. 28, Dugast, 1949, p. 113, and Poutrin, 1949, p. 42.
[2] Delarozière, op. cit., pp. 11–18.

population, the conquest and assimilation of which was very rapid. From the period of settlement onwards there was constant fighting among the different groups. Thus the chiefdom of Bandjoun sought to increase its power, and during his reign Fotso II brought under his authority the smaller chiefdoms of Bangam-Fokam, Bandrefam, Batoufam, and Bayangan to the south, and to the west those of Bahouan and Bandenkop. German occupation of the territory in the late 19th and early 20th centuries put an end to the growing power of the Bandjoun, and, with the exception of Bahouan, gave the conquered chiefdoms their independence.

Similar reports of conquest are found in Egerton's account of the history of Bangangte.[3] Nganteu, the founder of Bangangte chiefdom, is said to have come from Difum or Lifum to the east of the Mbam River. Egerton states that the old rulers whom Nganteu found were not entirely cast out or even completely deposed, so that there came into existence a dual system of sub-chiefship shared by the descendants of the original rulers of the country and the descendants of Nganteu's people. But there was a great deal of fighting when Nganteu and his successors sought to extend the chiefdom. Egerton lists the following chiefs who succeeded Nganteu in this order: Nenaton, Biatat, N'gassam I, N'jike I, Nya, N'gassam II, Yomi, Tchatchua, and N'jike II, the present chief, who succeeded in 1912.[4]

Besides these internal conflicts, the Bamileke were engaged in many skirmishes with the Bamum on the eastern fringes of the plateau. The Bandjoun and Baleng peoples not only defended their territory but also went into Bamum country to make reprisal attacks, even going so far as the walls of Fumban, where fortifications erected against these attacks can still be seen.

Raiding from the Bamum came to an end only with the arrival of the Europeans.

MODERN DEVELOPMENTS

For the purposes of administration the French have divided the territory into Regions, each one having a Regional head. These are again divided into smaller administrative units, the sub-divisions, each one having a sub-divisional head. Thus, there is the Bamileke Region, with its sub-divisions of Dschang, Bafang, Bafoussam, and Bangangte; Dschang is the headquarters of the Region. The number of chiefdoms contained within each one of these sub-divisions is as follows: Dschang 33, Bafang 30, Bafoussam 17, Bangangte 10.

Today the boundary of Mohammedanism starts at Fumban and follows a line roughly demarcating the end of the forest zone and the beginning of the savanna zone. All the trading centres in this southern part of the Cameroons have their Moslem quarter, occupied chiefly by Hausa merchants. The Catholic Mission has established three Apostolic Vicariates in the area, that of Douala comprising the western section, that of Yaounde covering the whole of the eastern section, and that of Fumban covering the northern section. Figures collected by the Catholic Missions in 1938 show that there are 60 principal mission stations within this area. A considerable number can be found in Bamileke country, for example those of Bafang, founded in 1926, Bandjoun, founded in 1929, and Bangangte, founded in 1939. The 1938 figures show that 37% of the total population in the Douala Vicariate were Christians.[5]

The French Protestant Mission is also established in the Cameroons; its Districts include Bafoussam and Fumban.

The Missions are in charge of a number of schools apart from those established by the Education Service. The latter service has established a special school at Dschang for the sons of chiefs; it is attended by Bamileke, Bamum, and Tikar.

[3] Egerton, 1938, pp. 92–4.
[4] Ibid., p. 110.
[5] Bouchaud, 1944, p. 40.

Roads

The Administration has built a number of roads in the area. One of these runs from Nkongsamba to Bafang where one branch of it continues to Dschang and on towards Bamenda country. Another road runs from Dschang to Bafoussam and Fumban. Others extend from Bafoussam and Bafang to Bangangte, where a further road leads to Ndikinimeki.

LANGUAGE

The Bamileke are often referred to as a Semi-Bantu-speaking people, but Greenberg maintains that there is no justification for this;[6] he classifies them as belonging to the linguistic sub-family known as the " central branch " of the Niger Congo family of languages; of the 24 generic sub-groupings within this central branch, Greenberg places the Bamileke languages in the Bantu sub-grouping. Westermann and Bryan consider that there is insufficient linguistic evidence for such a classification and prefer to regard the Bamileke language, with that of the Bamum, provisionally as an " isolated language group."[7] They add further that the name Bamileke is used by Europeans to designate a number of languages and/or dialects. These languages are sometimes referred to by Europeans as " Grassfield," which in Pidgin becomes *grafi* or *grafil*. The total number of languages and/or dialects is not known; Westermann and Bryan list the following:

Dschang (Dshang or Chang), spoken in Dschang Sub-division.

Babadjou, spoken in Babadjou chiefdom and neighbourhood.

Bagam, spoken in Bagam chiefdom.

Bamougoum, spoken in Bamougoum chiefdom. This language resembles those of Bameka and Bamendjou and also those of Bansoa and Balessing in the Dschang Sub-division.

Bafoussam, spoken in Bafoussam Sub-division.

Bandjoun, spoken in Bandjoun and the surrounding area; closely related to the speech of Baham chiefdom.

Babouantou, spoken in the north-eastern part of Bafang Sub-division.

Bafang, dialect cluster? Many dialects are spoken in the area surrounding Bafang. The name *fefe* is used to denote the language of the whole of Bafang.

Bakou, spoken to the west of Bafang.

Dialects of the Bangou, spoken in the Betchingou-Bamana area.

Dialects of the Bangwa-Batoufam area.

Bangangte, understood in the whole Sub-division, although other local dialects are spoken. Used in French Protestant Missions.

Dialect or language of Batongtou.

In all these languages there are noun classes; there also appears to be concord of a sort, e.g., with possessives. The vocabulary shows a considerable resemblance to Bantu. Tessmann classifies Bamileke " dialects " into those having many prefixes, few prefixes, and no prefixes, but Stoll says that all the dialects have prefixes, though some may be reduced to a nasal or to a vowel which is stressed only slightly. He also states that the speech of all the Bamileke dialects is extremely rapid, avoiding any polysyllabism and going straight to the radical with the least possible emphasis on prefix or suffix.[8]

[6] Greenberg, 1949.
[7] Westermann and Bryan, 1952, pp. 128–30.
[8] Dugast, 1949, p. 117.

PHYSICAL ENVIRONMENT

Bamileke country lies in an area which shows a gradual transition from the southern forest zone to the savanna zone of the north. It possesses none of the extremes of climate or vegetation characteristic of these two zones. The forest begins to thin out and savanna conditions begin to show themselves with greater frequency as one travels north above a line drawn roughly through Dschang, Bafia, Saa, Nanga-Eboko, and Batouri.

It is a country of undulating plateaux, bordered to the east by a deep valley, irrigated by the Nun River, and to the south falling away abruptly in a series of steep valleys from a height of 4,300 ft. Gallery forests stretch out along these valleys. To the north and north-west the Bambouto mountains extend along the British Cameroons frontier, rising to a height of 9,000 ft.

Dugast divides Bamileke country into three geographical zones as follows: [1]

(1) *The Dschang-Bana-Bangangte Upland Zone*

This is very hilly, uneven country. The altitude (the post of Dschang itself is 4,527 ft.) makes it a relatively cold area. Precipitations are caused by vapours coming on to the plateau from the low-lying humid valley of the Nkam and the Cross River basin and condensing there in violent showers. Laterite soils are found in the non-basaltic regions around Bangangte; these soils are almost entirely exhausted, though cultivation still continues.

(2) *The Bafoussam Upland to the North-east*

Volcanic elevations are characteristic of this region. It is fertile country and very little of it is left uncultivated. The Wood and Forest Service Authorities have shown that in spite of its appearance today this plateau was originally covered with dense forest. Kola and other species of forest trees still grow in gallery forest, and raffia-palms on the lower margins of the small rivers.

(3) *Southern Zone*

The Bafang mountain range, through which deep channels have been cut by the several tributaries of the Nkam River, is in this zone. The land is extremely clayey and far more thickly wooded than the rest of the country; there are also very fine plantations of palm-trees.

CLIMATIC CONDITIONS

Situated as it is between the equatorial forest and tropical savanna zones, Bamileke country (together with the neighbouring Bamum country) has its own distinct climatic features. These, however, are due not only to the intermediate position which it occupies, but also to its altitude—Bamileke country is roughly 4,000 ft. above sea level. There is little variation in temperature over the year, and the relatively cool climate has made Bamileke country one of the healthiest regions for Europeans in the Cameroons. Despois records the following temperatures for Dschang,[2] which is about 4,527 ft. above sea level; temperatures are of course higher in areas of lower altitude:

Maximum annual mean temperature .. .. 77° F.
Minimum annual mean temperature .. .. 58° F.
Month when maximum mean is greatest .. .. .. February (81° F.)
Month when minimum mean is least .. .. January (52° F.)

[1] Dugast, 1949, p. 113.
[2] Despois, 1945, p. 599.

96

Heavy showers, bringing down maximum temperatures, mark the beginning of the rainy season in March and they steadily increase until September. During this month Dschang receives over 12 ins. There is an abrupt decrease in rainfall—perhaps from 0.79 to 0.2 ins.—from October to November. Very little rain falls from November to February, and hardly any in December and January. Dschang receives an annual rainfall of approximately 36 ins. During the winter period an east or north-east wind, dry and dusty, blows almost continuously. Throughout the year the higher altitudes may frequently be covered in a heavy cold mist.[3]

VEGETATION

The thick forest to the south thins away in Bamileke country and, apart from some scattered patches, only the gallery forests remain, growing along river courses and streams. Apart from the raffia and oil palms, trees belonging characteristically to the forest zone but still found in this region include the *Canarium* and the *Pachilobus edulis*. Tall grasses common to the region are the *Pennisetum purpureum* (elephant grass), found wherever the soil is deep and fertile, and *Imperata cylindrica* which grows in poorer soil.

MAIN FEATURES OF ECONOMY

AGRICULTURE

The Bamileke are agriculturists and the small numbers of livestock which they possess play a very minor part in their economy. Some chiefs own small herds of cattle whose meat is consumed only on the occasion of certain ceremonies. Stranger Fulani groups herd cattle in mountain grassland areas and, in the dry season, in the Nun Valley. There is very little intercourse between these Fulani and the Bamileke. Most households possess a few sheep and goats, which are used as betrothal gifts, and as gifts to the chief, and are not generally eaten except on ceremonial occasions. They graze on uncultivated land and along pathways.

Hunting plays little part in the present-day economy of the Bamileke, although it was of considerable importance in former times. Despois reports that Bamileke living in the low-lying valleys to the south still hunt antelope, buffalo, and elephant.[4]

Staple crops grown by Bamileke are maize, cocoyams, and groundnuts; yam cultivation is not quite so widespread. Of secondary importance is the cultivation of sweet potatoes, cassava, and manioc. Products of trees such as the kola, banana, raffia, and oil-palm are all utilized. Certain valleys in the Bangangte Sub-division are particularly rich in oil-palms, and the main revenue of the peoples who live there is derived from the sale of their products to Bamileke and Bafia traders.

Seasonal Calendar

At the end of the dry season, in February, ridges or mounds are prepared ready for the planting in March when the rains begin. Contour farming is unknown to Bamileke and the ridges always follow the angle of the slope which is being cultivated. These ridges are roughly 19 ins. deep; each year when they are remade, any leaves or grasses are thrown into them, thus giving some fertilization to the soil.

Two or more crops are usually grown together on the same section of land, e.g., maize with groundnuts, cocoyams, or cassava. Maize is harvested in June-July, cassava and cocoyams begin to produce at the end of the rainy season in late October. Plots are used for three, four, or five years and then left fallow for one or sometimes two years. A married woman cultivates a plot of land of about 1¼ acres, allocated to her by her husband. The total area cultivated for a particular household will thus depend on the number of wives a man has. Plots in the vicinity

---

[3] Despois, op. cit., p. 599.
[4] Ibid., p. 621.

G

of dwelling-huts are enclosed by fences. Cultivated lands some distance away from the dwellings are not generally enclosed; sometimes, however, these are fenced in, and the fences are left in position even when the land is lying fallow. Wives of a chief co-operate a great deal in their work and the section of land allocated to each one is not delimited by fencing, but only by pathways and shrubs.

A woman usually produces more than is required for subsistence and she may dispose of the surplus in the market which is held every four days. Egerton writes that the market is primarily the women's affair, but that a man may go to market on his own account, taking palm or raffia wine, goats, and salt.[5] Nowadays regular traders are found at the markets selling European goods. Large numbers of people, perhaps between 4,000 and 5,000, assemble at the bigger markets, such as those held at Bandjoun. Great changes in the traditional economy were brought about by the introduction of coffee-growing in about 1928. Many Bamileke today work on coffee plantations which are mostly found in the Nun Valley, around Bamougoum, and in the Dschang Sub-division; men do the work on these plantations, whereas women are the agricultural labourers in the traditional system.

The agricultural services of the territory have introduced the quiquina tree; one species is more profitable but more difficult to cultivate and can only be grown under European supervision, but some Bamileke in the Dschang area have small plantations of a more robust species. The Agricultural Service aims at improving general methods of cultivation and also experiments with new methods at certain experimental stations, one of which is established at Dschang.

Division of Labour

Women and girls are responsible for planting, sowing, and reaping; there is a general belief that women can make the soil fruitful. Men may help with the initial work of clearing the ground; they erect fences, build and repair huts, and engage in trade.

CRAFTS

In order to preserve the traditional crafts and standards of workmanship, Raymond Lecoq visited the Cameroons in 1945 and spent several years founding craftsmen's schools, one of which is established at Bafoussam. Here sculptors and craftsmen of all kinds receive instruction from special teachers.

Most of the following account is based on Lecoq's book on Bamileke crafts.[6]

Domestic Architecture[7]

The Bamileke house has attracted much attention because it shows a unique combination of features, characteristic of structures of the savanna and forest zones. Thus its roof is conical and made of straw, while its clay walls are rectangular like those found in the forest area. Women's houses are about 12 ft. square and slightly smaller than those of the men. The walls are erected first, and the ceiling and roof, which are prefabricated, are attached by means of pegs and strands of bamboo bark. The framework of the whole structure consists of a lattice-work of bamboo, the interstices of the walls being tightly packed with mud and those of the roof being filled with straw.

The small doorway is a few inches above the ground and consists of four panels of wood which, if the house belongs to a chief or titled person, may be elaborately carved. Decorated pillars surrounding the doorway may also mark the house of an important person.

The main articles of furniture are a stool and a bed, usually made from the ribs of the raffia-palm. Only the chief has the right to a carved wooden bed.

[5] Egerton, 1938, p. 136.
[6] Lecoq, 1953.
[7] See also Chapoulie, 1931, p. 92; Malcolm, 2, 1923, pp. 21–7.

Sculpture and Carving

The equipment of the sculptor (*kam'jue*) consists of an adze (*t'chop*), hatchet (*d'jom*), chisel (*t'chop*), hammer (*kue*), and scraper (*kuon*). A sculptor usually works on freshly cut wood.

Statues most frequently represent the chief, but there are also small statuettes (*mupo*) of pregnant women which are held in the hand during certain dances. Sometimes sticks decorated with carvings of human and animal figures are placed outside a hut to keep away intruders.

Masks are always worn against the face and not placed on the head as among the Bamum. Both human and animal heads are carved and are often decorated with human and goat hair.

The horizontal *lam* drum, formerly used to summon people to war, is made from a large section of tree trunk and sometimes decorated with carvings of animal heads or the head of the chief. Other drums are the *n'ke deng*, which always has the figure of the chief carved upon it, the *nkak*, the *n'tem*, and the *ndükam*. All except the last are played by hand.

Horns, bracelets, and statuettes are all worked in ivory. Elaborately carved elephant-tusks are sometimes fixed in the ground for the performance of a dance.

Stools are carved from wood or made from the ribs of the raffia-palm. Certain wooden stools are reserved for special persons; thus nobody but the chief, his mother, the sub-chief, and certain notables may sit on the *kuo ketuok* stool. Wooden stools are always monoxylous and made from the *m'be* (*canarium*) or the *lem dje* (*polyscias ferruginea*); they may be elaborately carved with human and animal figures and are sometimes decorated with bead embroidery. A man is entitled to a particular stool according to his position in the hierarchically organized societies. A new member sits on the floor, but later acquires the right to sit on a small cylindrical stool (*n'tukuo*); those next in the hierarchy sit on slightly larger stools with three legs (*n'djata*); a larger stool of the same kind (*lengtchap*) marks the next grade, while those higher still are entitled to sit on a still larger four-legged stool; the largest stool is reserved for the chief and is often decorated with carvings of the panther.

Pottery[8]

Clay pots as well as baskets are made by women. Wooden pots decorated with carvings of animals are made by men. The woman potter works the clay into the required shape with her hands. Pots may be as much as 2 ft. high; globular and hemispherical shapes with single or double handles are made, and decorated by pressing plaited bamboo bark on to the moist clay. The sun gives them a preliminary drying before they are baked.

Metal-work

Lecoq mentions this only briefly. Despois reports that men forge working implements such as hoes and axes.[9] The hoe has replaced a type of spade which was used in agricultural work and which is now seen only in the performance of certain dances.

Weaving

This is the work of men. In the chief's village in Bangangte in 1938 there was only one weaver but he remembered a time when there had been six. A weaver's equipment consists of four twigs which he places in the ground about 1 ft. apart; at a distance of 6 ft. he places the other two sticks in a similar position. This forms the framework of the loom. A piece of wood about 9 ins. long, to which is attached a small comb-like structure, is placed in the middle of the frame, and the warp threads stretch from one end of the loom to the other, each one passing through the comb. A shuttle is used to pass the weft thread through the warp.

---

[8] Lecoq, 1953. See also Buisson, 3, 1931.
[9] Despois, 1945, p. 620.

LOCAL AND KIN GROUPING

VILLAGE, COMPOUND, AND LINEAGE

It appears that the only compact clusters of huts are those which mark the residences of chiefs, sub-chiefs, and, perhaps, important officials. These clusters are often termed " villages " in the literature. Apart from these, compounds vary in size and are scattered throughout the area, each one usually standing within its own enclosure. It is possible that the named administrative unit which is commonly termed " quartier " in the French literature may be considered as a dispersed village. (See below, p. 105, f.n. 14.) Within the compound itself each wife has her own hut and there may be one or more store huts; the largest hut is usually that of the compound head. The group most frequently found in a compound is the patrilineal polygynous family. Egerton writes that formerly children stayed with their parents until they were 15 years old.[10] Daughters leave the compound to go to live with their husbands on marriage. When a son wishes to marry and establish his own household, Egerton states that he leaves his parental compound and asks the official in charge of a *tang la* for land on which he may farm and build huts for himself and his wife.[11]

KINSHIP TERMINOLOGY

Malcolm briefly reports for the Bagam that " the head of the family (*n-gōn ndœp*) is the father (*te, ta,* or *ba*) in whom all the family authority and power is vested. Each family lives in a separate compound (*dzuo, zɔo,* or *nzuu*) and is quite independent of the others. . . . All children are unreservedly under the jurisdiction of the father."[12] He gives the terms of relationship (man speaking) as follows:[13]

Father	*te, ta, ba*	Father's father	*dɔ, dü*
Mother	*na, ma, me*	Father's mother	*ma ma, ka*
Son	*moŋ ma nko*	Mother's father	*ka*
Daughter	*moŋ mingwi*	Father's mother's brother	*ni m-ban*
Brother	*moŋ ma m-fœd*	Son's son	*mundzœd*
Elder brother	*ni*	Wife's father	*n-tse, n-tsi*
Sister	*moŋ ma mingwi, m-fœd*	Wife's mother	*n-tsi, m-vwɔo, n-gom*
Elder sister	*ma*	Wife's brother	*moŋ ma ng-mbi, n-dūp moŋ ma, n-tsi*
Father's brother	*moŋ moŋ me ta, ba m-bod*	Wife's sister	*moŋ ma n-gwii*
Father's sister	*moŋ moŋ me ta mingwi, ngwii moŋ ma ta, ta(n) n-gwii*	Wife's sister's husband	*moŋ ma ng-mbi*
Brother's son	*moŋ moŋ ma moŋ ng-mbi*	Wife	*mingwi*
Sister's son	*mundzœd*	Daughter's husband	*n-tsi*
Husband (w.s.)	*n-gōn*	Brother's wife	*moŋ ma n-gwii*

THE PATRILINEAGE

No detailed kinship study has been made in the area and our present knowledge is very inadequate, but the existence of patrilineages can be confirmed from the information given by Labouret on the cult of the ancestral skulls.[14] The patrilineal group consists of all those who trace their descent agnatically from a common ancestor and who share a common allegiance to their ancestral skulls. It appears that such patrilineages have only a shallow depth. Thus Egerton writes, " the attention [to the skulls] seems to become less as the ancestor is more remote. In

---

[10] Egerton, 1938, p. 235.
[11] Ibid., p. 136.
[12] Malcolm, 1926, p. 236.
[13] Ibid.
[14] Labouret, 1935, p. 139. See also below, p. 127.

many cases the father's and grandfather's skulls are known but the rest are confused and dismissed as not particularly important.''[15]   This may not be the case with chiefly lineages, however, for large numbers of ancestral skulls are preserved in a special hut in the chief's village and more attention is paid to them.

The lineage is a localized group and the homesteads of the adult male members tend to be found adjacent to each other.   The senior male member is the head of the lineage.   Unlike the succession to all other titles and goods, Labouret records that succession to lineage headship and the inheritance of lineage skulls go to the oldest male member of the oldest generation.   The lineage head makes offerings and sacrifices to the skulls on behalf of the lineage; he consults the diviner when any lineage member is ill and, if it is found necessary, he will placate an irate ancestor who may be causing the illness.   Adult male members of the lineage must come together to carry out any necessary communal work in connection with the ancestral cult, such as the building of a hut for the skulls.

[15] 1938, p. 256.

POLITICAL AND SOCIAL ORGANIZATION

Most of the following information is taken from the work of Delarozière[1] and Malcolm,[2] who carried out researches within the chiefdoms of the Bafoussam Sub-division and the Bagam chiefdom respectively.

As previously indicated, the term Bamileke does not refer to a people who form a single political unit, but to a collection of peoples who are divided into a number of more or less autonomous chiefdoms.[3] In pre-European days a hierarchy of chiefdoms could develop through processes of defeat and victory, segmentation, and through alliances formed for security measures. Owing to the frequency of warfare, however, such political structures showed little stability, and the status of component chiefdoms was constantly changing.

SUB-CHIEFDOMS

From the information which Delarozière obtained within the Bafoussam area, he was able to classify sub-chiefdoms in the following manner:[4]

(1) *Arising through Conquest*

Conquered chiefdoms lost much of their independence and were reduced to the status of sub-chiefdoms. The skulls of the ancestors of the conquered chief, the symbols of his position and chiefly authority, were brought to the village of the victorious chief and placed there. His title was changed from that of *Fon* (chief) to *fonte* (sub-chief), and he was obliged to show the customary signs of respect to the *Fon;* thus he could not sit in his presence nor speak to him without placing his hand over his mouth. All leopards killed on his territory had to be handed over to the *Fon.* Many of his sons, including his heir, were placed under the guardianship of the *Fon.* Succession to office remained hereditary, but the new appointment had to be ratified by the *Fon.*

Apart from such changes, the administration of the sub-chief's territory was still largely in his own hands.

(2) *Arising through Voluntary Alliance*

Certain chiefdoms abandoned their independent political status in order to obtain the protection of a stronger chiefdom and thus avoid subjugation by another. Delarozière reports that the former chiefdom of Bapa, threatened by the chiefdoms of Batie, Baham, and Bandenkop, preferred to place itself under the protection of the chief of Bandjoun rather than be conquered. Delarozière states briefly that this type of sub-chiefdom had a greater independence than any of the other types.

(3) *As a Result of a Rise in Status of One of the Administrative Units into which a Chiefdom is Divided*[5]

It appears that there was a tendency for a chief to give the status of sub-chiefdom to one or more of those administrative units which were situated on the borders of his chiefdom. It has been suggested that this was expedient in the event of attack

---

[1] Delarozière, 1949, *passim.*
[2] Malcolm, 1926.
[3] The current term both in the English and French literature is " chefferie," which, however, is often used to denote both the chief's village and the entire territory over which his rule extends. To avoid any confusion which may arise through adopting this term, " chiefdom " is substituted here.
[4] Delarozière, 1949, p. 30.
[5] Delarozière calls these units " quartiers " or quarters; this terminology is discussed later.

from a neighbouring chiefdom; the greater independence which the sub-chief enjoyed enabled him to act quickly without waiting for the orders of the chief.[6]

A hierarchy of chiefdoms may furthermore have been established by a process of segmentation as described by Delarozière. He states that some of the present-day chiefdoms are offshoots of another, older chiefdom; thus the Bandjoun and Balengou chiefdoms were first established by peoples of the Baleng chiefdom. At a later date Bahouan similarly developed from Bandjoun. Chiefdoms such as Baleng are often referred to in the literature as " mother-chiefdoms."

The bond between a chiefdom and that from which it has arisen is shown particularly in matters relating to succession to important offices and to arbitration. Thus it is the right of the chief of Baham, a " mother-chiefdom," to come to the funeral ceremonies of the *mafo* (chief's mother) of Bayangam, her " daughter-chiefdom," and furthermore to select another *mafo* from among the daughters of the Bayangam chief. The Baham chief also knows in advance the name of the successor to the Bayangam chieftainship and he may receive this boy into his chiefdom until the time comes for him to take his father's place. He advises and helps this boy, who in turn honours and respects his guardian.

" Mother-chiefdoms " often acted as mediators for their " daughter-chiefdoms " when these were in conflict with another chiefdom. Delarozière cites Raynaud who states that peace could be established if the neutral chief walked on to the fighting area holding blades of the sacred *fɔnkey* grass, and requested the parties to stop fighting.[7]

POLITICAL ORGANIZATION OF THE BAGAM AREA[8]

The Counsellors

The chief is assisted by five counsellors (*m-pfōsē*). On his accession the head-chief usually appoints two of his personal friends to this office, the other three having been in attendance on the late chief. One of the older *m-pfōsē* acts as remembrancer and is always in attendance on the chief at important ceremonies. One *m-pfōsē* attends the chief at all times and is furnished with quarters in the chief's compound. All five *m-pfōsē* are present whenever the chief officiates at any ceremony or judicial trial, but as a rule only one or two are present when minor complaints are being heard.

Attendants (*cuo fon or cinda*)

These include free-born men selected to be in attendance on the chief, sub-chief, and their counsellors. As well as being in personal attendance, they also have the duty of supervising work on farms. There are also a number of freemen whom Malcolm terms " honorary " attendants (*m-bwa pworo me*); these have no special duties to perform. They are selected by the chief for this distinction and may have *n-de* (a title of honour) prefixed to their names.

Boy Messengers (*monkofon*) and the taman dop

These live in a special hut (*n-dǣp n-ge n-gyii fon*) to the north of the main entrance of the chief's compound. Two or more of these messengers are always in close attendance on the chief.

The *taman dop* are special messengers who are employed to carry messages from the chief to his sub-chiefs (*fon tiu*); they are provided with food and dwellings by the sub-chiefs.

[6] Delarozière, 1949, p. 33.
[7] Ibid., p. 27.
[8] Ibid., *passim*.

Other Officials

Other officials, whose functions are described by Malcolm, are as follows:

(1) *The mɔpo, or Constable.* The mɔpo is also an attendant and receives his orders direct from the chief. All offenders against the law are apprehended by him and confined in the detention hut (*ndœp n-gœŋ*). As a sign of his authority he carries a stout wooden staff. He wears a long coarsely woven gown with the head-covering attached to it.

(2) *The tsaa tuŋ, or Herald.* The herald issues the instructions of the chief to the people after they have assembled in the market place. On such occasions he is attended by a number of other officials, and in his right hand he holds three spears, points uppermost, which he flourishes as he speaks.

(3) *The n-gaŋe fɔo, n-gwii fɔo, or Accoucheur.* This official also holds the status of an attendant, and is generally held in great esteem. His badge of office consists of a long steel chain which is carried over one shoulder and to which are attached three small ivory human figures.

Administration of the Chiefdom (Bagam)

Malcolm reports that Bagam is composed of numerous scattered compounds which are spread over a fairly wide area. The administrative unit is the *pfi* and it is made up of a number of compounds in a certain area. The man in charge of a *pfi* (*tera pfi*) is ranked as an attendant (*cuo fon*) on the chief. The actual work of administering a *pfi* is undertaken by a subordinate (*saa pfi*) who does not rank as an attendant. All orders to the members of the *pfi* are given to this man by the *tera pfi* or come direct from the chief; he also supervises any work allotted to his group of compounds. For the purposes of administration the territory of the Bagam is divided into two areas, each with about an equal number of compounds. These are called *m-ba pot* and *m-ba pfie ogoŋ* respectively and two of the senior attendants (*mwɔo fɔo m-bi* and *mwɔo n-kwii*) are responsible to the chief for their administration. If the chief wishes to have work done in any part of his territory he notifies one of these men who in turn instructs all the *tera pfi* concerned. When clearing and other work has to be done on behalf of the European Administration each *pfi* is allocated a definite section for which it is held responsible.

The chain of communication between the chiefs and the *pfi* is very simple. Sometimes the chief may communicate direct with a *saa pfi* when any urgent work is required to be done. In attendance on the chief there is always a number of boys and men whose sole duty it is to carry messages and these are under the control of a head *cuo fon.* The boy messenger receives his orders from this man and passes them on to the *tera pfi* or *saa pfi* as occasion demands.

Political Organization of the Bafoussam Area

The Chief's Advisory Council, the kamvə[9] *(Literally: "Descendants of the Ancestors")*

The body of persons known as the *kamvə* are stated to be the descendants in the paternal line of the nine founders and creators of the chiefdom who are believed to have emerged from the earth. Theoretically it consists of eight titled men together with the chief, but Delarozière found instances where membership had considerably increased. The office of chiefship is thought to have been vested in one of their members by the original *kamvə* and the reigning chief is considered to be this man's lineal descendant. A *kamvə* member holds his office of adviser to the chief by virtue of hereditary succession and cannot be removed from such an office. *Kamvə* members help and advise the chief on all important issues; the chief consults with them when he is about to choose his heir, and if he should die before making the

[9] Delarozière also speaks of the *kamvə* as a society. See Section on Associations, p. 110.

choice the *kamvə* members select his successor.   The *kamvə* control the activities of all the societies within the chiefdom.[10]

The Chief's Servants and Officials

Those placed at the top of the servant hierarchy are generically termed *wala*. The *wala* category is itself hierarchically sub-divided as follows:

(1) *Wala nka.*   Their duties are administrative and religious.   They are the members of the *pontiə* or priests' society, and are in charge of the cult of the chief's ancestors.   Delarozière reports that the chief himself cannot pour libations of palm-wine on to the skulls and that *wala nka* must do this for him in his presence. Egerton, however, states that the chief of the Bangangte made these offerings himself.[11]

A group of administrative units into which a chiefdom is divided may be put under the control of a *wala nka;* this means that he is responsible for the mainten-ance of order within this group and acts as adviser to the officials in charge of the administrative units comprising his group.   These *wala* also supervise collective work in the chief's village, such as the construction of huts and the upkeep and clearing of pathways.

(2) *Wala nza.*   These are members of the *paŋgop* society.   Their duties are largely domestic and they keep an inventory of all the chief's possessions.

(3) *The nge or bakam.*   These are adolescents who are being instructed in the duties of the *wala*.   Delarozière does not state on what basis they are recruited.

Lower down in the hierarchy are placed those servants (*tchinda*) whose duties are mainly domestic.   They act as messengers of the chief and watch over his wives. A young *tchinda* must sleep on the floor and is not allowed to cut his hair.   He becomes a *me tandia* or principal *tchinda* by paying the principal *tchinda* for the right to cut his hair and to sleep on a bed.   When he becomes a *tandia* he can if he wishes obtain permission to leave the chief's service.   Albert reports that he must remain a *tandia* for another four years, at the end of which time the chief will give him a wife or wives and permission to depart.[12]   The chief enjoys all rights over any children of the marriage.   The chief may confer a title on him and give him an administrative post.

As long as they remained in the service of the chief, these servants were celibate; the practice of giving wives to retiring servants whose children were of the same servant status led to the development of an hereditary servant class.   Delarozière also reports that children were sometimes placed in the hands of the chief as pawns if the father was unable to pay his debts; furthermore, children for whose mothers bridewealth had not been paid were liable to be placed in the chief's service.

Administration of the Chiefdom (Bafoussam)

Delarozière states that for administrative purposes a chief divided his territory into units of varying size, and that at the head of each one was usually placed one of his relatives or loyal servants.   Despois writes that a chief tended to create a large number of these administrative units so that no official in charge would ever be in a strong enough position to oppose him.[13]

These administrative units were named and the inhabitants of each one knew its boundaries.   Such units (termed " quartiers " in the French literature)[14] were

---

[10] See below, pp. 110 ff., for a description of these societies.
[11] Egerton, 1938, p. 253.
[12] Albert, 1943, p. 66.
[13] Despois, 1945, p. 611.
[14] Egerton (op. cit., p. 123) reports for the Bangangte that these " quartiers " are known as " *tang la.*"   He himself sometimes refers to them as villages.   Perhaps they may be con-sidered today as dispersed villages, but Despois states that formerly these were administrative units with relatively fluid boundaries, and that a chief could enlarge or decrease their number when it was politically expedient.

often grouped together to form a larger administrative unit, and each such group was placed under a *wala*. There are eight such groups within the Bandjoun chiefdom. The *wala* in charge of a group is responsible for keeping order within it, and for the smooth running of its markets. He also acts as adviser to the heads of the smaller units comprising his group.

TITLES

Delarozière states that any individual, even a slave, who has distinguished himself in the service of the chief may acquire a title.[15] Titles are bestowed by the chief[16] and inherited by a man's chosen successor. Once acquired, a title cannot be lost except when the holder is banished. To each title are attached certain privileges, such as the right to enter certain societies or to have carved doorways. The titles are ranked in an order of precedence, but a title lower down in the scale will not necessarily be dropped on the acquisition of a higher one and an individual may thus collect several titles. Delarozière lists the following titles according to the ways in which they are obtained:[17]

1. Held by the *kamvə* members, the descendants of the nine founders of the chiefdom: *nzədie*.

2. On the installation of a new chief the following titles are given. *Tafo*: held by the maternal grandfather of the chief or his successor; *kuipi*: held by a paternal half-brother of the chief—he is the chief's first minister; *sob* (*sup*): held by a younger paternal half-brother of the chief—one of the chief's close advisers; *moafo* (*wafo*): a uterine brother of the chief who acts as a close adviser; *nzəmafo*: held by the maternal uncle of the chief—one of the chief's advisers.

3. Titles conferred as a result of services given to the chief. *Fonte*: subchief; *wambo*: held by all brothers of the chief and by all those who have shown particular devotion to him. Many of the administrative units into which the chiefdom is divided are placed under the control of a *wambo* title-holder; *ndambu*: granted to some person who is particularly favoured by the chief.

4. Titles conferred as a recognition of war services. *Mbu* (*ben, mbu, mbəku*): those who, in time of war, enrich the treasure of the chiefdom; *sandia* (*sugang, sa safondop, sandə*): given to ex-*wala* who have distinguished themselves in combat; *wantu* (*watu*): reserved for those *wala* who are placed on the frontiers of the chiefdom in the face of the enemy.

All the above title-holders are known as the *m'kem*, the " notables," or important men.

5. Titles held by women. *Mafo*: held by the mother of the chief; *djukam*: the first wife of the chief. She is placed under the authority of the *mafo* and controls all those wives who live to the right of the chief's residence; *kuhon*: the second wife of the chief. She controls those wives who live to the left of the residence.

6. " Secondary " titles. *Mengkep*: conferred on one whose ancestors were slaves, but who has himself risen in the social scale, becoming rich and influential.

Variant forms of titles held in other chiefdoms of the Bafoussam area are listed by Relly as follows:[18]

---

[15] Delarozière, 1949, p. 63.
[16] Ibid.
[17] Ibid., p. 65.
[18] Relly, 1945.

Ba-Ngu (Bangou)	Ba-Ham (Baham)	Ba-Mungum (Bamougoum)	Ba-Yangam (Baya(n)gam)
1. *Fo :* chief.	*Foeh*	*Fo*	*Fo* or *Foe*
2. *Fon'toe :* sub-chief.		*Fontoe*	
3. *Wamba :* held by loyal men who have given the chief long years of service. Chief's sons may also hold this title.	*Wamba, Wambo, Wambe*	*Wamba*	*Wambo*
4. *Tschuipu, tschui :* receives his title at the time chief is installed. Close adviser to chief.	*Kuipu, Kui*	*Kuetche, Kuinefo*	*Kuipu*
5. *Tafo :* held by chief's maternal grandfather.	*Tafo*	*Tafa, Tanga*	*Tafo :* the new chief lives with this man nine weeks before his installation.
6. *Mafo, Wafo :* mother of chief, or brother of mother of chief.	*Wafo*	*Moafo*	*Mwafo, Mafo, Wafo :* held also by chief's daughters.
7. *Sob :* sons of chief or brothers of chief.	*Sob*	*Sob*	*Sob :* the most important of the chief's sons, thus titled on their father's death.
8. *Zzomafo :* "who inherits from the mother of the chief."	*N'zoemafo*	*N'zoemafo :* (a) chief's maternal uncle; or (b) another man if the *mafo* is dead and if there are no daughters to inherit the title.	*N'ziemafo :* brother of chief's mother.
9. *M'boe, M'bu :* adviser to chief principally in war-time. Held by one who is entrusted with the education of the future chief.	*M'boe, M'bu*	*M'boe :* (also held by the *N'zoemafo*).	*M'boe :* chief's "aide-de-camp."
10. *N'dimbu, N'di :* trusted henchman of the chief.			*N'dambu*
11.		*Saa*	*N'sa, N'sandio :* descendant of a *wala*. Adviser in time of war.
12. *N'diffo, N'zoeffo*	*N'diffo, N'deffo*	*N'deffo*	*N'diffo, N'zieffo :* trusted servant who buries the chief.
13. *Kwate :* "strong boy"; *Kepso :* sorcerer.			
14. *Talom*			
15. *Wala :* a high category of servants.	*Wala n'gue :* young *wala* who will receive a title after a trial period of several years.	*Wala*	*Wala*
16.		*M'ba, N'Tamba :* ex-*wala* who have left chief's service to marry hold this title.	

POSITION OF THE CHIEF

In many dialects the word for chief is *fo, fon,* or *fong.* Delarozière states, in his work on the chiefdoms within the Bafoussam Sub-division, that the first chief is thought to have been one of the nine founders, or *kamvə,* of the chiefdom who emerged from the ground. Malcolm was told during his research in the Bagam area that there had been 20 chiefs who had reigned over the Bagam people, the first of whom was Mbomvei, or " creator."[19] The divine powers attributed to an ancestral chief are thought to be bestowed by him on the reigning chief, his descendant in the male line. The chief is the living representative of this ancestor, the intermediary between the living and the dead, and the principal priest of the ancestor cult. All the beliefs relating to the cult are centred and focused on the chief.[20] For the Bagam area again, Malcolm writes: " Not only is he the . . . chief, he is also the chief priest. There are no priests as such in the Bagam area,"[21] and " This man [the chief] is the pivot on which the whole tribal law and order revolves. He is the representative of the tribe for all things, whether for good or for evil."[22]

As a consequence of his sacred character, the Bamileke chief is thought to be able to control the elements and regulate the seasonal rhythm. He is sometimes found to play a central role in agricultural rites, for example in the first-fruit rituals held at Baleng, when he must eat the first cocoyams of the annual harvest.[23]

The chief is the custodian of the land and he is ultimately responsible for the allocations of land. He is the supreme judge and only he has the power of life and death over his subjects.

The belief is generally held in the Bafoussam area, and is probably widespread in Bamileke country, that chiefs can at will become leopards, boas, elephants, and buffaloes; a chief thus transformed is thought to make long excursions into the bush. The chief alone has the right to possess leopards killed on his territory. Delarozière reports that the hunter who hands over a leopard to the chief is honoured with a title and given a wife.[24] There is a similar identification of the chief with the python, an idea also current among the Bamum (see above, p. 70). Python skins must be handed over to the chief.

There are in the chief's possession the insignia of chiefship and its sacred attributes: these, known in the Bafoussam area as *tchifong,* include:[25]

1. The skulls of the ancestral chiefs (*matu mpofong*).
2. The raised stones (*mola, tondem*) representing the ancestors. They stand before a chief's residence and on the frontiers of a chiefdom. The *mola* of a conquered sub-chiefdom are taken to the residence of the conqueror.
3. The cult objects, particularly the double-mouthed gongs (*kuefo*).
4. The chief's raffia bag (*kuanfong*). If this should be taken by the enemy or burnt, then the authority of the chief is thought to be destroyed. It is always kept in the chief's hut or in his bed, and is always packed with charms and medicines. It is believed to have the power to cause an adulteress to reveal the name of her lover, and to wreak vengeance upon a stranger who injures a member of the chiefdom.
5. The drums.
6. Arms (knives, matchets). These have been inherited from the ancestors and cannot be sold.
7. Leather and clay pipes. The chief's own pipe is never entrusted to anyone.

[19] Malcolm, 1925, p. 375.
[20] Delarozière, 1949, p. 41.
[21] 1925, p. 373.
[22] Ibid., p. 402.
[23] Delarozière, op. cit., p. 44.
[24] Ibid., p. 43.
[25] Ibid., p. 167.

8. The clothes and finery worn at the dances of the societies. These also are inherited from the ancestors and must not be sold or destroyed.

9. Trinkets and ornaments (the *mokuanfong*); these consist of bracelets, necklaces, and the dancing-masks. The chief must not sell or dispose of any of these; if he should do so, then his authority would diminish and his life would be in danger.

10. The thrones and stools inherited from the ancestors.

11. Horns made of ivory.

12. Calabashes decorated with beads.

13. Leopard and python skins.

14. A small breed of cattle. These are inalienable, but the chief may slay them whenever an important society has a feast.

The Chief's Village

This contains the huts for the chief's wives and servants, those housing the ancestral skulls, the meeting-huts of the societies, and those containing the drums which call society meetings. In the Bayangam chiefdom, Delarozière found that there were 70 buildings in the chief's village, including huts and granaries.[26]

Selection and Installation of a Chief

Delarozière gives the following report for the Bafoussam area.[27] Sons of the chief live with their mothers until they are eight or nine years old. After this they live together in a special hut looked after by the *dipofong* (a *tchinda*).[28] Later they are sent away from the chief's village to a maternal or paternal uncle, or to the chief of a " related " chiefdom. The heir, who may not necessarily be the eldest son, is chosen by the chief, his name being known only to the members of the *kamvɔ*, the *wala nka*, his mother, and the man in whose charge the boy has been placed. If the chief has no sons, he will choose a brother to succeed him. On the death of the chief the successor is taken to the dwelling of his maternal or paternal grandfather where he stays for a period of nine weeks. Egerton reports for the Bangangte Bamileke that the heir stays at this time with the chief-maker whose position is hereditary and who is the descendant of the first chief-maker to come to Bangangte with the first chief.[29]

At the end of the nine-week period the new chief is led back to the chief's village. In the *fam* (the chief's burial ground) the new chief sits on the trunk of a freshly cut banana-tree between his two brothers, the *sob* and the *kuipu*, who will be his close advisers. All three are veiled and smeared with red wood (*pɔh*). Later the chief is unveiled and proclaimed the new ruler in front of the crowd to whom he is presented.

An account of the accession of the chief is given by Malcolm for the Bagam area.[30] When the chief realizes he is going to die he sends for his five counsellors and nominates his successor (*n-zo n-dœp*). Nearly always this is the eldest son, but a chief reserves the right to nominate any of his sons. The eldest brother is selected if there are no sons. After the death and burial of the chief, and when all the members of the chiefdom are assembled at the meeting ground (*izan fon*), the newly elected chief sends for the attendants who officiated at the burial of his predecessor. All the people perform a circular dance on the *izan fon*, moving from left to right in short shuffling steps, and wailing continuously.

---

[26] Delarozière, 1949, p. 160.
[27] Op. cit., pp. 45–6.
[28] See above, p. 105.
[29] Egerton, 1938, p. 127.
[30] 1926, pp. 237–8.

The chief, accompanied by his counsellors and attendants, makes his first appearance to his subjects near the burial hut of an attendant whose ghost is thought to be in attendance on those who are dancing. He makes his way to a carved wooden stool (*dzuŋ*) which is in the middle of the meeting-ground, holding in his hands an iron-bladed spear (*kuun fon*) and a small square shield (*ngop ntso*). After sitting on the stool for several moments he performs a short, warlike dance and then retires to the hut where sacred instruments are kept. He eventually comes out and makes a speech, in which he promises to protect his subjects.

It is obligatory for all members of the chiefdom to see the newly elected chief on this day.

Two of the new chief's friends are appointed counsellors about five days after his accession. The wives of his predecessor are placed under his protection and his mother is installed in a hut near to his own.

The Chief's Mother, or Queen Mother[31]

In the chiefdoms of the Bafoussam Sub-division she is known as *mafo*. If the mother of the chief is dead his eldest daughter or eldest sister holds this position. Albert states that even during the lifetime of the chief's mother, one of his daughters is also given the title of *mafo* and enjoys the corresponding privileges.[32] The queen mother has her own separate dwelling and huts for her servants. Her house is a place of refuge and not even the chief himself can seize anyone who seeks protection there. She selects her husband herself, and he has no rights over the children of the marriage. She can commit adultery with impunity and she is free to leave her husband when she pleases. She is surrounded with as much respect as the chief himself. She is the president of the women's societies and is the only woman member of certain men's societies. She may also take part in *kamva* discussions.

ASSOCIATIONS

There is no adequate information about Bamileke men's associations or societies, though it is apparent that they are of extreme importance to the political structure of the chiefdom. This is not brought out sufficiently in the literature and there is also a lack of information on their working and internal organization. Thus it is stated that a " quartier " or dispersed village is the administrative unit within which the sections of the societies, particularly the *mandjon* society, are organized, but precisely in what manner these various sections are coordinated over a whole chiefdom is not described.

Each society has its meeting-house, and the house where the drums are kept; these drums are beaten to call members together. Access to the meeting-house is forbidden to non-members. Apart from the meetings, which are held every eight days, each society has a general assembly every two years. This takes place in the chief's village and the members of the society in question appear in their most elaborate garments and dance. Non-members are spectators. At this time the skulls of the chief's ancestors are brought out and the *pontia* (see below) parade with them. The general assembly would seem to be an occasion when each society in turn is formally recognized by the members of the chiefdom, and its position within the chiefdom reaffirmed.

Labouret noted the hierarchical structure of a society in his examination of the societies existing at Bandjoun, a member's place in the hierarchy being marked by the privilege of sitting on a particular type of stool.[33]

The following information is taken from Delarozière, whose study relates particularly to chiefdoms within the Bafoussam Sub-division.[34]

[31] Most of the information here is taken from Delarozière's work.
[32] 1943, p. 266.
[33] Labouret, 1935, p. 136.
[34] Delarozière, 1949, pp. 128, 160.

Associations Primarily Religious in Character

(1) The *kamvə*[35] (lit., descendants of the ancestors). This is one of the oldest societies and is believed to have existed at the time when the chiefdom was founded. It consists theoretically of eight titled men together with the chief; in certain chiefdoms the *mafo* is a member. The *kamvə* are the direct descendants in the paternal line of the nine founders and creators of the chiefdom who are thought to have come up out of the ground and chosen a chief from amongst their members. At Bandjoun there are 29 *kamvə* members, since for some time chiefs have tended to include the *kuipu* and *moafo* of their predecessor.

The *kamvə* is the chief's advisory council; it helps the chief to choose his successor, and if he dies before so doing, it is for the *kamvə* members to make the selection. It will decide upon the policy of the chiefdom; whether, for example, to make an attack upon another chiefdom. It constitutes the supreme tribal council, and its members are the high priests of the chiefdom, controlling and directing the activities of the other societies, particularly the *kungaŋ* society. In times of drought, it is for the *kamvə* to call upon the *kungaŋ* society to make sacrifices which will bring rain. No *kamvə* member can be removed from his position by the chief. The badge of the *kamvə* is a feather bracelet worn on the left wrist.

(2) *The kungaŋ.* Members are placed under the direct authority of the chief and *kamvə*. *Kungaŋ* members are the descendants of those *wala* who have been in the chief's service for a considerable number of years; right of entrance is hereditary, passing from father to chosen successor.

It is the duty of the *kungaŋ* to perform rites which will protect crops and bring rain in time of drought. When the maize is about to be sown they sing incantations to ensure the safety of the crop.

Associations Primarily Warlike in Character

These societies are often temporary, developing in times of conflict with other chiefdoms and dissolving in peace-time; unusual events within the chiefdom may lead to their rapid reappearance.

(1) *The kuosi.* In some chiefdoms (Bahouan) this is a recent development, in others (Bandjoun, Baham) it has been in existence for a long time. Besides the warriors, the *kuosi* accepted as candidates those who had sufficient means to pay the admission fee. Those eligible included all the members of the chief's family, certain of his servants, and important titled men. In more recent times the fees thus collected served to buy the necessary arms.

In peace-time the membership was reduced, and the society had certain administrative duties, such as allocating among villages and families the taxes and services due to the chief.

(2) *The kemdje.* The members are always veiled when they attend meetings which take place on the day of the week known as *nzə;* on this day the chief does not leave his residence, nor must anyone visit him; all normal activities must stop. It is for *kemdje* members to see that these rules are respected.

Its membership is restricted to rich men, whose admission fees are used in time of war to provide arms.

(3) *The kuentaŋ.* At Bandjoun this is a recent society whose members include the *kamvə*, the *moafo*, the *kuipu*, and the descendants of these. Its duty is to levy the warriors in time of war. According to Delarozière, it also acts as a kind of police force, executing the chief's orders and punishing recalcitrants,[36] adulterers, and thieves; it is generally feared.

---

[35] Delarozière calls this a society; it may be questioned whether it is anything more than the tribal council.

[36] Delarozière, op. cit., p. 82.

(4) *The kom.* Members are the sons of chiefs and their descendants, and trusted servants. It is their duty to protect and guard the arms and munitions of the chiefdom.

Associations of Servants and Officials

(1) *The pontiǝ.* The members are the *wala nka;* they are the priests of the cult of the chief's ancestors, and the custodians of the ancestral skulls. They live near the *fam,* which is the enclosure where these skulls are kept, and where their meetings are held.

They are also in charge of the finery which is worn by the members of the societies on occasions such as the general assembly, or when a dance is held for some specific event.

Delarozière relates to the *pontiǝ* the *komfam* society of Bangou chiefdom, and the *diŋkem* of Bayangam chiefdom.[37]

(2) *The paŋgop.* The members are the *wala nza.* These are in charge of the insignia of the chieftainship, and organize collective work.

Other servant societies of much more recent origin than either the *paŋgop* or the *pontiǝ* are listed by Delarozière as follows:[38]

(*a*) The *taŋkom* (Bafoussam chiefdom); (*b*) the *kommenyu* (Batoufam and Bandrefam chiefdoms); (*c*) the *samola* (Bangou chiefdom); (*d*) the *komkuosi;* (*e*) the *mbukem* (Bangam chiefdom).

Associations of Recent Development

(1) *The kambuin.* This society has developed quite recently and was founded in Bamendjou by the ruling chief. Members include the chief, the rich, influential, and notable titled men. Great prestige is attached to membership of the association and members are able to benefit considerably from it economically. There are no rituals connected with it. Meetings are held once a week in a hut in the chief's village; all members wear veils and their equality with the chief is shown by their being allowed to remain seated in his presence. All drink palm-wine from the same dish and then the affairs of the country are discussed. The chief, the president of the society, is assisted by a council which may consist of titled men and sub-chiefs who have contributed much of their wealth to the *kambuin*.

A member must tell the *kambuin* which of his sons he wishes to take his place in the society after his death. He chooses a fellow member as a sponsor and hands over to him the necessary sum for his son's admission. The fee will eventually be distributed by the council among the members. A son who does not take his father's place in the society is thought to incur his wrath and any illness he may suffer is diagnosed as the vengeance of his father. If a member fails to attend a meeting without previously giving reasons for his absence he is punished by a fine. He may even be obliged to give a wife to the chief and chickens to the other members.

The *kambuin* attends the funeral ceremonies of its members and receives gifts from the deceased's successor.

(2) *The kafafa or kafatcha.* This association is very similar to the *kambuin* and people may frequently belong to both. The same prestige and economic benefits are attached to membership. Its insignia are a plumed conical hat and a panther skin. A member will indicate his rank within the society by the number of panther skins he wears.

Associations for the Sons and Daughters of Chiefs

(1) *The nia.* The duties of this society consist of protecting and keeping in good condition the musical instruments which are used in the course of certain ceremonies. Members are the sons of chiefs.

(2) *The muenkem.* This group includes both the sons and daughters of chiefs.

---

[37] Delarozière, op. cit., p. 146.
[38] Ibid.

The makem

Delarozière says very little about this society, but he compares it to the *nia* society, though it is in charge of less important musical instruments.

The mandjon

All boys become members when they are 12 years old. The society is divided into two sections:

(a) The *maŋkui*, which includes young men between the ages of 12 and 18. The head of the *maŋkui* is a *tandia* of the chief.

(b) The *mandjon* proper, which includes all adult men of the chiefdom.

There is a third section, the *laliŋ*, but it has no peace-time activities; in time of war its members are the élite of the warriors.

The *mandjon* of a sub-chiefdom remains independent of that of the chiefdom.

The head of the *mandjon*, the *tandia mandjon*, often has a special meeting-house for the members near his own compound, but sometimes the meeting-house is in the chief's village itself. Attendance at meetings, which are held weekly, is obligatory and the projects and duties of members are discussed.

The chief's commands are carried out by the *mandjon;* they collect taxes due to him and guard his prerogatives. The chief consults the *tandia mandjon* and the four *mandjon* council members when he needs any particular work done, such as the building of huts. The work will be allocated to certain *mandjon* members and if any of them fail to appear the *mandjon* will take reprisals, damaging crops and stealing livestock. A member who is absent from a meeting without first seeking permission to stay away is punished in the same way.

Old men usually cease to be members of the *mandjon*. Neither they nor women are admitted to the meetings.

Nowadays the activities of the *laliŋ*, the section composed of the bravest and strongest men, are confined to dancing.

Women's Associations

(1) *The mandjon.* The women also have their own *mandjon* society, the president of which is the *mafo*. They function in much the same way as the men's *mandjon*, and assist each other in agricultural work.

(2) *The mue su.* This is the association of the best women cultivators. Members assist each other in their agricultural work, and they have the right to carry a large knife which is used in the clearing of the land.

Egerton states that among the Bangangte Bamileke the chief's mother and his principal wife each have their own society whose members are responsible for the agricultural work on their fields, for neither the chief's mother nor his principal wife does any agricultural work herself. The society of the principal wife is known as the *mason* and consists of about 50 members, most of whom are the wives of wealthy title-holders. It meets each week, when the principal wife states what work she wishes to be done. The society of the chief's mother may have as many as 100 members; it is called *n'dala*. The duties of members are the same as those of the *mason* members. " When the chief's mother decides to invite a new member she sends two of the existing members with a special emblem of wood which they take and set up outside the woman's house. If the woman feels she cannot support the expenditure of time and material, she goes to see the queen mother, taking the emblem with her, and begs to be excused."[39] Egerton reports that these are the only two women's societies in the Bangangte chiefdom.

LEGAL PROCEDURE AND SOCIAL CONTROL

The head of the polygynous household exercises authority over its members and settles minor disputes between them. His authority over them is not absolute; thus

[39] Egerton, 1938, p. 139.

H

Delarozière reports that although he could sell members into slavery, he did not have the power of life and death over them.[40]

Supernatural sanctions support the authority which a lineage head wields over its members. Any offences committed within the lineage are thought to incur the wrath of the ancestors, and Labouret states that if one lineage member should curse another he is excluded from the activities of the lineage. After a time this exclusion forces him to repent, and in order to atone for his behaviour he has to enlist the aid of the lineage head. The latter seeks the advice of the diviner and, if the signs are favourable, he agrees to co-operate with the offender, who brings him two hens to be sacrificed to the ancestors. The lineage head then announces to the ancestors that harmony is once again restored among their living descendants.[41]

Delarozière states that in the chiefdoms within the Bafoussam Sub-division the heads of the administrative units into which a chiefdom is divided have the power to inflict punishments for minor offences. In cases such as adultery they can only act as examining magistrates.[42] The chief is the supreme judge. Only he has the power of life and death over his subjects, or can inflict banishment upon an offender. He intervenes in all litigation involving one of his subjects and a foreigner from another chiefdom. The *kamvə* acts as the supreme tribal council which assists the chief in dealing with the most serious cases. The societies may settle certain disputes and punish certain offences committed by members.[43]

Malcolm states for the Bagam[44] that if a man is wronged by another, he generally attempts to settle the matter by his own efforts, or with the assistance of friends. The individual wrongs thus avenged are mainly thefts, slanders, and personal assault. As a rule the personal property of the offender is appropriated. Very rarely an assault is attempted, although it has happened over disputes in the market place. In the case of farm or land disputes, murder, or marital disagreements, the attention of the chief is drawn to the matter, who causes the offender to be lodged in the tribal detention hut.

Heads of compounds have the power to try and punish offenders against "family law" in their own compounds.

The chief is the sole judge of all offences against tribal law and of such cases that might be brought to his notice. He has the power of life and death over his subjects. With the assistance of his five counsellors he judges the cases in his court-yard. He sits in a carved wooden chair (*dzuŋ fon*) and the counsellors sit on the ground on either side of it. Whenever a man gives evidence he approaches the chief in a crouching position, holding his hands before his mouth. The salute *n-de*, *m-bomve*, or *zaki* (which is Hausa for lion) is given when approaching, and also when the chief makes any pronouncement.

Methods of Establishing Innocence or Guilt

The following methods have been reported in chiefdoms within the Bafoussam Sub-division:[45]

(1) Trial by tortoise. The two parties come before the chief, bringing a tortoise with them. Each gives his view of the case and the accused holds the tortoise in his hands as he makes his defence. After this he spits on the tortoise and puts it on the ground with its head before the chief. The tortoise acts as a jury; if it moves towards the chief the accused is guilty; if it moves in the opposite direction, then he is innocent. Albert reports that if the accused wishes to assert his innocence even further, he may tear out the heart of the tortoise and eat it. If he is guilty he will die as a

[40] 1949, p. 36.
[41] Labouret, op. cit., p. 139.
[42] Delarozière, loc. cit.
[43] Ibid., p. 37.
[44] Op. cit., pp. 239–40.
[45] Albert, 1943, pp. 79–80.

result, but his innocence is proved if he suffers no ill effects, and in this case the accuser himself is believed to die as a result. Trial by tortoise is reported for the Bangangte by Egerton,[46] who gives the following account: sometimes the defendant holds the tortoise in his hands while making his statement, and then sticks a sharpened piece of bamboo through the carapace. As he does this he says "If I am guilty, may this tortoise destroy my household." The defendant then hands the dead tortoise to the complainant who places it where his maize is stored. If any relative of the defendant now falls ill, it is believed to be caused by the tortoise, and the defendant is obliged to ask his accuser to stop it. The accuser may demand cash and women as payment, and the defendant must supply two goats, two fowls, and two calabashes of palm-oil. With the help of the medicine man the complainant then attempts to stop the avenging process by cooking the tortoise and sprinkling over it the blood of the two goats and fowls and some of the palm-oil. He gives certain medicines to everybody concerned, the complainant, the defendant, and the defendant's family. In this way the anger of the tortoise is appeased. Egerton also reports one special type of tortoise judgment which is used when the chief himself is accused.[47] He states that chiefs are held responsible for any calamities which may afflict their subjects collectively. These are generally epidemics of sickness, droughts, and plagues of leopards. In such a case the chief is accused. As a response the chief divides a tortoise into two halves and cuts the heart into small pieces; these pieces are given to the chief's sons, his chief henchmen, and some of his brothers. These people "answer" for the chief, and they eat the pieces of heart. If no misfortune befalls them, the chief is considered innocent.

(2) Another method is that of eating a particularly hot and bitter kind of bark. If the accused is guilty he is assailed by a raging thirst and death follows; if he confesses his guilt then an emetic is administered.

(3) The tongue of the accused may be pierced with a needle and if no blood appears then he is considered innocent.

(4) The accused may be made to hold a red-hot axe over which special leaves have been rubbed; if he is innocent he will suffer no burns.

(5) Egerton mentions the trial by oath which was taken on what he calls the stone of justice. A woman accused of adultery may be required to swear her innocence upon it; anyone who perjured himself on this stone was thought to suffer extreme ill effects.[48]

(6) Malcolm reports for the Bagam that oaths may be taken by using the name of the high god, *Mbomvei*.[49]

Punishments

An account of punishments within the Bagam area is given by Malcolm.[50] In general the punishment awarded is carried out immediately after the trial. For a petty offence the offender is usually confined for several days in the stocks or is flogged, the flogging being administered by one of the chief's attendants. In former times, serious offences against tribal law were punishable by death, the offender being beheaded in the market place. Offenders against the personnel of the chief's compound were sold as slaves in the open market. Adultery was punished severely, the woman being sold as a slave and the man beheaded in the market place. Another

[46] 1938, pp. 242–4.
[47] Ibid., p. 244.
[48] Ibid.
[49] 1925, p. 241.
[50] Ibid., p. 240.

method of punishment is to tie a man's hands high above his head to a pole in the detention hut and to keep him in this position until he is in a state of collapse.

Albert states that among the Bandjoun a man guilty of adultery was burnt alive or stoned to death. An adulteress was sold as a slave. A man guilty of *lèse-majesté*, which included serious disobedience and injuring or insulting the chief, was punished with death.[51]

Egerton reports for the Bangangte that the punishment for murder was death by hanging. If a man assaulted another man and did him bodily injury, the chief put him in prison for a time and fined him five goats. For offences due to negligence or carelessness, the offender was reprimanded. Sometimes an adulterous queen and her paramour were punished by being tied together and thrown into a deep latrine and left there to perish by suffocation. A chief's daughter who committed adultery was banished. In other cases the guilty parties were sold.[52]

SUCCESSION AND INHERITANCE

This is determined by patrilineal descent. Succession to lineage headship and inheritance of the paternal skulls of the ancestors is reported by Labouret to pass to the oldest male member of the oldest generation.[53] It appears that succession to other titles and goods follows a different rule; Albert states that " according to custom " the eldest son is the heir, but that a father may choose any one of his sons to succeed him.[54] Similarly Malcolm reports for the Bagam that it was not always necessary that the eldest son should be nominated as the heir, but that it was " country-fashion " to do so.[55] An heir takes his dead father's name, inherits any titles held by his father and the right to take his father's place in any of the societies to which he belonged; he also inherits his father's wives and goods. The rights in land held by his father will now be conferred upon him subject to the approval of the chief. The heir is not obliged to share his inheritance with his brothers but he may do so when it is of a considerable size. Albert reports for the Bandjoun that if a man dies leaving an only son who is too young to succeed his father, the chief appoints a guardian who will treat his inheritance as his own until the heir is old enough to take possession of it. Rights over any female children born to the guardian and the dead man's wives will be enjoyed not by the genitor but by the heir.[56]

Malcolm states that among the Bagam the eldest brother is the heir if a man has no children.[57]

LAND TENURE

Most of the information on the system of land tenure in the region is taken from Delarozière's studies in the Bafoussam Sub-division.[58]

All land within the chiefdom is under the titular ownership of the chief and all rights to the use of land ultimately derive from him. The responsibility for allocating land is delegated to the heads of the administrative units into which the chiefdom is divided (Delarozière's " quartiers "). It is to these men that a man needing land, perhaps a stranger to the chiefdom, will make application; no land can be allocated, however, without the approval of the chief. It is from the produce of the land within this unit that tithes are paid to the chief.

A man distributes plots to his wives, who exercise cultivation rights over them. The chosen heir inherits his father's plots, and though the chief has the right to take these plots from him, it seems that the right is rarely exercised.

[51] 1943, p. 82.
[52] 1938, p. 241.
[53] 1935, p. 139.
[54] 1943, p. 229.
[55] 1926, p. 236.
[56] Loc. cit.
[57] Loc. cit.
[58] 1949, pp. 28–9.

Land is inalienable; thus the gifts which a man may make to the chief on receiving land are not thought of as payments for the purchase of that land. It is a usufructuary, not an absolute right of ownership which is granted.

The chief has his own plots on which his wives grow the produce necessary for his own use. Exclusive rights are exercised by the chief over groves of bamboo trees in certain valleys.[59] Certain trees may be considered as the personal property of the man who planted them and the oil-palm, the raffia, and the kola come within this category. The chief, however, has the right to a share of palm-wine, kola nuts, and raffia-palm products.[60]

Egerton reports for the Bangangte that the land cultivated by a man and his wives is referred to as *la*, and is usually enclosed. A number of these enclosures form the *tang la*[61] (Delarozière's " quartier "); attached to the *tang la* is a certain amount of uncultivated land from which allocations are made by the man who is placed in charge of the *tang la*. Egerton writes: " There are two kinds of land in the *tang la*, that which is available for anyone who likes to ask for it, and that, directly under the control of the king himself, which is always reserved for the members of the men's societies which meet regularly at the chefferie [i.e., chief's village]."[62]

Though all the land is nominally owned by the chief, there is a category of land over which he exercises more direct rights;[63] these lands are known as the *tsafon* and they include: (1) land on which stands the residence of the chief; (2) all vacant or uncultivated land; (3) areas known as *fiala* or *miala*, which are generally grazing lands or small forested areas. *Fiala* are often situated on the boundaries of chiefdoms; Delarozière noticed that land granted by the chief to the Administration or to the Missions is usually *fiala* land; (4) market places; (5) pathways.

With the exception of the land on which the chief's residence is built, members of the chiefdom may freely cut the grass on *tsafon* land, and may graze their livestock there. It is not obligatory to seek the chief's permission before exercising these rights.

SLAVERY

Malcolm gives the following account of slavery in the Bagam area.[64] " In principle all slaves are the property of the chief, whether they are in his compound or not. There are, or were, two methods by which slaves were acquired—by capture or purchase. Slaves are rarely purchased outside the tribal area at the present day, and then only girls are bought. The method of obtaining a girl slave in the tribal area [is as follows] . . . a bead bracelet (*kwɔoŋ*) is placed on her wrist by an attendant and because of this she must leave her home and attach herself to the man who has claimed her. A present, either in cash or kind, is given to her relatives before she leaves her compound. Girls prefer to be slaves in the chief's compound as they say they do not have to work so hard there. From time to time the chief may transfer some of his female slaves to one or other of his attendants, and at the same time he obtains others from within his tribe. A girl may be presented to the chief by the chief of a neighbouring tribe not for purposes of marriage but for slavery. In certain cases the chief may purchase girls from neighbouring tribes in order to give them in marriage to his own male slaves. Any children born of such wedlock are counted as slaves and are not allowed to participate in tribal ceremonies, except in a subordinate capacity.

" Young men and boys may be claimed as slaves by the chief in order to do forced labour, and to work on the farms. A number of slaves will make their

[59] Société des Nations: *Rapport Annuel du Gouvernement Français sur l'Administration sous Mandat des Territoires du Cameroun*, 1922, p. 47.
[60] Ibid.
[61] 1938, p. 123.
[62] Ibid., p. 136.
[63] Delarozière, op. cit., p. 29.
[64] 1926, p. 235.

appearance at the market place when all the townspeople are assembled, and all the boys of about 12 years of age are captured and taken under guard to the tribal prison hut (*ndœp n-gon*). They are placed in the charge of the hut-keeper (*te ndœp n-gon*) who is held responsible for their safe-keeping. Later on they are put to work on the chief's farms, or else sent to assist the various tribal craftsmen. In all cases these boys are provided with clothing, food, and lodging by the chief.

" Slaves have no individual rights, but may possess property. They are solely at the disposal of their masters, who may transfer them at will. In practice there is very little difference between the status of a free-born man and a slave. The slave may move about the tribal area without any restraint being placed on him whatever."

WARFARE[65]

Violation of tribal boundaries was the main cause of inter-tribal warfare. An act of violence against any member of the tribe also constituted a *casus belli*.

In order to decide upon an offensive, the chief called a meeting (*pfür*) of all males capable of bearing arms, on the tribal meeting ground. After deciding to attack, all the warriors armed themselves with spears and sword-knives, and assembled at the chief's compound. The war leader (*ta ma n-joŋ*) marshalled the men and, led by the chief, they proceeded to the attacking ground singing and dancing and flourishing spears. Men who had distinguished themselves in former fights wore red feathers on their heads. They advanced in single rank; before beginning the fight, the chief took a place in the rear and the war leader stood at the head of the attacking party.

When one side was defeated, the chief of the vanquished side sent two or more messengers (*n-go n-top*) to the chief of the victors. As symbols of their mission they carried branches (*kuŋ kuŋ*) which they waved as they approached. They were met by an attendant (*cuo fon*) who led them to the chief and his counsellors. They approached the chief in a crouching position and remained thus until their mission was fulfilled. The chief and counsellors determined the terms of peace, which were generally adhered to by both the contending parties.

Formerly the dead were decapitated and their heads carried off to the compounds of the victors. In tribal ceremonies such as the accession of a chief they were displayed. The weapons and livestock of the vanquished were handed over to the followers of the victorious chief and later apportioned to the tribal warriors. Prisoners were confined in the chief's compound. When the fighting was over all the members of the chiefdom were assembled and, if victory was theirs, a dance of victory was performed in the market place in which everyone joined.

POSITION OF WOMEN

Because the women toil in the fields all day while the men are the relatively leisured sex, it has often been assumed that the women in the area are necessarily degraded and abased.[66] This view ignores the existence of many rights which a wife has over her husband; moreover Egerton states that a woman cannot be compelled to marry a man if she dislikes him. After marriage, if a husband does not perform certain duties for his wife, she will not stay with him. It is for him to provide her with a plot to cultivate, with tools and utensils, and with a hut to live in. If he does not fulfil his obligations towards her, then she is free of her obligations towards him. These consist of working in the fields for five out of the eight days in the week. If a man has more than one wife, the one with whom he is going to sleep prepares food for him in the evening.

The reverence with which the chief's mother is regarded tends to confute general statements as to the " low status " of women.

[65] From Malcolm's account of the Bagam (1926, pp. 242–3).
[66] Albert, 1943, p. 155.

MAIN CULTURAL FEATURES

PHYSICAL AND MENTAL CHARACTERISTICS

Buisson notes three distinct physical types within Bamileke countr̲y there are the peoples whom he calls " pure " Bamileke living withir̲ roughly circumscribed by a line drawn through Dschang, Bafoussam, Bangangte, and Bana. These are of medium height and have dark brown skins; their faces show medium prognathism. His second group live in the north-eastern part of Bamileke country and show certain Bamum characteristics. They, like the first group, are dolichocephalic, but are much taller; prognathism is very pronounced; skins are light brown. The third group live to the south and show a mixture of Bamileke and Mbo physical features; they are of medium height and have dark brown skins. Buisson states that they are not so muscular in appearance as the first two groups.

The extreme aptitude which the Bamileke peoples have shown in all kinds of commercial activities, their intelligence and adaptability have been noted by many ethnographers and administrators, and they are often referred to as one of the most promising peoples in the Cameroons.

ORNAMENTATION AND DRESS

The only article of clothing a woman usually wears is a piece of material hanging from a string waistband; men may wear a simple loincloth. Often they do not wear any garment, but nowadays European cotton dresses are favoured and obtained whenever possible. The traditional costume of the chief consists of the cloth wrapped round his head, and the loincloth whose fullness is a mark of chiefly rank and upon which hang small bells. He also wears ivory bracelets and necklaces. After marriage women are adorned with a kind of cicatrization, which may reach from the breast to the abdomen.[2] Egerton states that the Bangangte women are cicatrized on the back only, usually after their second child is born.[3]

A married woman who does not conceive is cicatrized after some years of barrenness to make her fruitful. Other ornaments are ivory bracelets and earrings; the ears are pierced when the girl is about eight years old. As a mark of their rank chiefs' wives wear circles of cowries on their heads.

THE LIFE CYCLE

BIRTH

Albert reports that the toad and the snake are thought to be not only the protectors but also the creators of children.[4] If a child is born lame the misfortune is held to be due to the mother's hurting a toad or snake while she was digging in the fields. Pregnant women work right up to the time when the child is to be born. According to Egerton there are no specialist midwives among the Bangangte, but two older women, experienced in delivering children, are usually present at the birth. They receive gifts of palm-oil, wood, or salt from the husband in return for their services.[5]

Great care is taken of the mother after the birth of the child. Egerton states that her own mother may come and look after her for as long as five months.[6] A name is given to the child immediately it is born. The length of time a mother

[1] 1, 1931, p. 86.
[2] Buisson, 2, 1931, p. 108.
[3] 1938, p. 247.
[4] 1943, p. 147.
[5] Egerton, op. cit., p. 236.
[6] Ibid.

ckles her child varies; she may wean a child after 18 months or after five years. Sexual intercourse is forbidden during the suckling period.

Soon after birth a baby is taken to be shown to neighbours and friends, who also visit the mother and bring gifts. Offerings of meat and palm-oil are made by the father to the ancestral skulls.

The birth of twins is considered particularly desirable. Delarozière states that twins are sacred;[7] they come under the chief's special protection and he has a right to one of them. The first-born twin is always known by a special name (m'bakom in Bangangte); the mother and father also receive special names (manyi and tanyi in Bangangte). The next child to be born receives a name meaning " he who comes after the twins." Twins are honoured and respected all their lives.

As they grow older boys and girls play together and learn to fetch wood and water. Between the ages of 8 and 10 girls begin to go with their mothers and help them in their agricultural work. A child whose mother dies when it is still a baby is usually given by the father into the care of its mother's people; if the child is a girl the father retains the right to the bridewealth on her marriage.

Malcolm obtained the following information on childbirth among the Bagam.[8] His informant was the tribal accoucheur, n-gaŋe fɔo. When a woman expects the birth of a child there is little visible preparation; she does not work on the farm, but remains in or near her compound. About three months before the child is expected the accoucheur gives her an infusion (mapod) to drink made from the leaves of a vine and palm-wine or water. Immediately before the delivery, another infusion is prepared and drunk from the open palms of the accoucheur.

Together with two women (kwei mon) experienced in such matters the native accoucheur remains in attendance until the delivery is complete. After the birth he severs the umbilical cord with a small iron-bladed knife which is used for this purpose only. As a rule the mother rises at the end of the second day.

The newly born child is rubbed all over with wood ashes, after which it is washed with warm water. It is then anointed with a mixture of palm-oil and cam-wood powder and a cord with pendent amulets to ward off evil influences is placed round its neck.

As a sign of motherhood, the mother carries a small woven square bag with short plaited handles. If twins have been born, a leaf (mbw pot) of Alchoruea cordata is attached to a piece of string and worn by each of the twins on his fore-head; the leaves are sprinkled with camwood powder from time to time. The father wears five feathers of the ngw bird in his front hair, and these are also sprinkled with camwood powder. In addition, he carries two small square grass bags with blue vertical borders.

MARRIAGE

A girl usually marries at the age of 15, young men when they have been circumcised, which is usually at the age of 14 or 15. Egerton reports, however, that they seldom marry until they are at least 18.[9]

A girl may become betrothed when she is only a few months old. A man may ask her parents if they are willing to accept him as their future son-in-law and, if they show their approval, he brings them a present of two goats. When they have received the second goat, similar presents must also be made to the grandparents of the girl. When she is older, she and her mother regularly visit her future husband, taking him prepared food, and he gives the mother a present on each visit. When the girl reaches puberty she is ready for marriage and the question of bridewealth is discussed between the girl's father and his future son-in-law; the gifts already made to his fiancée's family are considered as part of the bridewealth.[10]

[7] Delarozière, 1949, p. 55.
[8] 3, 1923, pp. 388–9.
[9] Egerton, 1938, p. 310.
[10] Rapport Annuel du Gouvernement Français sur L'Administration sous Mandat des Territoires du Cameroun, 1922.

Egerton reports for Bangangte that before cowry currency was replaced by coinage the bridewealth varied between 10,000 and 30,000 cowries together with seven goats; when marks came into use the bridewealth varied between 150 and 250 marks together with seven goats. By a decree of February, 1935, the Administration fixed the maximum bridewealth at 500 francs, though larger amounts were sometimes paid.[11] Egerton states that the chief does not pay bridewealth for his wives if they are his subjects, but he must do so if they come from stranger chiefdoms.[12]

The parents' choice of bridegroom is not entirely binding on their daughter. She cannot be compelled to marry a man she dislikes. If the bridegroom chosen shortly after her birth displeases her, or if he has displeased her parents, she is then entitled to find another fiancé who will return the betrothal gifts to the ex-fiancé.

Egerton reports for the Bangangte Bamileke that a woman does not occupy the hut which her husband builds for her until she becomes pregnant. She will live with him in his hut until this time.[13]

For marriages other than those of the chief there is a special ceremony which Egerton describes for the Bangangte as follows:[14]

" The parents of the bride fix a day. On the evening of this day they go with their daughter to the bridegroom's parents. They do not go alone. At least 10 others, members of the family and friends, go with them. Before they arrive, friends of the bridegroom begin a dance before the house of his parents. When the bride arrives, her escort is singing the marriage song, ' We must go quickly; the night is coming.'. . . When they reach the bridegroom's village they stop singing . . . and they wait for the bridegroom's father to come out and meet them. The bride is taken to the hut of the bridegroom's mother and everybody joins in the dance. The next day . . . both sets of relatives take the bride and bridegroom to the father's house. The bridegroom stands outside the door and the woman inside. They face each other and put their feet together on the threshold. The bride's father then pours water over their feet. After this the bride's parents go home. The girl stays in her mother-in-law's hut until she is taken to her husband.''

Albert describes the marriage ceremony of the Bandjoun Bamileke.[15] Here, on the day of the marriage, the bride, accompanied by her brothers, is taken to the hut of the bridegroom. When they approach it the brothers raise their voices to announce their arrival. Friends of the bridegroom thereupon leave the bridegroom's hut and ask them what they require. At this, the bride and her brothers keep silent. The friends of the bridegroom then return to his hut, telling him who have arrived. For this news they receive a reward, consisting today of about 50 francs. Meanwhile the bride and her brothers stand waiting in front of the hut; after a series of gifts have been handed over to the brothers, they enter the hut and eat food specially prepared for them. After the presentation of more gifts to the bride's brothers, they leave. The bride attempts to leave with them, but when her brothers have received yet another gift, she consents to remain. Eight days later, the bride's mother arrives at the hut of the bridegroom together with certain friends; she carries a large basket containing yams, and the friends carry another, smaller basket. After gifts (nowadays consisting of francs) have been presented to the bride's mother and her friends, the bridegroom takes away the yams and the visitors depart. This procedure finally establishes the marriage.

Marriage of Chiefs' Daughters in Chiefdoms of Bafoussam Sub-division

Delarozière makes the following brief statements about the marriage of chiefs daughters.[16] These girls are betrothed when they are about eight years old, and

[11] Egerton, 1938, p. 311.
[12] Ibid., p. 304.
[13] Ibid., p. 308.
[14] Ibid.
[15] 1943, pp. 165–7.
[16] Delarozière, 1949, p. 52.

not at birth according to the usual practice. Gifts given to the chief on the marriage of one of his daughters are not thought of as bridewealth, and he has all rights to the children of the marriage. The marriage festivities are held in the village of the bridegroom and the chief, his wives, and servants are present. When these festivities come to an end, the bride is led to her husband; on the morning of this day, the *mandjon* society and friends of the bride go in procession through the market place in the chief's village. The husband is the instructor and guide of any offspring of the marriage, but he can exercise no rights over them; they are treated as the sons and daughters of the chief.

The Principal Wife

Egerton reports that the " first wife," or principal wife, has the following rights and duties. She gives the first fruits of the harvest to her husband, and she may help to apportion lands, over which her husband has rights, to his other wives. If her husband wishes to have more wives it is her duty to find suitable ones for him.[17]

Marriage by Exchange

Egerton reports that marriage by exchange, i.e., where men exchange sisters or daughters and marry the women so received, is seldom practised by the Bangangte Bamileke but is more frequent in the Bafoussam area.[18]

Betrothal and Marriage among the Bagam[19]

A girl may be selected as a future bride while still an infant and she lives with her parents until she is claimed by the bridegroom. This may happen a few months after she has reached the age of puberty, which varies between 11 and 15. Cohabitation during the period between puberty and marriage is strictly forbidden.

The time chosen for the marriage is during the moon's first quarter. The prospective bridegroom (*sifo mon nda*) goes to the compound of the girl's father and gives him the bridewealth (*nkaap tse*). This is generally in the form of goods or money to the value of about £5. In some cases it is paid in instalments, the first payment being made about two months after the girl has reached puberty. Presents (*nkaap mve mwo*), such as goats and other livestock and palm-oil, must be given to the girl's immediate relatives. The bride's father decides the actual day on which the ceremony is to take place. In his compound the bridegroom makes all preparations for the event by laying in a stock of foodstuffs and palm-wine.

On the appointed day the mother of the bride covers her with a lotion made from powdered camwood and water. Her marriage clothing consists of a loincloth, a waist-cord made from twisted string which supports a pubic cloth, a necklet of coloured trade beads, armlets of brass or iron, and anklets. The bridegroom's body is smeared all over with a mixture of palm-oil and camwood powder and he wears a loincloth and a sleeveless gown.

The groom goes to the bride's father and announces that everything is ready, and is then informed that she will go to his compound after sundown. A proxy for the bride's mother (*me iyun*) and one for the father (*te iyun*), together with the bride and a number of small girls, then proceed to the bridegroom's compound. On her arrival the bride immediately goes to the hut prepared for her. The bridegroom and any wives he already has are not allowed to approach this hut during the marriage festivities. The guests assemble in the bridegroom's compound and indulge in dancing and singing. Later, food is taken to the bridegroom who has remained in his hut, to which the bride is eventually led. Here she is presented

[17] Egerton, 1938, p. 308.
[18] Ibid., p. 312.
[19] Malcolm, 3, 1923, pp. 389–93.

with the marriage stool by her husband. When she is seated, the proxy for her mother is given a present either in money or in kind; this woman then returns to a hut temporarily allotted to her, where she remains for seven days. The bride remains in the bridegroom's hut for the first night.

Marriage festivities are generally continued for three successive nights. No special ceremonies are held if a slave woman is married.

Marriage of the Chief among the Bagam

Before succeeding to chiefship the heir is allowed to marry in accordance with the usual customs. After his accession additional wives are acquired either by purchase or as presents. In these cases there is no ceremonial form of marriage. A woman may be obtained from a neighbouring tribe, and is handed over to the care of the chief's mother (mafo) or one of his head wives (miyo). The chief is informed when there is any suitable girl for him within the chiefdom. Instructions are issued for her to be handed over to the chief's mother; his wishes must be obeyed even if the girl is already betrothed. When a woman who was formerly betrothed has a child, the chief gives presents of livestock and palm-wine to her former fiancé and her father. To acquire the status of a head wife (miyo) a woman must be free-born and have borne several children to the chief.

Marriage of the Chief's Daughter or Relative among the Bagam

A procession is formed at the compound of the bride's parents on market day. It is led by an attendant known as mbe. Two attendants playing the double bell and pluriarc follow, and after these come the proxies for the mother and father and the bride, wearing a skin belt instead of the string girdle worn by other brides. All the women carry grass bags on their left wrist, into which various small gifts of food are placed by the onlookers as the procession passes. Occasionally the bride's breasts are splashed with water carried by one of the women in a calabash. The procession returns to the bride's father's compound, and in the evening goes to the bridegroom's compound.

Figures for the total number of marriages in 1951 are as follows: [20]

Sub-division				Monogamous Marriages	Polygynous Marriages	Total
Dschang	..	..	..	229	158	387
Bafang	..	..	..	182	163	345
Bafoussam	..	..	..	175	160	335
Bangangte	..	..	..	71	56	127

Separation and Divorce

Malcolm writes for the Bagam that when a man and woman disagree, the matter is referred to the chief. If a dispute cannot be settled, the chief may transfer the woman to a man living some distance away. Such a woman is known as mingwi kepon.[21]

Egerton cites the following grounds for divorce among the Bangangte.[22] If a woman's child dies, her husband should sleep with her before he sleeps with any of his other wives. If he does not do this, then she is free to leave him. The first wife has the duty of presenting the first fruits of the harvest to her husband. If he takes these from another, the first wife may leave him for ever. Impotence, but not barrenness, is grounds for divorce. Infidelity on the part of the wife was the only reason for which a man could divorce her, so far as Egerton could discover. A chief could deal with an objectionable wife by sending her back home. Nowadays the Administration recognizes only three grounds for divorce: (1) if a husband does

[20] Figures received from Centrifan, Douala.
[21] 3, 1923, p. 394.
[22] Op. cit., pp. 312–13.

not maintain his wife properly; (2) if one of the spouses has been condemned to at least one year's imprisonment; (3) adultery.

The children follow the innocent party and the bridewealth must be repaid to the man if he is not the guilty party.

ILLNESS AND DEATH

Egerton gives the following information for the Bangangte.[23] If a man falls ill, it is always assumed that something or someone is responsible. If the illness continues, the relatives consult the spider oracle and the course of action is nearly always the same. The places of the ancestral skulls are swept and watered and offerings of fish, specially prepared with oil and salt, are set beside them.

When a man dies, relatives and friends at once begin to mourn for him. The man's friends dig his grave in front of his hut. The body is laid in the grave on its side, with the knees partly drawn up, and with the hands under the head, which is always placed towards the north. A commoner is wrapped in leaves before burial. A king has his forehead bound with some precious fabric and is shrouded in the same material.

If a man dies away from home, but not too far away, he may be brought back for burial. If this cannot be arranged, his heir will go to the place where he was buried and bring away the skull to bury it with the skulls of other members of the family.

A part of a man's personal belongings is destroyed and placed on his grave. Graves are not cared for. Skulls are later removed from the bodies, and each one is buried in a hole 18 ins. deep outside the wall of the hut.

Official mourning lasts two full days. Friends of the dead person come to chant, dance, and lament. Friends of the family come again, bringing gifts of palm-wine, cooked yams and bananas, goats and fowl, and the relatives give a feast. Women shave their heads and cover themselves with white earth as a sign of mourning, continuing for one or two months.

Whenever anyone dies there is always the suspicion of foul play. If it is a man, then his wives are suspected; when the lamentations are over they must go through a purification ceremony, which is also an ordeal. They go to the river, and the first wife enters the water, standing with her feet wide apart; between her legs she puts a cushion of banana leaves which she has been using as a seat during the mourning period. If the current carries it away, all is well. All the wives go through this performance. A husband, in the event of a wife's death, goes through the same ceremony.

If a woman dies in pregnancy, she is cut open, and the child is buried beside her. When a woman dies in childbirth, the child is allowed to die with her.

Death ceremonies among the Bandjoun are reported as follows by Albert.[24] Sacrifices to the dead are made whenever one of their descendants is ill. Lamentations begin immediately after death. In the case of a married man or woman who has children, or in the case of a first-born child, the burial takes place inside the hut; in all other cases it takes place in front of or to the side of it. The mother and father, if it is a child who has died, or a man and all his wives and children if a co-wife has died, may take no food for a week unless it is given to them by a special woman who is called in for this purpose. They must clothe themselves in banana bark and sleep on the floor stretched out on banana leaves. At the end of the week another woman who "chases away the mourning period" comes to wash them and to burn the banana bark and leaves. Ordinary clothing may now be worn, but old clothing and ornaments must be destroyed.

After a period of six months to two years, the grave is opened and the skull removed. This is buried inside the hut in a very shallow hole. Sometimes there are huts exclusively for these skulls.

[23] Op. cit., pp. 255–9.
[24] 1943, pp. 168–79.

Malcolm gives an account of death and burial among the Bagam.[25] The body is stripped of all clothing, and is covered with a mixture of palm-oil and camwood powder. It is then attired in the deceased's finest raiment. In almost all cases, burial takes place on the day of death; the grave is dug close to the hut, about 4 to 5 ft. in depth. After the body is put in position the relatives are called to see it; they sprinkle camwood powder over it, saying as they do so that it is for the benefit of the ghost of the deceased. The grave is filled in by men. No mound is left and nothing is placed on top of the grave. Once buried, a body is never exhumed, unless there is a large-scale migration. The remains of former chiefs were carried from their original home on the eastern side of the Nun River and were re-interred at the place where the present village of Bati is situated; when they proceeded to Bagam some of these remains could not be found. Hence in the ceremonies in connection with the ancestral cult, visits are paid to some burial huts in which there are no remains.

Death and Burial Ceremonies of Chiefs

When a Bagam chief dies his body is prepared for burial by his immediate attendants (*mfosei*). He is robed in his finest ceremonial clothing, including the chief's cap (*tcuo fon*), and is placed in a sitting position, with the knees wide apart, in a large cane chair. In the left hand a chief's brass tobacco pipe is fastened, and in the right a carved buffalo-horn drinking-cup. The body is sprinkled with camwood powder and taken to the sacred instrument hut. The burial takes place on the day following the death. After the body is placed in the instrument hut, the attendants assemble outside his compound and signify to the people that all fires must be put out. This is the first official notification that the chief is dead. Lamentations then begin, and the women smear their bodies with ashes. The body is taken to the burial place and lowered into the grave by the five counsellors. When it is in position a clay tube reaching up to the level of the ground is laid on the dead man's head. A hut is built over the grave as soon as the body is buried, and an inverted clay bowl is placed over the clay tube. Later, a goat is slaughtered over the grave and the blood allowed to flow down the tube; the liver of the animal, chopped up finely and mixed with palm-oil, is also dropped down the tube.

The period of mourning lasts about a month, during which the attendants smear their bodies with ashes.

The death of a chief in the Bafoussam area is described by Delarozière.[26] It is believed that a chief does not die, but goes to live with his father in order to make room for his successor. All the societies assemble together on his death in order to perform warlike dances. He is buried in a shallow tomb; a hollow piece of bamboo is placed in the mouth of the corpse into which libations of palm-wine are periodically poured. A small hut is erected over the grave. Mourning for a chief lasts for six months; during this time his wives sleep on the floor, and it is taboo for them to shave their heads, to wear their bracelets and earrings, or to have sexual intercourse with the new chief. Albert states for the Bandjoun (within Bafoussam Sub-division) that the skulls of chiefs were kept in special huts.[27] According to Egerton this is done among the Bangangte also.[28]

[25] Op. cit., pp. 394–9.
[26] 1949, pp. 47–8.
[27] Op. cit., p. 36.
[28] Op. cit., p. 253.

RELIGION AND MAGIC

THE SUPREME BEING AND OTHER GODS

Raynaud states that the cult of the ancestral skulls has completely eclipsed the worship of the Supreme God, *Si*, and that the first chief, the founding ancestor of the chiefdom, has in fact become the principal *Si* or *Si Ta*.[1] Albert also writes that such phrases as *si-ta*, *si-ma*, or *si-yon* (i.e., god of my father, of my mother, of my country) all allude to the founding ancestor.[2] Similarly, the High God of the Bagam is the first chief and creator of the chiefdom, *Mbomvei*.[3]

Egerton states that throughout the Bangangte chiefdom there are places called *m'ben*, " sacred to the god of the country, a force unknowable, intangible, more in the nature of a fate than a god."[4] Albert also notes among the Bandjoun the existence of local gods, one of whom played a part in the traditional history of the founding of the chiefdom.[5] One of the sons of the chief of Baleng came into the country on a hunting expedition with his servants. As he was taking some refreshment he noticed a number of ants swarming on to his food. Since ants are thought to be the messengers of a god, he understood that a god was present asking for food and shelter. He therefore planted a tree where the god could take refuge, and from that time the god watched over the country. The son of the chief of Baleng continued on his way and later founded the Bandjoun chiefdom. The god is of little importance compared with this founding ancestor, who stands at the top of the hierarchy of spiritual beings.

ANCESTOR WORSHIP AND ANCESTRAL SKULLS

In his work on the Bandjoun Albert states that there is a general belief that the spirit of a dead man takes refuge in his skull; unless care and attention are given to the skull, the spirit will be a malevolent force, seeking vengeance upon those who are neglecting it.[6] Offerings made to the skulls will result in positive blessings falling on the living descendants. If the skulls of former chiefs are lost the power of the reigning chief is undermined and the prosperity of the whole chiefdom is thought to be endangered.

Among the Bagam there are priests in charge of the cult of the chiefs' ancestral skulls, which may be kept in a separate hut in the chief's village.[7] Labouret writes that every two or three months the chief consults the diviner to find out what offerings he should make to the ancestors; a priest sacrifices a goat and pours libations of palm-wine over each skull and places salt at its side.[8] On all these occasions the ancestors are invoked to protect the community, to keep order within it, and to make its women fertile.

Malcolm recorded several ceremonies,[9] in all of which the chief took the principal part, assisted by his attendants and an old man who acted as remembrancer. The announcement of a forthcoming ceremony by the chief's attendants was known as *su* and consisted largely of displays of mimic warfare and masked dances. The chief's mother appeared, wearing a small scarlet cloth and bead anklets, and sat on a small stool to the right of him. This was the only occasion, apart from *ndop*, on which any woman was seen to play a prominent part. The object of *ndop* was the planting of seed for the use of the tribal ancestors. The chief's women pre-

---

[1] Delarozière, 1949, pp. 41–2.
[2] Albert, 1943, p. 45.
[3] Malcolm, 1926, p. 241; 1925, p. 374.
[4] Egerton, 1938, p. 227.
[5] Albert, op. cit., p. 40.
[6] Ibid., pp. 34–45.
[7] Malcolm, however, states that " there are no priests as such in the Bagam area." (1925, p. 373.)
[8] Labouret, 1935, p. 138.
[9] Between July and December, 1917. See Malcolm, 1925, pp. 373–404.

pared the garden in which he and his attendants planted seeds and seedlings. The ceremony of visiting the burial huts of former chiefs was known as *maa sie*, and the whole procedure as *zepon*. The first hut to be visited was that of the living chief's father, and the last was that of *Mbomvei*, the first known chief. Accompanied by his attendants, some playing on sacred instruments, the chief proceeded to the burial hut, where he sacrificed a kid and heated palm-wine was distributed to the company. Dancing followed in the enclosure of the burial hut and the chief and his attendants then went to the burial hut of the deceased attendant whose ghost was responsible for supplying the needs of former chiefs. Libations of palm-wine were poured on his grave. At the hut of *Mbomvei* a sheep instead of a kid was slaughtered, and calabashes of palm-wine and goods brought by craftsmen were distributed to onlookers and attendants.

Other ancestral cult ceremonies recorded by Malcolm are: *nzo ngon, su ngon,* and *su fon mbeivi,* which involve dancing and the sacrifice of a goat or kid to the ancestors. During *nzo ngon* the women are enjoined to work on the farms and the chief forbids his subjects to quarrel with neighbouring villages. *Ndurro, mba ngon,* and *ngan* consist mainly of dancing.

Paternal and Maternal Skulls[10]

All members of the patrilineage are united in their allegiance to the same ancestral skulls. The senior male is the ritual head of the group and has the skulls in his possession. If a patrilineage wishes to move its place of residence, the new dwellings are first erected and there is a special ceremony before the skulls are finally transferred to them. A fire is lit and food prepared which is offered to each skull by the ritual head; the diviner who is called in then offers fruit to the lineage members in order of seniority. The skulls can then be taken to the new dwelling. Formerly a diviner was paid 90 cowries for this service.

It may happen that a lineage member dies some distance from his home so that it is not possible to preserve his skull. To neglect an ancestor would be dangerous, for his anger would fall upon the living members of the group. The ritual head, therefore, accompanied by a diviner seeks to appease it in the following way. He sets out in the direction first taken by the dead man and, after walking a considerable distance, selects a suitable place where he pours libations of palm-wine, proclaiming that it is destined for the ancestor. Finally he collects some of the soil and this will in future represent the skull of the dead man.

There exists also a cult of the female ancestral skulls, but this is not adequately described in the literature. Labouret states that " each heiress takes to her hut the skull of her mother and of her grandmother." She buries them near her bed so that they will protect her household and makes sacrifices to them when the agricultural work begins. Offerings may also be made to these skulls to render a woman fertile. The illness of a child may be attributed by a diviner to a particular maternal skull, and in this case the mother goes to the guardian of the skull, who touches the sick child with mud taken from the shrine of the skull, to which the mother makes offerings.

Albert states that the remote dead are not entirely forgotten, even if their skulls are not in the possession of the living. Their spirits are thought to wander over the country as malevolent forces, since they are homeless and neglected. Often small houses are built, a tree is planted or a large stone erected where the spirit is able to reside and where offerings will be made to it.[11]

The first chief and founder of the chiefdom, however, is not thought of as belonging to this undifferentiated collection of spirits; he stands out as the most important figure in the ancestor cult, the guardian and protector of the chiefdom. He has the power to cause drought, famine, or rainfall and bestows his divine attributes upon his " son," the living chief.

---

[10] The account of paternal and maternal skulls which follows is taken from Labouret, op. cit., pp. 135–40. [11] Albert, op. cit., pp. 38–9.

RELIGIOUS ASSOCIATIONS

In his work on the chiefdoms of the Bafoussam Sub-division, Delarozière describes as being " primarily religious in character " the *kamvə* and the *kungaŋ* societies, the organization of which has already been described.[12] The *pontiə* society also has specific religious functions, since its members protect the chief's ancestral skulls and make offerings to them.

OTHER ASSOCIATIONS

Albert[13] records the existence of secret societies of leopard-, chimpanzee-, and snake-men, in which a man makes an " alliance " with the animal on becoming a member.

The society of leopard-men is generally feared, since its activities are mostly malevolent and the identities of its members are not explicitly known, though certain individuals will be suspected. A single will, intelligence, and soul are thought to be shared by the member and his animal double. When a leopard-man dies, the double lives on, but without a soul, and is known as a " dead " leopard. Leopard-men are believed to harm and kill not only livestock but also men and children. Unlike the other societies, described below, women can become members.

There are no longer chimpanzees in Bamileke country, but Albert states that the Bandjoun have come to identify them with the baboons on the right bank of the Nun River. Meetings of the chimpanzee society are held weekly. A new candidate is either recommended and presented by a member or is the son and chosen heir of a member. The entrance fee is a goat and a ram, seven hens, and, nowadays, a cash payment of about nine francs. Albert was not able to obtain information on the rites of initiation. The paraphernalia of all members consists of an antelope-horn filled with various grasses and crushed wood which are believed to have magical properties, and small human images which are held in the fist and thought to confer physical strength equal to that of the chimpanzee. Membership of the society gives a man protection against damage to his livestock and crops by the leopard or if he is being threatened by a member of the leopard society. Non-members will seek the aid of members of the chimpanzee society against such dangers.

The society of snake-men has a head at whose house the meetings take place and where libations and sacrifices are made to the sacred stone in which the soul of the founding ancestor is thought to reside. A man inherits an alliance made by his father and the right of entry to the society. There is a period of initiation, and the initiate pays an entrance fee of a white chicken and, nowadays, several francs. On the day when he is received into the society he has to eat seven grains of a special plant after which he is believed to have the power to turn into a snake or at least to accomplish acts of vengeance. When a man is bitten by a snake he believes that a man belonging to the snake society is taking vengeance upon him; he must therefore seek out a snake-man whose power may be greater than that of the aggressor. The snake-man shapes a cassava leaf into a snake form and tells it to seek out and kill the offending snake; if, in spite of this, the man dies it means that the " cassava snake " has not been successful.

Albert states that membership of the snake society is a necessary qualification for entrance to any of the other societies in which alliances are contracted with animals.[14]

MAGICIANS

Masson lists the attributes of medicine men and diviners from information collected in the Dschang region.[15] Both categories of magicians are usually referred to in the literature under the general term *ngan-ga* (*nga:* man, *ga:* magic). Masson

---

[12] See above, p. 111.   [13] Albert, 1943, pp. 100–16.   [14] Albert, op. cit., p. 101.
[15] Masson, 1939–40. He uses the term " sorcerer " to describe both medicine men and diviners; sorcerer is here used, however, to describe one who possesses bad medicines and employs them illicitly.

points out that this term properly belongs to the diviner who employs the spider oracle. The *ngan-ga* goes at night to the spider's hole, covers it with blades of grass and surrounds it with small variously shaped pieces of calabash; finally, to isolate the spider from all external interference, he covers the area with a shelter of small twigs. He returns in the morning when the spider has disturbed the grass and pieces of calabash; according to the patterns they make the diviner is able to interpret the spider's answers to the questions which he has asked. Masson also lists two other diviners, the *ngan-ken*, who is able to divine the whereabouts of lost goods and the *mankuini* who is consulted particularly when a man wishes to know in advance the result of a lawsuit.

Medicine men may be called in on the occasion of an illness, birth, or death. Masson lists the Dschang terms for them as follows: *ngan-fou; ngantchi; ngan-tsangang; mankwi; kamsi; gni-tem-wa; mba-toum-feu.*

All receive fees for their services. The first three diagnose and cure illnesses with special medicines, which, in the case of the *ngan-fou,* may possess real therapeutic properties. The *ngantchi* is thought to cure his patient by injecting into his blood a certain powder possessing magical properties. The *ngantsangang* usually effects his cure by extracting a stone or other object from the body of the patient.

The *mankwi,* who may be a woman, is called in at the birth of a child. If the birth is a difficult one the *ngan-fou* may be called to minister to the patient. The *kamsi,* who also may be a woman, is called in at the birth of twins; she washes them with a special medicine and murmurs incantations over them as soon as they are born.

The *gni-tem-wa* is called to perform a post-mortem examination in order to discover the cause of a man's death. He may perhaps claim that the death was caused by the absence of a vital organ; he will then prepare a powerful medicine capable of discovering who is to blame, and of punishing the offender fatally.

The *mba-toum-feu* is called upon to exhume the head of the dead man. This is done in the region of Dschang about a year after the burial. He washes the skull and pours palm-oil over it before placing it in a shallow grave in the hut. He is also called upon when any exceptional sacrifices are to be made to the spirits of a particular lineage.

Sorcerers. Masson states that the *ngan-lefang* and the *ngan-sia* are magicians who can use their powers and medicines for illicit purposes. He also reports that the *ngan-sia* form a secret society about which very little is known. They are thought to be responsible for many kinds of atrocities. The *ngan-lefang* is believed to control thunder and to have the power to send it anywhere in order to bring destruction upon his enemies.

The *nto-beng,* the rain magician, has the power to control the rain. If a man wishes to prevent rain from falling on a particular day he goes to the *nto-beng* and pays him a fee for performing the necessary rites. Masson reports that the chief often requested the *nto-beng* to keep rain away on market days. Egerton also reports the existence of a rain magician, whose position was an hereditary one.[16]

The minnyi. A category of magicians is found among the Bangangte Bamileke which does not seem to be reported by Masson for the Dschang region. These magicians are known in the dialect as *minnyi*. Egerton writes of them as follows: "A *minnyi* is a mixture of fortune-teller and healer, possessed of occult powers, beneficent powers. . . ." The powers of the *minnyi* are not inherited, a man or woman becomes aware that he possesses them if he falls down in a fit. He may afterwards go to a recognized and established *minnyi* with whom he stays for two years learning about medicines and the arts of healing, but this is not essential. A chief may call upon several *minnyi* if certain events are troubling him in the chiefdom, for example if there is an undue amount of sickness. They may then direct the chief to pour libations of palm-oil on certain of the sacred stones.

---

[16] Egerton, op. cit., p. 229.

I

BIBLIOGRAPHY

Albert, A.
  Au Cameroun Français Bandjoun. Montreal: Editions de l'Arbre, 1943.

Baumann, H., and Westermann, D. [trans. L. Homburger]
  Les Peuples et les Civilisations de l'Afrique. Paris: Payot, 1948, pp. 332, 454.

Bouchaud, J.
  Histoire et Géographie du Cameroun sous Mandat Français. Douala: La Procure du Vicariat Apostolique, 1944.

Buisson, E. M.
  1. " Présentation d'une carte ethnographique du peuple Bamiléké comparé aux groupements en ceinture." *Togo-Cameroun*, 1931, pp. 83–7.
  2. " Tatouages Bamiléké." *Togo-Cameroun*, 1931, pp. 107–16.
  3. " Céramique Bamiléké." *Togo-Cameroun*, 1931, pp. 117–22.
  4. " L'art chez les Bamiléké." *Arts du Cameroun à L'Exposition d'Art Colonial de Naples*, 1934.

Capponi, A.
  " Le Lignite de Dschang." *Bull. Soc. Et. Cam.*, 7, 1944, pp. 75–86.

Carton, C.
  " Etude démographique comparée des Bamiléké et Bamoum." *Ann. Medic. et Pharm. Colon.*, XXII, 1934, pp. 350–63.

Chapoulie, H.
  1. " La case Bamiléké." *Togo-Cameroun*, 1931, pp. 92–105.
  2. " Chefferies Bamiléké." *Togo-Cameroun*, 1931, pp. 102–5.

Chauleur, P.
  " Esquisse ethnologique pour servir à l'étude des principales tribus des territoires du Cameroun sous Mandat Français." *Bull. Soc. Et. Cam.*, 3, 1943, pp. 9–66.

Delarozière, R.
  1. " Structure sociale des populations dites Bamiléké." *L'Afrique et l'Asie*, Paris, 1948, pp. 50–5.
  2. " Les institutions politiques et sociales des populations dites Bamiléké." *Et. Cam.*, II, 1949; 25–6, pp. 5–68; 27–8, pp. 127–75.
     (These two articles are published together as *Mém. I.F.A.N., Centre du Cameroun*, No. III, 1950.)
  3. " Etude de la stabilité de la population Bamiléké de la Subdivision de Bafoussam pendant les années 1946 et 1947." *Et. Cam.*, 31–2, sept.-déc., 1950, pp. 138–87.

de Pedrals, H.
  " Contribution à l'établissement d'un inventaire ethnique du Cameroun." *Bull. Soc. Et. Cam.*, 15–16, 1946, pp. 28–9.

Despois, J.
  " Des montagnards en pays tropical Bamiléké et Bamoum." *Revue de Géographie Alpine*, 4, 1945, pp. 595–635.

Deutsches Kolonialblatt, 1912, pp. 76–7. " Bericht des Oberleutnants von der Leyen über seine Erkundung des Nun."

Dugast, I.
  Inventaire Ethnique du Sud-Cameroun. Mém. I.F.A.N., Série: Populations, No. I, 1949, pp. 113–22.

Egerton, F. C. C.
  African Majesty. London: Routledge, 1938.

Gèze, B.
  " Géographie physique et géologie du Cameroun occidental." *Mém. Mus. Nat. d'Hist. Nat.*, XVII, 1943.

Greenberg, J. H.
  " Studies in African Linguistic Classification." *South-Western Journal of Anthropology*, V, VI, 1949, 1950.

Jacques-Félix, H.
  " Une réserve botanique à prévoir au Cameroun: le sommet des Monts Bambutos." *Bull. Mus. Nat. d'Hist. Nat.*, 1945.

Labouret, H.
  " Les populations dites Bamiléké." *Togo-Cameroun*, avril-juillet, 1935, pp. 135–41.
Lecoq, R.
  Les Bamiléké. Paris: Présence Africaine, 1953.
Léger [Adm.]
  " Contribution à l'étude de la langue Bamiléké." *J. Soc. Afr.*, II, 2, 1932, pp. 209–27.
Malcolm, L. W. G.
  1. " Notes on the Cameroon Province." *S.G.M.*, XXXVI, 1920, pp. 145–53.
  2. " Huts and Villages in the Cameroon, West Africa." *S.G.M.*, XXXIX, 1923, pp. 21–6.
  3. " Notes on Birth, Marriage and Death Ceremonies of the Eyap Tribe, Central Cameroons." *J. Roy. Anthrop. Inst.*, LIII, 1923, pp. 388–401.
  4. " Notes on the Ancestral Cult Ceremonies of the Eyap, Central Cameroons." *J. Roy. Anthrop. Inst.*, LV, 1925, pp. 373–404.
  5. " The Socio-political Organisation of the Eyap Tribe." *Anthropos*, XXI, 1926, pp. 233–43.
Mann, O.
  " Die geologische Untersuchung des Dschang-Bezirk vom Januar bis Juni 1911." *Mitt. v. Forschungsreisenden u. Gelehrten aus d. Deutschen Schutzgebieten*, 1912, pp. 217–32.
Masson, G.
  " Médecins et sorciers en pays Bamiléké." *L'Anthropologie*, XLIX, 1939–40, pp. 312–32.
Mitteilungen von Forschungsreisenden und Gelehrten aus den Deutschen Schutzgebieten, 1908, pp. 160–2, 189–99. " Erster Bericht über die Landeskundliche Expedition der Herren Prof. Dr. Hassert und Prof. D. Thorbecke in Kamerun."
Mueller [Oberst.]
  " Die Manenguba-Expedition." *Deutsches Kolonialblatt*, 1905, pp. 501–2.
Olivier, G., *et al.*
  " Documents anthropométriques pour servir à l'étude des principales populations du Sud-Cameroun." *Bull. Soc. Et. Cam.*, 15–16, 1946, pp. 17–86.
Portères, R.
  " Climat et végétation sur la chaîne des Bambutos." *Bull. Soc. Bot. Fr.*, 93, 1946, pp. 352–60.
Rausch [Leutn.]
  " Die Nkam-Nun-Expedition." *Deutsches Kolonialblatt*, 1910, pp. 690–3.
Relly, H.
  " Quelques notes sur les noms et titres du Grassfield." *Bull. Soc. Et. Cam.*, 10, 1945, pp. 77–83.
Sanmarco, V.
  " Les Bamiléké du district de Dschang. Exemple de l'influence du climat sur la vie indigène au Cameroun." *Ann. Géogr.*, tome LIII–IV, 1945, pp. 223–5.
Société des Nations: *Rapport Annuel du Gouvernement Français sur l'Administration sous Mandat des Territoires du Cameroun*. Paris. (Particularly 1921, 1922, and 1923.)
Strümpell, F.
  " Expedition in den südostlichen Teil des Bezirkes der Station Bamenda." *Deutsches Kolonialblatt*, 1903, pp. 84–6.
Tessmann, G.
  " Die Völker und Sprachen Kameruns." *Petermann's Geogr. Mitteilungen*, 1932, No. 5–6, pp. 113–20; No. 7–8, pp. 184–90.
Westermann, D., and Bryan, M. A.
  Languages of West Africa. London: Oxford University Press for International African Institute, 1952.
Weulersse, J.
  " Un exemple d'adaptation à la vie tropicale: la tribu des Bamiléké (Cameroun)." *Comptes Rendus du Congrès International de Géographie*, tome III, 1931, pp. 501–5.

IV. THE BANEN, BAFIA, AND BALOM OF THE FRENCH CAMEROONS

INTRODUCTION

The names Banen and Bafia really refer to two small but distinct groups of peoples whose total population is no more than 80,000. To the north of these two groups live peoples speaking semi-Bantu languages: the Bamileke, Bamum, and Tikar. To the west and south their immediate neighbours are various Bantu-speaking Basa tribes, while to the east are some small scattered groups, remnants of a vast population, the Bati, whose language in the past influenced that of the Bafia group.

With some minor exceptions, the general cultural features of the Banen and Bafia groups are very similar, while they show more divergences from those of their immediate neighbours to the north and west. It was for this reason that Tessmann called them the " Mittel-Kamerun Bantu," in spite of the linguistic differences between the two groups.

The Banen group consists of the Banen, Nyokon, Yambeta, and Lemande; the Bafia group includes the Bafia, Bape, Yambasa, and Balom. Originally the Banen group probably inhabited the territory on either side of the Nun River somewhat to the west of its junction with the Mbam, partly in the area which would now be described as the southern part of Bamum country, and partly in the area south of the Nun. At that time the first of these areas had probably not been overrun by the Bamum and was inhabited by Bamileke. It thus seems reasonable to suppose that the Banen group was driven southwards at the time of the onslaught of the Bamum and the flight of the Bamileke. Some of them met other Banen already settled on the south bank of the Nun and broke up into three small groups which moved forward fanwise. One of these groups, the Banen-Pokek, settled not far from the Nun, near the Yambeta with whom they shared many linguistic resemblances. Farther west, the Banen-Ndoghok infiltrated among the other Banen, and still farther west again, other small groups spread themselves out in the area between the north-western Banen and the Bamileke. All these groups speak a common language whose sentences begin with the words *nyɔ kɔ a* and they are able to understand that of the Banen. They are today called Nyokon which may be derived from *nyɔ kɔ a*. In the course of their migration, or after having settled in their present habitat, these Nyokon may have come into contact with the neighbouring Bamileke, because they have to a certain extent adopted their culture and it is for this reason that Europeans usually classify them with the latter.

It appears that the Yambeta and Lemande have always lived south of the Nun. Their speech may be considered a dialect of that of the Banen with whom their customs are more or less identical. The Banen group is thus homogeneous in origin and language.

The Bafia group is less homogeneous than the Banen because its component peoples do not share a common origin. According to Tessmann, who made a close study of them 40 years ago, the Bafia, Bape, and Yambasa were once part of an autochthonous population in an area close to their present habitat, but were frequently disturbed by nearby invasions. At the time when the Fulani were advancing southwards, the large group known as the Bati were forced to retreat, thrusting the Bafia back. The Bati even began to cross the Mbam and settle on its right bank, thus coming into direct contact with the Bafia whom they influenced in many ways, especially linguistically.

The Yambasa tribes, also fleeing before the Bati, advanced a little farther to the south, crossing the Sanaga River from the east and the Mbam from the north.

The Bafia group emerged from all these collisions with their original culture more or less intact, though their language underwent some change.

A group of tribes known as the Fak were also fleeing southwards from the Fulani at this time. Today these Fak are referred to as the Balom. They came down the Mbam Valley, crossed the river and settled near the Bape and Yambeta. After living for a time among these peoples, the Fak went northwards to their present habitat. According to Tessmann, they speak a language which is merely " a dialect of the Bafia language "; if so this would appear to be a case of language borrowing.

To sum up, there is linguistic unity within the Banen group, and also within the Bafia group, while there is cultural uniformity between both groups, certain variations being shown on the one hand by the Nyokon and on the other by the Balom, although the exact extent of these variations has yet to be determined.

Very little is known about any of these peoples except the Banen proper and the Bafia proper. Existing information is partly derived from the observations made by the first expeditions to penetrate this area, originally rather difficult of access. Military expeditions into the area were made in 1892 by Captain H. Ramsay, in 1901 by von Schimmelpfennig, and in 1904 by Captain Dominick, who was the first to penetrate deeply into Bafia country. It was not until 1911 that Major Puder was able to obtain the surrender of the Bafia and Banen and to subdue the area by setting up administrative centres. In 1913 Tessmann made a field-trip in the area, providing a most valuable account of the region. Since then the numerous reports written by administrative officers have provided useful though somewhat uncoordinated information.

THE BANEN

LOCATION AND DISTRIBUTION

NOMENCLATURE

The name " Banen " is said to mean " the rich men," but no satisfactory explanation of it has ever been obtained. In his linguistic study of the Cameroons Tessmann gives " Banen(d)." Koelle called the peoples " Penyin " or " Penin."[1]

LOCATION

The Banen belong to three different administrative sub-divisions, one section of them being in the Ndikinimeki Sub-division in the northern part of their country, the most populous zone. The southern Banen belong to the Yabassi Sub-division. Finally, in the extreme north-east, the Manoui River, an important tributary of the Nun, was chosen as a natural boundary of the administrative region, with the result that some very small groups of Banen—the Kibum, Ponek, Niŋgesen, and Ndigbisum, numbering less than 1,000 persons all told—were included in the Bafia Sub-division, together with the Yambeta and Lemande tribes.

The territory of the Banen is shaped like a quadrilateral drawn out obliquely from north-east to south-west, with a large area jutting out westwards among the Basa and Bandem peoples. The area occupied by the Banen and the Yambeta is bounded on the north by the Nun River, a tributary of the Mbam, which is itself an important tributary of the Sanaga. To the east the Yambeta occupy the Mbam Valley, a few miles from the river itself, their immediate neighbours being the Balom. Towards the south, the Lemande occupy the uplands whose mountainous summits overlook the Yambasa Plain. To the south, the boundary of Banen territory follows the edge of the uplands in a north-east/south-west direction, without any marked natural boundaries between the Banen and the Basa-Bibimbi peoples. In the extreme south-west corner the Banen occupy the mountains of the upper reaches of the Ekem and Ebo Rivers, which join lower down to form the Dibamba River; here the Basa tribes are their near neighbours. To the north they occupy the valleys of the tributaries of the Upper Wouri (Wuri) and are in direct contact with the Bandem; the territory of the Nyokon extends along the deep valley of the Nihep, a tributary of the Makombe or Upper Wouri. Beyond this lies Bamileke country.

PHYSICAL ENVIRONMENT

The country within these boundaries is uneven and mountainous, scored by deep valleys where torrential rivers run. The few rivers which are wider and calmer are cut by rapids and are therefore not navigable.

The traveller coming from the low-lying Yabassi country towards Ndikinimeki or along the tributaries of the Upper Wouri and through Nyokon country towards Bamileke territory comes upon two steep rock faces in the middle of the forest, which raise the country to a height of 815 metres. Near Ndikinimeki the hills rise again, covered on one side with forest, on the other with savanna, and culminating in Mount Ehola, 1,200 metres high. These mountains form the watershed between the Sanaga and Wouri basins and are an important hydrographic centre for the tributaries of these two rivers.

The thick vegetation covering the mountains includes some fine strips of primary forest in the Inubu valley. The grassland area inhabited by the Itundu, Eling,

[1] See Johnston, 1919, vol. I, pp. 698–710.

Yambeta and Lemande is by far the least wooded and trees grow only on the mountain peaks. The mountains are granitic, the soil is very much weathered, and has become pure laterite throughout the savanna zone. In the forest country of the Nyokon, however, it is remarkably fertile.

The climate is typical of the sub-equatorial zone, with four seasons of unequal length. The main dry season lasts from the middle of November to the end of March, then storms begin and the peak of the first rainy season is in June. This is followed by a few weeks of extreme drought, from July to the middle of August, after which the rains gradually start again, becoming very heavy in September and October, a period during which the rivers are very full and hard to cross. The uplands enjoy an agreeable climate, with cool nights throughout the year, the heat being tempered by the altitude and an average degree of humidity.

TERRITORIAL GROUPING AND DEMOGRAPHY

The territory occupied by the Banen covers about 4,475 sq. kms. (c. 1,800 sq. miles) and has a population of 28,326 inhabitants, the average density thus being 16.3 per sq. mile.

Within the population as a whole it is possible to distinguish certain groups of people claiming a common ancestry. Thus from north to south there are the following:

	Men	Women	Total
ITUNDU, consisting of the Itundu, Nefande, Nomale and Buturu groups	554	729	1,283
YAMBETA, with the villages of Kon, Bongol and Di			1,984
NDIKI, consisting of the Bonyanya, Ndignimeki, Ndegten, Ndegnelemb, Ndogpɔmbus, Ndogbɔkɔk, Nebɔlɛn, Mafɛ, and Ndigtɔlɛ clans	1,117	1,426	2,543
ELING, consisting of the Neboya, Ekondj, Mafut, Nebatshel and Nituku groups	986	1,317	2,303
LEMANDE, with the villages of Tshekos, Osimp, Ndang, Tobany, Bunyuguluk, Nyambay			1,916
NDOGBANOL, consisting of the Ndogbek, Etong, Ndignyok, Ndogbekom, Ndogbasiomi, Ndogtok and Ndigbil groups	698	816	1,514
LOGONANGA	631	617	1,248
NDOGBIAKAT, consisting of the Ndogbien, Ndogminokon and Ndogbaembi sub-tribes	959	1,203	2,162
YINGI	419	452	871
NYOKON, including the Mbalmasi, Ndogmakoŋ, Ndogmaloŋ, Bwa and Huŋ.			3,002

Small, scattered groups gradually attached themselves to one or another of these tribes. The Ndoghok, already mentioned (p. 132), are an example of such a group. Population figures are as follows:

Ndoghok, Ndogmios, Akut, Ndigtiek, Ndogmaï, 704; Ndokoko, Ndigyel, Ndema, 1,866; Ndognonoho, Ndokalende, 956; Ndogwanen, 206; Ndogbasaben, 375; Ndogbilak, Ndogbakumek, 834; Ndokon, 86; Ndogbu, 351; Ndogmba, Ndogmandeng, 440; Ndogmiol, 208; Ndongol, Ndogmem, 152.

In addition to the above, some of these small Banen groups, breaking up into even smaller groups on their way down to the western valleys, travelled through the primary forest along the various tracks which lead to Yabassi. Once in the more open lowlands, some of these people settled close to or even among the Basa and Bandem, forming communities such as that of the Ndogtuna, with its 1,288 members.

There is also a considerable colony of Banen in Douala itself, numbering about 2,000 members.

The Banen, whose density of population is already low, show clear signs of decreasing in number. The main reason for this is probably the isolation of their country, which makes medical care impossible, except in the extreme north and south. Throughout this area of mountains and dense forests it is almost impossible to combat sterility, venereal diseases, and infant mortality. Only the Nyokon, healthy and prolific, are increasing in numbers.

The Banen are a homogeneous people. Only in the extreme south-west corner of their country is there any mixture with the neighbouring Basa and Bandem. It may be added that the territory of the Lemande is peopled not only by autochthones but also by fragments of various Bekke (Bafia) clans and by Banen proper who were pushed back eastwards. Finally, some Bamileke traders have established themselves around the administrative centre at Ndikinimeki. Moreover, since 1940 a colony of Bamileke planters has grown up at a spot some 10 miles north-west of this centre. Their numbers are increasing rapidly. From five or six in 1940 they had grown to 250 in 1946 and today this colony of young men, who are developing large areas hitherto uncultivated, numbers over 1,000.

TRADITIONS OF ORIGIN AND HISTORY

The Banen have no general idea of their history as a single large group. The most northerly section admit that before the European occupation they knew nothing of the existence of the southern tribes. Similarly, the southern people declare that their ancestors knew nothing of the existence of the northern tribes.

It is very probable that the original habitat of the Banen was a little to the north of their present territory, in the angle formed by the junction of the Mbam and Nun Rivers, or even on either side of the lower reaches of the Nun.

The Yambeta and the Lemande say that they have always lived on the right bank of the Nun. The Ndiki and the Itundu (the most northerly Banen tribes) state that they originally lived on the left bank of the Nun and that they crossed this river 13 generations ago, a period of roughly 300 years. When they reached the right bank, they found some Banen there already and displaced them, usually acquiring the desired territory in exchange for a compensatory payment, after which the displaced group always moved off in a westerly or south-westerly direction. After the Itundu had arrived, the Eling tribe (which split off from them) settled in the savanna-covered uplands, driving out the Ndogbanol. The latter moved westwards and settled in territory formerly occupied by the Ndogbiakat, whom they displaced. Driven back in this way, the Ndogbiakat attacked the Basa, of whom they still say today " they planted the palm-trees of our country."

The Yingi are a branch of the Eling which broke away from the main body and continued to move westwards, by-passing the other Banen tribes and finally settling among the Basa. They also infiltrated among the Bandem.

The only outstanding event which the Banen remember with any clarity is a war against the Bamum in the time of King Mbuembue of Fumban. The Bamum, coming from four different directions, at first routed the few Banen, Ponek, and Kibum whom they encountered near the Nun, but then a sort of coalition was rapidly established among all the Banen who felt themselves endangered by the Bamum horsemen. The battle took place a few miles south-west of the present site of Ndikinimeki, at the foot of the first mountain spurs, and the Banen managed to draw the enemy cavalry into a trap from which they were unable to escape. These events took place about 100 years ago and nothing similar has occurred since.

Later, in the time of the Bamum king Nsangu, grandson of Mbuembue, a new war drove the Nyokon from the left bank of the Nun. They fled in an east-west direction, followed the course of the Nde River, and settled in the savanna surrounding the present-day Hausa villages of Tonga and Kargachi. Their traditions speak of the acts of vassalage which they owed annually to the king of the Bamum. They later freed themselves and went into the rich forest country shortly before the area was occupied by Europeans, the first of whom arrived in 1901. On the approach of von Schimmelpfennig's expedition, the Ndiki, incited by their chief Somo, took up arms. The chief himself was wounded, a few others were killed, and the people very quickly surrendered.

MODERN DEVELOPMENTS

Roads

No road has ever been made into the wild Banen country, since every attempt has been prevented by the two great cliffs which rise up in the depths of the forest to form the Ndikinimeki Plateau. The only large trade route is the road from Yaounde to Nkongsamba in the north on the edge of the forest. It is joined by two road sections, one of which, from Ndikinimeki to Nituku (7 miles), was completed three years ago. It is to be extended as far as Yangben (Yambasa) where it will join the projected main road from Bafia to Eseka. The other leads out of this in a south-westerly direction as far as Ndogwanen, where it stops on the edge of the forest close to the first great cliff of Ndogbanol country. Finally, far to the south among the Yingi, there is the end of the road from Yabassi. This also stops at the cliff, and these two road sections, one from the north and one from the south, are linked only by footpaths.

Medical Services

The northern zone of Banen country is served by the hospital at Bafia, whose chief medical officer supervises the dispensaries of the area. There is a dispensary near the Ndikinimeki administrative centre which deals with 20,000 to 30,000 cases a year, and another at Nituku, among the Eling, which deals with about 9,000 cases a year. There is a leper colony for about 50 lepers not far from the Ndikinimeki dispensary.

Educational Services

In the north, at Ndikinimeki, there is a small three-class school supervised by the Administration. There are three African teachers for the pupils whose numbers vary annually from 145 to 175. Here also the Catholic Mission runs two schools with a total of 324 pupils. The Protestant Mission has 390 pupils. At Nituku, among the Eling, the Administration has just opened a school with an estimated total of about 100 pupils. The Catholic Mission, with nine teachers working in the bush, has another 308 pupils. Finally, there are the small very simple schools run by the Protestant Mission, where reading, writing and the elements of arithmetic are taught to about 1,100 pupils.

LANGUAGE

Ever since the publication of the first Banen vocabularies, the language has been classified as semi-Bantu. But in fact this classification is incomprehensible and quite erroneous. The Banen speak a Bantu language, with all the characteristics of the group, viz., a complete system of noun-classes; the standard system of pronouns; a full complement of verbal derivatives; a complicated tonal system similar to that known throughout Bantu. In the realm of phonetics, however, the presence of the neutral vowel ə should be noted.

The Banen proper all speak the same language. A few words differ in the boundary areas: certain expressions showing Basa influence are found among the Eling, and the Ndogbiakat use a number of pure Douala words, all these influences being of course due to trading connections. Only with reference to the speech of the Yambeta, Lemande, Ndoghok and Ponek is one justified in using the term "dialect."

Because of the limited expansion of their country, the Banen people's only means of communication with neighbouring groups is pidgin English.

MAIN FEATURES OF ECONOMY

AGRICULTURE

The Banen are primarily an agricultural people. In former days, hunting was practised on a fairly large scale, but today this is no longer the case. Moreover, the local rivers are so small that except in the Inubu Valley fishing is only a minor source of food.

For the most part farmers have to work a very poor laterite soil, and they have adapted themselves admirably both to their land, from which they get maximum crops, and also to the climatic conditions.

During the dry season, from mid-December on, the edges of the small river beds are farmed and the damp earth is planted with everything necessary to provide adequate food supplies until the main harvest season. During December the men start clearing the bush where the women will work as soon as the first storm has broken, and the land has been burnt over and the ash dug in. When the rains begin, yams, maize, groundnuts, *wandzou* peas, melons, early and late beans, calabashes, cassava, and green vegetables are planted. Several different crops are sown in the same circular mounds of earth. In May the cultivation of cocoyams and macabo begins.

During the August rains, sweet potatoes are planted in the plots from which the crops have already been harvested (*wandzou* peas, groundnuts, maize, etc.) and also in plots which have lain fallow for some time. At this time, also, there is a second planting of maize, *wandzou* peas, and early beans which will ripen before the dry season starts and before the heavy work of yam harvesting begins in November. Then the new agricultural year opens, with the men clearing the bush and the women harvesting cocoyams and sweet potatoes.

The Banen practise strict rotation of crops: a different crop is grown in each field every year, and after five or six years of cropping the land is left fallow for two or three years.

By working on the damp soil of the rivers, forests, and savanna in the spring, and by means of a second sowing in the rainy season, the Banen achieve as many as three harvests of maize, groundnuts, *wandzou* peas, and beans in one year, in addition to their plentiful harvest of tubers. This means that their diet is a varied one and that it is not possible in their case to pick out any particular staple foods, since in addition to the foods previously mentioned, the Banen consume large quantities of bananas and many different "wild" foods. They have no periodic food shortage.

Men use matchets and axes for bush clearing, and women use a short-handled hoe. All work is done in teams. Everyone—man or woman—belongs to a small team of friends (8–12 members) and each team (*yumwə*) works in turn for each of its members.

Crops are stored in different ways: cocoyams and yams in small granaries next to the dwelling-house and of similar construction; *wandzou* peas and groundnuts in baskets hung from the kitchen roof; maize hung directly from the roof beams; beans and melon seeds in stoppered calabashes. Yams are stored in the fields in rectangular fenced enclosures.

Measurements made on farms show that among the Banen a woman farms an average area of from $\frac{1}{2}$ to $\frac{3}{4}$ of a hectare ($1\frac{1}{4}$ to 2 acres) annually; in a polygynous family the senior wife assisted by her co-wives may harvest nearly 2,000 kilos of yams and almost 1,000 kilos of other tubers. Junior wives harvest much less.

In addition, a woman prepares a yam plot for her husband's personal use, when his friends come or when he wishes to help a woman who needs seeds. The harvest from this plot will amount to about 500 kilos and is kept in the husband's personal store.

In addition to their food farms, nearly all Banen own a few hundred cocoa-trees, and a certain number are on the list of planters owning several thousand coffee-shrubs. Coffee, and more especially cocoa, as well as the magnificent palms from which the Nyokon gather large quantities of oil, are cash crops whose sale enables the people to buy such luxuries as small articles of furniture, clothes, etc.

The Banen raise very little livestock. Every household keeps hens but only a few families own goats and sheep which they rear not so much for food supplies as for the fulfilment of certain social obligations, especially on the occasion of marriages and funerals. Finally, one often sees guinea-pigs kept under the kitchen shelves: they are fed on grass and fattened for eating.

TRADE

Local markets are held, either near a chief's home or at a much-frequented crossroads, at regular intervals (every four, five, six, or eight days) and wherever possible on different days, to allow produce to circulate from one market to another. Men and women bring the produce peculiar to their own district, and oil, salt, and blacksmiths' products are thereby made available everywhere.

Hausa butchers also attend these local markets. It is from these men that the people obtain the small amount of meat which they consume and it is mainly owing to their presence that hunting has almost died out.

In certain bush-markets money is not used in any transactions, goods either being bartered or exchanged for certain quantities of palm kernels. These kernels are sought by European traders and are eventually centralized in the large markets near the coast, but they are also used to make the oil with which the natives smear their bodies.

Large markets are held only on the borders of the country, on the Nkongsamba-Yaounde road in the north, where the lorries from the big trading centres can pick up goods, and in the south among the Basa people on the Yabassi road, and on the Sakbayeme-Edea road. Today, the Banen themselves have opened a new trade-route eastwards towards Yambasa country. Only a few years ago the people thought nothing of carrying over 100 lb. of cocoa or palm kernels several times a year on a six or seven days' journey westwards to the trading centre at Yabassi. Today, owing to the intensification of European and native trade, which in a few years has put a considerable number of lorries on the road, the people feel themselves much closer to the distributive centres for their goods; they are never more than one or two days' walk from the big outside markets.

In the big northern markets—at Ndikinimeki, Nituku, and Tonga—trade is above all a transit trade in palm-oil; this is brought from Basa and Babimbi country and then sold from market to market on its way to the Bamileke Plateau.

DIVISION OF LABOUR

Both men and women play their part in the annual work-cycle of the Banen. After the men have spent several weeks clearing the land, the women begin to cultivate it, sowing crops as the men's work proceeds. This simultaneous work of the two sexes goes on for about two months. The women have scarcely finished ridging before the first yam shoots make their appearance. This means more hard work for the men, who go into the forest and cut branches to stick into the ground as supports for the yam stalks. This work lasts a good month. Meanwhile the women weed and hoe the plots. The men now begin building new huts and repairing damaged roofs and granaries, and when this work is completed, the women, working in large teams, plaster the walls and partitions with earth, and beat the floors smooth.

In addition, the men, in readiness for the approaching harvest, prepare the baskets necessary for gathering, carrying home and storing the ripened crops. Both men and women take part in the harvest.

Men carry out minor carpentry and rope-making tasks in the evening after the day's work, while the women are preparing the meal. On their way home from the fields, their baskets filled with food, the women gather firewood for cooking, and they and the children also fetch water.

During the dry season some women work as potters.

After the maize harvest, the women make beer. Throughout the year they crush palm-nuts and make the oil, after the men have cut down the nuts with their matchets and brought them to the homestead. Men collect palm-wine.

CRAFTS

Women use only a hoe in the fields, and men only a matchet and an axe in the forest.

Fire is made with a sort of tinder box (*mokwas*): a flint is held in the left hand against some inflammable dry fibres and is struck by a sliver of metal held in the right hand: the resulting spark sets fire to the fibres. Once they have made fire the Banen do their utmost to preserve it: their forests provide them amply with wood which burns without going out. At night they always cover the log on the kitchen hearth with ashes, so that it only needs blowing on the next morning to produce a flame.

Wood-work

For making beds, stools, mortars, pipes, spoons, and drums the main tool used is the matchet, supplemented by small two-edged or hooked knives of varying sizes.

Basket-work

Carried out by men, basket-work is of a very simple type. Cane and rushes only are used, whether for baskets or sleeping-mats.

Weaving

An exclusively masculine craft; only raffia is used. The loom (*neŋaŋ*) is simply a vertical frame, without a harness, and has only a single row of heddles. The weft is made by hand. Weaving serves only to produce small carrying bags. The edges of these little bags are sewn together with the help of a needle (*musiononi*) made from the rib of an oil-palm leaf.

Rope-making

This is practised by both sexes, is quite rudimentary, and consists simply in plaiting three strands together. Some women know how to plait eight strands together to make necklaces and belts.

Pottery

Only cooking pots are made. It is an essentially feminine craft and involves the shaping of a lump of earth to which rolls of earth are attached spirally by polishing the surface. Shaping is done without a wheel: the woman simply moves round the pot, which is finished off by being drawn out at the bottom and is fired in the simplest possible way in a heap of burning logs.

Iron-working

Formerly iron-working included both smelting ore in blast furnaces (*bub*) and the use of the forge (*hilun*). Smelting was done in two stages. The ore, extracted either from surface rock or from mine galleries, was first smelted in blast furnaces, and the iron thus obtained was melted again on a hearth heated by means of a wooden bellows. This technique, forgotten during the last 40 years, was revived during the second world war. The smelters were mostly Eling tribesmen, members of the Niboya clan. The iron they produced found its way through the markets to smiths in neighbouring tribes. Today, smiths only work with old iron of European origin. The smithy is very simple, consisting merely of a hearth dug in the ground, bellows made of wood and banana leaves, some water, a stone anvil, and a hammer, or simply a large stone.

House Construction

A house is built by fixing large posts in the ground and attaching long raffia-palm ribs to these by means of thin creepers. The sloping roof, made next, consists of a framework of similar construction to which are attached raffia-palm mats. Among the southern Banen the roof is put together on the ground, each side being made separately, and then dragged up on to the walls so that the top rests against the ridge-pole. After the roofing is completed, the wattling of the walls is daubed with clay so that all gaps are filled in. Often windowless, the houses built today are provided with a crude wooden door and a padlock.

None of these techniques involves any decoration. There is no carving on houses, furniture, or drums. Only a few relics of former days, such as stools and wooden headrests, are decorated with incised lines. Old people remember that in their youth calabashes were decorated with poker-work or rows of beads or coloured raffia. Today, only wooden spoon-handles bear line decorations, and the upper part of cooking pots is ornamented before firing by means of a roller of plaited straw.

The art of dyeing has today been more or less forgotten in most areas.

Masked dancing is unknown among the Banen, who have thus lacked one of the incentives for wood-carving.

Since the European occupation, some of the people living within a few miles of the administrative centres have learnt to use European wood-working tools and to make household equipment.

SOCIAL ORGANIZATION AND POLITICAL SYSTEM

Social Grouping

As has been indicated above (p. 132) only a few of the Banen tribes exist as organized functional units, owing to the fact that the people's migrations through dense forests tended to split them up into very small groups.

Among those groups which are not yet disorganized, there is still a feeling of unity within the tribe (bonɔŋ) under its chief. The term bonɔŋ refers equally to the social group and to the territory it occupies. The chief is " he who commands " (momanɛn). The only authority in the eyes of the people is the chief legally chosen according to customary law; title and functions go from father to son. It is not necessarily the eldest son who inherits the function of the chief, his father. The heir is chosen by the father, but this choice is guided by a small private council and is in any case only really valid if approved by the group as a whole. There have been occasions when the administration has agreed to the appointment of young chiefs without the approval of the people, who have then refused to accept these men as their true chiefs; order was restored only when there was a return to the rule of ancestral custom.

A chief is not addressed by his title of momanɛn, but is called munɛn (rich man), just as are those whose power derives from their wealth. Authority does in fact depend to a great extent on economic power.

The basis of social grouping is the patriclan (hitik), that sub-division of the tribe whose members are the descendants of a common ancestor, close enough for them all to be conscious of the blood tie which enforces exogamous marriage: it is in fact by the rules of exogamy that the clan may be defined.

Descent is normally reckoned patrilineally, though there are in fact sometimes exceptions. All the male members of the clan consider themselves brothers, and as a general rule they occupy a common territory, their dwellings being loosely dispersed over this area. The territory occupied by the clan includes not only the homesteads with their surrounding kitchen-gardens, but also more distant fields and the land necessary for extensive cultivation. It is the whole of this extremely dispersed settlement which is loosely referred to by Europeans as a " village."

A man related to the clan through his mother may join it. If the maternal nephew (*umbieny*) gets into trouble with his father's family he may run away and demand help, protection, and support from his mother's family. The nephew who knocks at the door of his maternal uncle (*isen*) is always welcomed and will never meet there with the difficulties he has known elsewhere. If no urgent necessity forces the *umbieny* to return to his own family, he may remain with his uncle and found a family, and his children will say that they belong to the clan of his *isen*.

The head of the family, whether joint family or elementary family, is known as the *isə* or father, and the close patrilineal ancestors are also known as " fathers " (*bisə*) as are all the male members of the family of the same generation as the father. The mother is referred to as *inyə,* and all the women of the family, sisters, cousins, aunts, etc., are the *embɛn.*

All the members of a joint family (*nikul*) descended from a common grandfather think of themselves as brothers. The simple elementary family consisting of a man, his wife, and their children is the *nɛkɔ* or hearth, home.

THE HOMESTEAD

In the clan territory, each family head builds his huts round a central quadrangle (*ombɛl*). The husband's hut (*mim*), larger than those of the women, occupies one side of the courtyard. At right angles to his hut, and on its right hand, is that of his senior wife and her children. Next come those of his other wives and their children, the whole forming a closed square. The wives' huts are not necessarily built very close to each other; in fact, they are usually separated. Nowadays, a 6-ft. fence is still often built between the huts so as to enclose the courtyard completely, only a single entrance being left in the fence.

A son lives with his father until he marries, when he goes off and builds his own compound (*ombɛl*) of small rectangular huts of puddled clay, with sloping roofs made of palm-leaves. His own hut usually has two rooms of unequal size. In the larger one he receives his friends, in the smaller one he rests. A woman's hut consists of a single room serving as both kitchen and bedroom: the hearth and shelves are on one side, a rough bed on the other. In practice a woman's hut today usually has two or sometimes three rooms: the kitchen, in the centre, is separated by partitions from the bedroom on one side, and from a small storeroom on the other.

RIGHTS OF INHERITANCE AND SUCCESSION

On the death of the family head his heirs are his sons: his daughters have no rights of inheritance. The eldest son is more favoured than his brothers, and it is in fact he who divides the property and keeps the largest share for himself. The father's wives and daughters, his land and domestic animals are all inherited, but the homestead is not, because among the Banen it is even now seldom built of durable material. The son only takes the father's wives if they are willing to remain with him. Nowadays, if they prefer to return to their own families, they cannot be prevented from doing so, but the daughters remain with their father's family. If the heir has brothers, each will receive his share of the sisters, because each brother will have to give one of his sisters in marriage when he wants to get married himself. Disputes may later arise if the eldest son refuses to give their shares to his brothers. The same is true of land. When it is a question of sharing out cocoa-trees or simply the profits of the cocoa crop, or when coffee-shrubs are involved, over which there are proper land rights registered with the Administration, then all the skill and tact of the new family head, or his senior, the clan chief, will be called into play, otherwise the dispute may continue throughout his lifetime.

If the family head has no male heir difficulties may arise, because normally the dead man's brothers have the right to inherit. Very often, however, a man who has no son does not wish his property to pass into other hands, so when his daughters reach marriageable age he keeps one back. She must bear children in her father's house, and her son will be proclaimed heir to the property of his grandfather. Once the heir is born the father may give his daughter in marriage.

SLAVERY

Today slaves cannot be inherited, as they have all been freed. However, every member of the community knows which men and women are free-born, and which were once slaves.

In former times slaves were of several kinds. There was the slave man or woman who had been bought in the market-place, someone whom a neighbouring tribe wanted to get rid of, known as a *yɔnd*. The female *yɔnd* became a wife; the male *yɔnd* became the property of the family, who would increase their wealth by his labour. There was also the *mutɛka*, a man or woman who was handed over by one group to another as a conciliatory gift to bring peace after disagreement had led to bloodshed. Other categories of slaves were the *muyɔŋ* or captive, *mukom*, the prisoner of war, and *yɔlɛ*, a general term describing anyone taken by force in whatever manner.

The bought slave (*yɔnd*) occupied the lowest position, but a female *yɔnd* was often highly respected in the household. Even today the son of a slave, if in need, can look to his former owner for help and the master still feels a certain responsibility towards a son of the family's slave; he may even give him a wife. Nevertheless, if there is a quarrel, a descendant of a slave is sure to be insulted because of his birth and will be made to feel the stigma of his lowly origin.

STATUS OF WOMEN

On the whole there is respect for women among the Banen. A woman may obtain a certain authority within the family if she is intelligent and industrious. Her husband is very dependent upon her help in farming and takes good care not to annoy her in any way, for a Banen woman will threaten to leave her husband over a trifle. If she delays at all in returning from a visit to her own family he is very worried. A woman will often wait for her husband to come and fetch her back from such a visit.

Among the Banen a woman is able to make the most of her physical capacities, since there is a strict rule—though now being undermined in certain Christian families—that she may not bear children more than once every two and a half to three years.

A woman is free to market all the crops she grows; the money earned in this way belongs to her and her husband is ignorant of the total. She is free to spend the money as she wishes and may even save enough to get another wife for her husband.

In certain chiefly families a daughter may return to her father if she is left a widow and may acquire wealth and prestige in the following way. Her father gives her land and she accumulates savings; she may then become a family head herself by " marrying " one or more women, giving the requisite bridewealth to their families. These wives, while helping her with her work and sharing her life, will also bear male heirs to her.

AGE-SETS

Men and women are not grouped in age-sets. The only living link between people is that of kinship. It seems most unlikely that mutual aid groups ever existed among the Banen, and if they did, there is no evidence of them today in any sphere of life.

Organs of Local Government

The prestige of the chief is today much lower than it was in the past. Formerly his authority was inherent in his position as head of the whole community; he was chief, judge, guide, and counsellor. Today he is still the chief, in that he is the intermediary between the Administration and his people, and he is the heir of the ancestors; he is judge, because many minor disputes are brought before his personal court, but it is doubtful whether he is still guide and counsellor.

In former days the chief's primary concern was the increase, prosperity, and general well-being of the whole community; because of his religious power he could act as intermediary between his people and the forces of nature. Today, however, he is not only regarded with some suspicion because of his constant contacts with Europeans, but Christianity has undermined his religious authority. In order to regain this authority, he tends today to make himself feared by intimidation. Thus the community looks for its well-being and prosperity rather to the clan chief, or to the head of the joint family (*nikul*), who acts on the whole as a paterfamilias, in our sense of the term. This clan chief or joint family head is the pacifying element in the community. It is he who receives the first fruits of crops and of palm-wine, the main portions of animals killed in hunting, etc. In return he sees that peace is kept in the community, he acts as counsellor, and it is to him that a young man will go for financial help towards a marriage which is beyond his means.

Judicial Procedure

We have seen that the chief of the tribe is its judge, but only those cases that cannot be settled within the family come before the chief.

The chief's court is held almost every day, and in any case on market days, near his house. He is surrounded by the elders, the old men who know customary law, and who sit in judgment with the chief. They act as assessors, whose advice the chief may and should take. The chief delivers the verdict with the approval of his elders.

These elders are all that now remains of a very exclusive circle which in former times revolved round the chief of the tribe. He was always surrounded by a small council (*eŋɔŋ*), whose members were known as *bahik* (sing. *muhik*). These men never left the chief. Plaintiffs would come to them at night, bringing presents to gain their goodwill, and asking for immediate vengeance on the accused, who would then be brought along and given a hearing, before being confronted with his accuser.

Offences dealt with by the chief's court were of many kinds, but the majority fell, as they do today, under a few main heads: sorcery, theft, debt, sexual offences.

Cases of sorcery are numerous and of many different kinds. They involve the preparation of " medicines " (*beha* and *misiɔŋ*), some of which act as true poisons while others are believed to cause death by magical means. A person might also be accused of being possessed by an evil spirit (*nelemb*) which could leave his body without his knowledge in order to kill. A curse spoken in anger could cause death. Finally, there was the crime of straightforward armed murder.[2]

Theft of agricultural products is a most grave offence. Stealing from a field or from a yam store is so serious that a guilty woman is immediately suspected of having been driven to it by an evil spirit, whose presence in her had hitherto been unsuspected.

---

[2] A leopard-man who commits murder is not prosecuted. The leopard-man is not a member of a secret society, as among other tribes elsewhere, nor does he play the part of executioner. Among the Banen, being a leopard-man simply consists in paying a high price for a certain " medicine " (a plant, probably one of the *Liliaceæ*), which is hidden and kept alive somewhere in the owner's compound. At night, the owner's spirit can escape from this plant (*nenyaŋɛ nɛ mɛkɔ*) in the shape of a leopard which goes off to kill whom it chooses. If the leopard is wounded by a hunter, its owner will bear similar wounds; if the leopard is killed, its owner will die unless he eats the liver of the dead beast within three days. The Banen claim that by refusing the liver to those who ask for it they are gradually ridding themselves of leopard-men.

Sexual offences include adultery, but also incest within the clan and the breaking of the taboo on sexual intercourse with a woman during the two years following the birth of a child. The last two offences have very far-reaching consequences: the guilty individuals have broken a taboo (*embak*) and this may bring misfortune to the whole community.

When cases were difficult to settle, recourse was had to ordeals, which alone were infallible.

The type of penalty imposed depended on whether the guilty person was a powerful free man, or a slave, or a woman.

There were always extenuating circumstances in the case of the rich man who had given many propitiatory gifts to his judges, but blood money (*nem*) had nevertheless to be paid. A man could be sentenced to death or to banishment, which meant being sold as a slave to a foreign tribe. As it was taboo for a free man to be killed by a free man, he had to be captured in the forest and killed far away from his home by a slave. His property was then confiscated and his wife and children scattered.

A slave or a woman found guilty was far more severely punished, even for minor offences, because in such cases no extenuating circumstances existed. The death penalty, mutilation, or banishment was the rule.

Today all serious offences come before the Administration. Most of the cases heard by the Administration's courts are concerned with suits for divorce and claims for the custody of children (because of the civil registration of marriages), as well as land disputes and occasional murder cases. Other matters and disputes within the village and the family are brought before the chief, in spite of the awkward situation created by his present-day inability to take stringent action, according to ancestral custom, in such special cases as the activities of *balemb* (evil spirits), curses, the use of *beha,* and certain sexual offences. Recourse may still be had to ordeals, some of which are dangerous, since they involve the use of poisons, though the most frequently used is swearing on a tortoise. Nevertheless the people today feel defenceless, because the severe penalties of former times are no longer possible, since the chief is not allowed to pass sentence of death or banishment.

LAND TENURE

The tribal chief is the custodian of the land, but the community enjoys the free use of it and owns the usufruct. Only a stranger who joins the community has to ask the chief for permission to farm. Within the community, everyone is free to farm the plots of his choice, each plot belonging to its first occupant—the people commonly say " I have this land " or " Someone else has it." " Family land " is not enclosed but is delimited by natural boundary marks such as rocks, trees, paths, etc. Land is occupied as and when it is needed by the family, and whether it is in the forest or in the savanna, or on the edge of a stream, everyone knows the portion he has chosen, whether it is in use or lying fallow. These plots are widely scattered and very small. Everyone also knows who owns the plots which do not belong to him. Today it is necessary to walk a long way from a settlement, sometimes for as much as an hour, before coming to land available for new clearing.

As noted above (p. 136), all the Banen tribes occupied other territory before settling in their present habitat: these ancestral lands are known as *behalal*. When these are unoccupied, like the *behalal* of the Ndiki near Mount Ehola, palm-trees there have become the collective property of the members of the various clans, each of which knows the boundaries of its own territory. Clan members are free to cut palm-nuts, but only on their own territory.

K

MAIN CULTURAL FEATURES

PHYSICAL AND MENTAL CHARACTERISTICS

The Banen are of medium height and thickset. Chiefs' families are taller with longer limbs. The cranial index is mesocephalic, with numerous examples of brachycephalism. The nose is only slightly flattened. Pigmentation is variable but in general rather dark and sometimes very dark. The Banen are of a very independent but friendly nature.

ORNAMENT AND DRESS

The Banen often decorate their bodies with tattoo marks (*beban*) consisting of small cuts made blue by being rubbed with soot. Raised tattoo marks (*bembaka*) are only seen on women of about 50 or over. In former days, the face, the trunk (chest or back or both), or part of the trunk, and the arms were tattooed. The decorations are not family or tribal marks, but with few exceptions, every Banen, young as well as old, has, just above the nose, a small circle of blue cuts, less than an inch in radius; very often, also a few small cuts are made on the cheekbones. As everywhere, tattooing is gradually dying out.

In former days also, the lobe of a woman's left ear was pierced with a hole large enough to contain aromatic plants and a pipe.

Teeth are filed. Today many young people still have their upper median incisors broken off slantwise, but in former days all four upper and lower incisors were cut vertically along both edges so as to leave a small space between the teeth. The operation was and still is carried out with a knife, a stone being used as a hammer.

In the bush the people are almost naked, men wearing a small loincloth and women a small belt of coloured beads in which are stuck, back and front, bunches of leaves or ferns. Everyone likes to wear narrow bracelets of iron or brass on the wrists. These replace the huge bracelets of former days which are still sometimes worn by women in remote villages, where some also wear heavy brass rings round their calves.

Near European centres men wear a larger loincloth and a small shirt, and similarly, when they attend mission services, women usually wear a long straight dress and men wear trousers.

THE LIFE CYCLE

BIRTH

The Banen have no really precise idea of the mechanism of conception and they combat many cases of sterility by carrying out a special ritual ceremony (*esay ohɔ*) in the course of which the husband and wife are given a great deal of moral advice urging them to lead a regular life. The people assert that many conceptions take place during the three months following this ceremony.

Birth takes place in the woman's hut. The husband is never present. The pregnant woman is assisted by other women and particularly by some older woman whose competence is well known. The umbilical cord is cut with a knife (it may even be bitten through) and the placenta is buried behind the hut.

After two or three days (though sometimes on the day of birth itself) the mother gets up, and after five days is allowed to bathe in the river and to take up her usual tasks again.

The baby is not washed but on the fifth day is wiped with leaves smeared with a mixture of palm and cabbage-palm oils. Some time later it is smeared with a reddish mixture made of the powdered bark of the *padouk* tree. This is believed to protect the baby against skin diseases, especially scabies. Very often the baby is laid on a tiny bed of palm-leaf ribs coloured with *padouk* powder. Among pagans, at the time of the second new moon after the birth of a child, it is customary for an old man of the family to say over the child: " As the moon grows, so may this child grow." Then he spits on the child as a sign of benediction.

The child is named a few days after birth. This may be done by the midwife (who will give it the name of a member of her own family) or by its parents, who may name it in memory of a well-loved or dead relative, or in commemoration of some special event which has just occurred in the family. The Banen insist that naming a child after another member of the family does not in their case imply a belief in the reincarnation of this relative in the child. The name given at birth is not necessarily the final name; this is sometimes given when the child is circumcised, or even later.

Twins

The birth of twins (*embwasalɛ*) is an event both welcomed and feared. Welcomed because the family thus gains two new members, but feared because twins may be the cause of all kinds of misfortune. Parents are obliged to take endless precautions to avoid annoying or angering the twins, and thus incurring these misfortunes, known as *nɛhas*, which may be illness or any other unpleasant happening.

If at birth there is only one placenta, then all is well; but if there are two, this means that the woman is inhabited by an evil spirit (*ibuŋɔ*) now revealed for the first time.

As soon as the twins have been born the medicine man (*ɛmwɛn*) is summoned. He recites spells over the parents and gives them the appropriate medicinal plants to eat. He then orders the father to fix a curtain of palm-leaves in front of the hut door, because the twins may not see daylight or the outside world in case they are tempted to return " whence they came," i.e., to die. From now on, any relatives or friends who come to visit the twins during the next 23 days (5 + 9 + 9) are forbidden to speak in a normal voice: the slightest word spoken by or to them must be chanted. As soon as the *ɛmwɛn* has gone the special dances for the twins begin and continue for five days. On the fifth day the celebration reaches its height. All the participants—members of the family as well as guests—wear short skirts of ferns and thick garlands of leaves round their necks; their heads are wreathed with leaves. The final celebration takes place on the ninth day, when gifts are offered by friends to the children who are still kept in total darkness. Everyone arrives shouting and singing; dancing goes on for the whole day and incantations are repeated over the twins. At a certain moment, to the accompaniment of loud shouts from the crowd, the parents climb up the back of their hut and appear on the roof, where they dance for a moment and then leap down. At the end of the day the *ɛmwɛn* returns and a light meal of plantains is prepared, which will be served to the guests gathered in groups of five. The *ɛmwɛn* brings his medicine plants and the father has his talisman, which is simply a piece of *cereus*. When the medicine plants have been specially cooked and he has recited the appropriate incantations, the *ɛmwɛn* makes all the company take part in a sort of communion-feast, starting with the parents. This is the final event of the celebration and all the necessary rites have now been accomplished.

On the occasion of the next yam harvest, every woman of the large family group must give two yam tubers to the twins' mother, who will eventually plant them in a special plot, from which everyone will be free to gather what he needs.

When the twins start to walk there is another celebration, in the course of which two goats are killed. One of these belongs to the twins' mother and the other is offered to the whole village.

If one of the twins dies it must be buried at a crossroads.

Twins have special names. If they are both boys, the first-born is named *Somo*, the second *Lumu*. If they are girls the elder is named *Sen*, the younger *Sɔl*. If they are a boy and a girl they are named *Somo* and *Sɔl*, or *Sen* and *Lumu*, according to whether the boy or the girl is born first.

Bringing up twins is a delicate task for their parents, because throughout their lives, but especially until they reach adulthood, they must never be displeased or angered. They are believed to be able to revenge themselves on anyone who displeases them.

CIRCUMCISION

This used to be performed when a boy reached manhood or sometimes even after he was married. It was not accompanied by any initiation ceremony, and although it was an occasion for celebration, there were no preparatory rites, no period of confinement, no special training: the boy merely received his final name at this time. Today, a boy is named at birth or soon after, and is circumcised, without any initiation rites, when still a small child.

MARRIAGE

In the past the customary form of marriage among the Banen was by exchange of brides between two families. This was the only form possible for the daughter of a free man (*ifəy*). To the Banen, marriage involving the payment of cash or goods was equivalent to buying a woman, who thereupon became a *yɔnd* or slave. Finally there was the debt-marriage, in which a man unable to repay a debt gave a woman of his family instead. In this case the woman was not a *yɔnd* but a *nikinə* or relative.

For the past 20 years or so, exchange-marriage has been illegal, and today the only surviving form is marriage involving bridewealth, the payment of which is officially registered.

The Banen regret the suppression of exchange-marriage, and the women feel strongly about the matter. They commonly say: " Nowadays, we are bought." In their eyes, exchange-marriage was a dignified institution. There was absolute equality and bargaining was impossible. Moreover, in the opinion of the people, the stability of marriage was greater, a break being more difficult because often the " exchange " (as she is called) and her husband would refuse to separate if their union was happy and fruitful, and the fickle wife was therefore obliged to remain with her husband. Moreover, if one of the wives died, and her "exchange" refused to return to her own people, her husband would give another wife to the widower.

Among the Lemande the idea of equal exchange is carried to extremes, concern for the interests of the two contracting parties extending even to the fertility of their marriages. If one of the wives is barren, whoever gave her in exchange must give one of his own daughters to the childless husband, who, thus compensated for his wife's barrenness, will be able to exchange the child for a new wife.

The Yambeta and the Lemande, who have direct contact with the Bafia, borrowed from the latter the custom of marriage by capture, described below. The Yambeta and Lemande form of this custom differs in one important feature from the Bafia form, however, and this difference is obviously due to the influence of exchange-marriage, a custom which the Yambeta and the Lemande share with the other Banen. Among these two groups the captor-husband had to give to the girl's father, or to her husband if she was already married, a daughter born of the new union.

Exchange-marriage does not seem to have existed among the Nyokon. This people had only two forms of marriage, that in which a marriage-payment was made by the husband to the wife's family being the more common. The other, marriage by capture, was much rarer and today no longer exists.

Among all these Banen, including the Yambeta, Lemande, and Nyokon, a wife goes to live with her husband immediately after marriage, but she continues to regard herself as belonging to the clan of her birth. All the men of her husband's family are allowed access to her, if they wish and if she agrees: her husband cannot object. All children born of the union belong absolutely to the husband, and they will remain with him if the marriage breaks up. On the same principle, a child born before marriage belongs to its mother's family, as has already been stated in connection with the rules of inheritance (p. 142).

In the past a girl went to her husband's family at an early age. She was entrusted either to him or to one of his wives, usually the senior wife, who would bring her up with her own children. A wife's arrival at her husband's home was the occasion for a big celebration, with dancing, during which the entire clan, as well as the two families, pronounced the incantations necessary to make the union happy and fruitful. In the case of a young girl, the marriage was consummated without further ceremony a few months after she reached puberty. Today this ceremony, known as *esay*, still takes place more or less secretly in Christian families. Even though it is not carried out with all its former pagan ritual, nevertheless a young girl never enters her husband's house for the first time without being accompanied by a crowd singing and shouting the appropriate formulæ.

FUNERAL RITES

When a person is at the point of death, family and friends gather round his bed, but no loud or prolonged lamentations are uttered at that time. A corpse is laid out with its cheek resting on its hand: a woman on her right side, a man on his left. The top of the head must always face east. The widows, completely naked, sit on the bare ground near the body, and there is absolute silence. Burial must take place on the day of death, if this occurred in the morning, or on the following day if it occurred in the afternoon. The day of burial is known as *manyən*.

A few hours after the death, women sitting on the floor of the mortuary hut start to chant monotonous lamentations (*imbey*) in which they recount events in the life of the deceased. At the same time a friend of the dead man brings a wooden drum (*iko*) into the courtyard and beats it to announce the death to everyone. Gradually the people gather, and meanwhile the work of grave-digging starts. As the crowd increases, lamentations start in the central courtyard of the homestead and dancing begins, becoming more and more frenzied and continuing for several hours. When the grave is ready, dancing ceases, and some of the dead man's relatives wash the corpse and wrap it in a shroud. Thereupon the eldest son performs a ritual dance in imitation of a leopard hunt. Holding a spear, he hops across the courtyard on his right foot, and at the door of the dead man's hut he mimes a hunter aiming at a leopard. The crossing of the courtyard and the miming must be repeated nine times, and then the hunting mime is carried out on the roof of the hut. While this is going on the dead man's maternal nephews arrive shouting to claim the gift which their maternal uncles owe them on behalf of the dead man. (In the past, the nephews would have carried off a young girl; today a goat or some other present is sufficient.) At this time the dead man's brothers have a kind of " looting right " over his possessions. The maternal uncles also arrive now, with presents (*befona*) for their dead nephew, and they too claim a last gift from him. He must now for the last time " give food " to his nephews, maternal uncles, and brothers. The " looting right " may extend to all objects inside the hut to the crops already harvested, and even to those as yet unharvested.

After these presents have been distributed, the corpse is carried to the grave by three men of the family. The widows follow in silence, walking hand in hand, and sit down by the grave. The grave consists of a trench about 3 ft. deep and a small mortuary chamber (*ikul*) made in its north side. The *ikul* is about the same size as the corpse and is enclosed by logs fixed vertically to prevent earth from touching the corpse. Some of the dead man's personal belongings are placed at the bottom of the large trench, which is then filled in and a small mound raised over it. Sometimes, a few days later, a miniature hut is built over the grave. This is an exact model of a dwelling-hut, and is doubtless intended to reproduce the old custom of burying a man in his own house.

After the burial the widows wash on the grave, and return to their husband's hut, where they remain in absolute seclusion for 20 days, seated on dried banana leaves. A widow from the village takes to each of them a small packet of herbs known as a *yɔt*, in which is wrapped some object, selected by consultation with an earth spider, which will prevent the *yit* (spirit) of the dead man from appearing and annoying the widows. During the 20-day period they must not go outside the hut, nor may they cook; food must be brought to them. During the first five days they must speak only in undertones.

The children of the dead man attach a little bell to their right arms in order to make their father's spirit believe that if it approaches them it will be attacked by hunting dogs. This concludes the rites connected with the actual burial.

Five days later, everyone gathers together in the evening to sing lamentations until sunrise. This is the *bwɔse bo alan* (fifth day): women sing and dance but there is no eating or drinking: it is a solemn occasion entirely given up to memories of the dead man. On the evening of the fifth day, the men of the family must choose the widows they wish to marry. In the darkness each man brings a small gift to the woman of his choice: if she accepts it, this means that she agrees to marry him: if she is unwilling, she will refuse the gift.

On the sixth day, just as dawn is breaking, the dead man's children gather up any articles they have used since the day of his death and break them at the nearest crossroads. They also break their *ilikəlik* belts and burn them. They are now free to go about once more and to carry on their normal life. From now on, also, the widows may raise their heads and speak in a normal voice. On the morning of this sixth day the children have another rite to perform: by ritual words and gestures they must ward off any illness which their dead father may send to them.

On the 20th day after the death the big celebration known as *hit* (20) takes place. In readiness for this occasion, the widows, who have hitherto remained entirely naked, prepare the special garments known as *bilikəlik* which consist of a short knee-length skirt of dried plantain leaves and a little wreath (*ekaŋ*) plaited of the same material.

The *hit* celebration is an important one. It lasts for 24 hours, and in order to give the dead man " a good burial " it is essential that all the numerous guests should be able to eat and drink in great quantities throughout the day. This entails very heavy expenditure by the heir and the other men of the family, but without it due honour cannot be paid to the dead man.

The celebration starts at nightfall and is divided into two distinct parts. First comes a night of vigil (*nisieni*) during which the women sing funeral dirges in the dead man's hut and the men dance frenziedly in the courtyard amid wild uproar.

At dawn the widows have their heads shaved and put on the *bilikəlik*, the skirt and wreath. They smear their knees, the top of the head, and the wreath with clay, take up a long thin walking-stick and clutch the protective *yɔt* under the left arm. They then return to their own huts and during the afternoon take part in the *hit* dances (there are special dances for men and women). There is much shouting and drinking of palm-wine and guns must be fired if the proceedings are to be successful and the dead man adequately honoured. Celebrating goes on through the night until everyone is exhausted. From then on, the dead man's wives are free to go about their ordinary domestic duties.

Burial rites are the same for both men and women, and in theory the mourning period lasts a year, during which time neither widows nor widowers may cut their hair or enter a market, since custom forbids them to take part in the merry-making and small talk of the neighbourhood. There is no absolute rule against re-marrying during the year of mourning, but such a marriage is frowned upon if it takes place too early.

Visitors to the bereaved family on any of the ritual occasions following a death are obliged by custom to take with them gifts known in these circumstances as *befona* (sing. *efona*).

Guests at the *manyɔn* day, 5th day, and 20th day celebrations never arrive empty-handed. Small baskets of yams, packets of salt, bunches of plantains, calabashes of palm-oil or wine, small sums of money, may all be brought as last gifts to the dead.

The heir is expected eventually—there is no fixed time-limit—to give in return presents exceeding in value those received. If he fails to do this he will incur general discredit: he has not given his kinsman a worthy funeral.

This *befona* custom is but one manifestation of the principle of unequal exchange which runs right through the Banen economic system.

During the 20-day mourning period, the heir, in any family of importance, must gather together enough palm-wine and food for yet another ceremony. According to custom, a few days after the *hit* celebrations the elders are supposed to come to his house and carry out on his behalf the *esay* ceremony, in the course of which he will be installed as family head, wearing various objects dear to his father and holding the walking-stick of the dead man. He must receive the blessings of the family elders who establish him in his new role in the sight of all. After this ceremony the heir gives a great thanksgiving feast to all his family.

RELIGION AND MAGIC

The Banen believe in a High God whom they call *hɔɛl, kolo*, or *ombaŋ*, this last word meaning " above, up above." The meaning of the other words is not known. The pure Bantu radical for " god " is found in the phrase *nyam indi*, " if God grants. . . ." As in many other regions of Africa, this High God plays no part in everyday life.

Of much greater importance is the belief in water and forest spirits and in survival after death. Spirits who dwell in the forest are known as *banyɔnyɔ*. From time to time a person working in the forest may be seized by them and carried off to their " village," where he sees many things which he is forbidden to reveal. A few days later he is released and returns home unharmed wearing an annular necklace. Such a person never speaks of his adventure and must observe various taboos thereafter. Spirits inhabiting rivers may be referred to by the generic term *biw fam*, " those who died and have come out again," which term may be applied equally to any dead person whom the living believe to have been seen alive once more. These water spirits are sometimes greatly feared and are often accused of causing death by drowning.

The dead survive for a limited time and then only in their own family; their spirits (*bit*, sing. *yit*) have nothing to do with families to which they are not related. They are to be feared because they come to annoy and not to help. In the place of the dead they continue to live as they did on earth. They survive only as long as people think of them, and when they are forgotten die a second time, completely, reappearing, it is said, in the form of small mushroom-shaped ant-hills in the bush. This time they are thought to be really dead.

The most important aspect of Banen religion, however, is of a very different order. Its essence is a belief in a vital force animating objects as well as living beings, which can reveal itself in dreams or by certain signs, such as the journey of a centipede, the cry of an owl, a meeting with a rat, etc., all of which are regarded not merely as random events but as having been placed in man's path by the mysterious life-force. While a man does his utmost to obtain the greatest possible happiness from this force, he is also able, by means of the spoken word and by spilt blood, to call up all the forces of evil.

The concept of the vital power of the spoken word has already been met with in the Banen life-cycle, as in the blessings spoken during the *esay* ceremony which are believed to be of help throughout life. Moreover, special words must be spoken over a child yet to be conceived, over someone about to marry, over a sick person, and over fields and animals in order that they may prosper. Such words are also necessary for someone who has broken a spell or transgressed some rule and from whom the weight of the *embak* taboo must be lifted.   In oaths and professions of allegiance blood is needed as well as words because, while the word is power, the blood of the sacrificed animal is the witness that will trap the perjurer.

The spoken word is supremely important in Banen religion, as is shown in many different practices.   Sometimes it is not a spoken formula or spell which transmits power, but a prayer in which the suppliant, instead of expressing a request, enumerates his virtues in a series of statements addressed to the unknown vital force. For example, if a father sees his child dying, he prays for its recovery by saying: " I envy nobody, I steal from nobody, I am the servant of all, I do not despise the old, etc."   Such a prayer is often recited facing the moon which plays an important role in human life, and is the means of reckoning time.   The growth of a child is often compared with the waxing of the new moon, and in its waning it is believed to carry away misfortunes and illness.

Generally, however, prayers are said over a highly venerated object, a piece of bark from the *eŋgal tree* (*Anopyxis ealænsis sprague*).   This piece of bark, which is referred to briefly as *eŋgal,* is obviously their most precious talisman.   It is not bought, but is simply detached from the tree with a blow from a matchet; after it has been assured that no harm is intended it is told that it has been taken to protect its owner against all possible enemies.   The *eŋgal* is not consecrated or made the object of any special rites, nor is any blood shed on it, but its power is explained in the following way: " The power of my *eŋgal* is as old as the creation of man on this earth, because as soon as men were created they began to pray and they understood that it is the *eŋgal* which helps them.   When I am in trouble, my *eŋgal* is my prayer."   There is an *eŋgal* in almost every family, and to give a piece of one's *eŋgal* to one's friend is to give him the most precious gift of protection against all misfortunes.   Nevertheless, no myth, legend, or proverb provides the slightest explanation of the origin of this belief in the *eŋgal,* and the tree whose bark is used is not itself sacred.

Besides the *eŋgal,* there are certain other protective talismans which are handed down from one generation to the next.   Examples are: pieces of rock crystal (*hinim*), a certain red stone (*mulol*), and small axes of polished stone of neolithic origin (*mahɔka ma bit,* " axes of the spirits of the dead ") which are sometimes dug up on a farm plot.   A prayer is said over these objects, while a few seeds of the *Aframomum* fruit (*helɔ he basa*) are chewed and then spat out on to them, because *helɔ he basa* gives power to the spoken word and spitting saliva on to an object establishes a living contact between the power of the object and the individual. Finally, there are talismans which are simply ordinary objects specially singled out by divination.

In divination we find yet another manifestation of the concept of a vital force. The diviner (*mondo w'eŋgamb*[3]) and the apparatus he uses do not achieve their results by mere chance, but because they are in direct contact not only with each other, by virtue of the words spoken when the apparatus was consecrated, but also with " life," because blood was shed on the apparatus and the diviner consumed a special portion of the sacrificed animal.   The diviner, his apparatus, his protective talismans (*bisiek*), and the vital force which permeates human beings and all the events of this world are so closely bound up together that they form one single entity; this is why divination is always infallible.

There are religious associations whose members aim to increase their wealth and prosperity.   Each association is grouped round a sacred object, knowledge of which is only acquired through a succession of initiation ceremonies.   There are no large men's societies among the Banen today.   All that remains is the memory of the terror they inspired and the crimes which were perpetrated when they passed noisily through the bush at night.   The *muŋgɔl, muŋɔn,* and *ulumu* societies were of this type, but no further information about them is available.   We know for certain,

[3] *Eŋgamb* really means " earth spider " (*mygale*), but the term is now used to refer to any kind of divination.

however, that the *eŋɔl* society of men and women—but especially of women—still existed 10 years ago among the Eling. The sacred object was a basket containing, among other things, some small polished stone axes and human figures roughly carved in stone. These sacred objects were only revealed to the initiates at the conclusion of lengthy dances and incantations.

It is reasonable to assume that these associations were originally of foreign, not Banen, origin, because in the *muŋgɔl, muŋɔn,* and *eŋɔl* societies the ritual language used was Basa and in the *ulumu* society, Bafia.

Christianity and Islam

The Catholic Mission of the Fathers of the Holy Spirit numbers 4,413 Christians and 1,418 catechumens, and the Protestant Mission has 3,121 Christians and 647 catechumens.

Finally it may be noted that among the Yambeta there are a few converts to Islam: these include the present Paramount Chief.

THE BAFIA AND THE YAMBASA

LOCATION AND DISTRIBUTION

NOMENCLATURE

The Bafia call themselves *Bekpa*. The name " Bafia " seems to have been formerly used by the Bati to designate the Bekpa and was a nickname, from *fia*, past participle of the verb *nfiak*, meaning " to take a chicken by the neck." The Bafia are thus " the people who were taken by the neck like chickens." Owing to its official adoption by the Administration, " Bafia " quickly came to be used for all the peoples in the area, and today it is applied to other tribes who are not, strictly speaking, Bafia, such as the Bekke, of Lemande origin and the Bape who, according to Tessmann, are really Balom.

The neighbouring Yambasa call the Bafia by their own name Bekpa, but the Banen call them Bafɛ.

According to Tessmann, the name " Yambasa " was given by the Bati to a congeries of peoples, not homogeneous in culture and speaking different dialects. The name was originally simply that of one of the clans of the Elip tribe. Here again it was extended by the Administration to cover the entire population of the area. Tessmann points out that the Bafia gave their neighbours, the Yambasa, the name of " Biambasa."

LOCATION

The 1913 edition of Moisel's map includes both the Bafia and the Yambasa peoples under the single name " Bafia."

The Bafia territory is in the Mbam Valley, on the right bank of the short section of this large river which runs in a north-west/south-east direction. It is quadrilateral in shape, covering an area of about 370 sq. kms. (*c.* 150 sq. miles), measuring about 14 miles from east to west and about 12 from north to south.

PHYSICAL ENVIRONMENT

The country is undulating, about 1,500–1,800 feet above sea level, with the Don mountain range in the west reaching a maximum height of 2,800 feet.

The soil is laterite but is well watered everywhere by the small tributaries of the Mbam, which do not dry up in the dry season. It is fertile savanna country cut by narrow strips of forest, and its wild palm groves are remarkably dense and rich. Today only the valleys of the Don range are covered with thick forest, which indicates that the forest once spread over the whole of the present savanna area and was destroyed by man.

The territory of the Yambasa is much larger, lying to the south of Bafia country. With an area of about 2,900 sq. miles it has natural boundaries on three sides: on the east and the south, the Mbam and Sanaga Rivers, and on the west, the Lihoua, a tributary of the Sanaga. To the north lies Lemande and Bafia country.

It is an area of gently undulating plain, which rises a little in the neighbourhood of the Lemande mountains and contains the richest and most fertile section of the region, consisting as it does of savanna covered with palm groves even denser than those of Bafia country.

DEMOGRAPHY

The peoples who today all call themselves Bafia actually consist of the Bekpa, the Bekke, and the Bape. The Bekpa, the most numerous, number 11,956, and are grouped into six clans, whose founders are said to be the sons of the legendary ancestor Pa and his wife Binkira. The six clans are:

Population

Ngam a Binkira, consisting of the present-day villages of Dang, Rionong, and Biamo 4,654

Sanam a Binkira, dying out.

Yakan a Binkira, consisting today of the villages of Yakan and Gbaram 749

Rum a Binkira, consisting today of the villages of Rum and Biamese 1,031

Guife a Binkira, consisting today of the villages of Bep and Guife 1,276

Koro a Binkira, consisting today of the villages of Gufan, Tchekan, Lable, Donengkeng, Niamsong, and Ribang 4,246

Total 11,956

The Bekke, who probably originated from the neighbouring Lemande, number only 3,879 and are divided into two sub-groups: Kiki and Bitang.

The Moko, who were driven from the left bank of the Mbam by the Balom, number 1,149.

Finally there are the Bape, who, according to Tessmann, are really Balom who settled in Bafia country and adopted their culture. There are only 1,412 Bape in the villages of Gaa, Nkeng, Lakpwang, and Denk.

There is thus a total population of 18,396 with a density of 120 per sq. mile and a rate of increase of 2.2

The Yambasa consist of four main tribes: *Population*

The *Mehele*, consisting of the Bokito, Benyi, Kedia, Yoro, and Ediolomo clans 2,020

Yangben, consisting of the Yangben, Omende, Bongo, and Batanga clans 5,008

Elip, with the villages of Yambasa, Kananga, Balemba, Boalondo, Bodombo, Basolo, Bombato, Kelgoto, Bongando 5,531

Kuono, with the villages of Yendzing, Esende, Ombesa, Baningoang, Baliama, Bunyabusumbi, Bogondo, Gefige, Gebobo, Bakoa, Assala, Bokaga, Bubaka 14,162

Total 26,721

The Yambasa thus total 26,721, with a density of 61 per sq. mile.

TRADITIONS OF ORIGIN AND HISTORY

The country now occupied by the Bafia seems to have been peopled in the following way:

The Bekke, coming from the Lemande mountains, were the first to arrive in this area which was already occupied by the Yambasa, whom they drove back. This change of habitat involved a migration of no more than a few miles, in a west-east direction. They were followed by the Bekpa, whose traditions suggest that they too migrated in a west-east direction. They themselves state that they came from the northern part of Babimbi territory and first entered the area through the gap between the Sanaga River and the Don mountains. They thus moved in between the Yambasa and the Bekke and finally met the Bape and the Fak (Balom). In this way the country was gradually taken over by separate clans of farming people seeking new land. It was not always a peaceful process, however, for the Bekpa say that they had difficulty in entering the plain, fighting the Bekke and the Yambasa, and driving back the Bape.

It is impossible to give even an approximate date for these events, and the historical record of these peoples goes back only to the middle of the last century. A raid by the Bamum took place around 1840. They came through Yambeta country and attacked the Bekpa in the Don mountains. The Bekpa at first fell back towards the south, as far as the territory of the Bekke. There the Bamum met with such strong resistance that they were forced to withdraw and never again attempted an attack on this area.

Later, towards 1880, there was an attack by the Fulani. They came from the north-east and crossed the Mbam with their cavalry. They were immediately attacked from the rear by guerillas and had to withdraw rapidly eastwards across the Mbam and take refuge among the Babute.

Finally, a few years later, there was a war with the Bati. They had been forced to retreat before the Babute who were themselves being pushed back by the Fulani. The Bati at first settled peacefully in the uninhabited forests south-west of the Mbam. There was then continuous contact between the Bati and the Bafia, the two cultures influencing each other in many ways, particularly linguistically. Soon, however, conflicts developed and the Bati advanced into the heart of Bafia country. After several wars, the Europeans finally intervened and drove the Bati out of the Bafia territory. Disturbances still continued, however, and the country was not finally pacified until 1911 when, after Major Puder's expedition, the Germans set up an administrative post there.

The Yambasa people do not form a single entity but appear to be made up of several heterogeneous elements. Indeed Tessmann, when he studied the area nearly 40 years ago, pointed out that the Yambasa did not think of themselves as a single group.

According to their traditions, the Mehele tribe were the first to establish themselves in the area. Formerly they were scattered throughout the savanna, but today, having been pushed back on the arrival of another element of the present population, these Mehele are massed along the upper course, and as far back as the source, of the Lebamo River, a tributary of the Sanaga.

A second population element, the Elip, who lived at first on the left bank of the Mbam, went southwards and crossed the Sanaga, to settle at first among the Mangisa. Then they crossed the Sanaga again, this time from east to west, and occupied the whole of the plain of the lower course of the Lebamo. They drove out most of the Bati-Tsinga people they found established on a small central range of hills, but a few remained in a small village which still exists today, a sort of Tsinga fortress in the midst of the Yambasa. The Elip prospered rapidly and spread not only over the lower Lebamo Plain, but also over the plain on the right bank of the Sanaga, over the Mbam Plain, and eventually came close to the Bafia. Here, however, they came up against another migrating group which had arrived from the north-east after crossing the Mbam and by-passing some Bati groups. These Kuono Yambasa (of which some elements continued to exist in the Dschim Valley and were marked on the 1913 edition of Moisel's map) were probably pushed back by the Babute at the time when the latter were jostling all the other groups in this area. The Kuono penetrated among the Bafia, the Yambasa who had come from the south, and the autochthonous Mehele. They occupied the plains bordering the Bafia Hills and watered by the small tributaries of the upper Lebamo.

MODERN DEVELOPMENTS (BAFIA, YAMBASA, AND BALOM)

Medical Services

The Administration's work in piping water from springs and in planting eucalyptus to reduce swamps (Bafia) is resulting in improved health conditions in the villages.

There is a large hospital at Bafia, with an African and a European doctor, and an adjoining maternity section. A few miles from Bafia, at Donengkeng, there is another hospital and maternity section, run by the American Mission, and headed by an American doctor. There are bush-dispensaries at Ombessa and Yangben (Yambasa), and four leper-homes, each with a small hospital. Finally, endemic diseases are combatted by mobile teams consisting of a European doctor and native assistants who travel about the country.

Education

The Education Department is very active in the Bafia region today. In 1947 there was only one official school at Bafia, with six classes and 300 pupils; besides this there was an American Mission school of six classes and 609 pupils at Donenkeng and a school with 500 pupils run by the Bafia Catholic Mission.

In the bush there are, in addition to the Government schools, three 3- and 4-class schools around Ombessa, eight schools around Yangben (Yambasa) and three schools among the Balom, all run by the Catholic Mission. The Bafia and Yambasa schools have 1,300 pupils, and the Balom schools 240. Finally, the American Mission has some 1,500 pupils in 18 schools, of which the most important are at Baliama, Kiki, and Yangben.

LANGUAGE

In the linguistic chapter of his book *Die Bafia*, Tessmann wrote that the Bafia language is related to those of the " neo-Bantu " type of which Fang is the most important. His opinion differs little from that of Dr. L. K. Anderson, the only person to have made a close study of this language, though Anderson feels that the Bafia language might best be classified as " semi-Bantu." Some years ago he explained why he considered it to be related to the Bulu language, and since then he has written: " The language is certainly Bantu in its grammatical structure. The principle of concord is immediately apparent. Nevertheless there are clear signs of non-Bantu influence." Among these non-Bantu characteristics Anderson mentions the following: many monosyllables of the pattern consonant–vowel–consonant; absence of certain nominal classes (he lists six classes, however); analogy between many Sudanese and Bafia roots; existence of the plosives *kp*, *gb*.

DISTINCTIVE ECONOMIC, SOCIAL, AND CULTURAL FEATURES

The economy, social organization, and material culture of the Bafia and the Yambasa are so similar that we shall continue to treat the two groups together. Even in 1907, Captain von Stein zu Lausnitz, who had travelled through the terri- tories of the Basa, Fang, Eastern Maka, Bamum, and Babute, was very much struck by the cultural features peculiar to the Bafia and Yambasa and commented that they differed materially from all other tribes of his acquaintance.[1]

Furthermore, as has already been pointed out, the main cultural features of the Bafia peoples are so similar to those of the Banen that it is unnecessary here to do more than point out the differences.

MAIN FEATURES OF ECONOMY

AGRICULTURE

The Bafia do very little hunting or fishing and agriculture is their main source of food. They have the advantage of a much richer soil than the Banen, but their agricultural implements are very similar—matchets and axes used by the men for clearing, thick stakes as levers for uprooting large gramineous plants, and hoes used by the women.

[1] 1908, p. 526.

Each family works its own plot of land, with the help of teams of friends, who go from one family to another in turn.

Crops grown are the same as those of the Banen, with millet as an additional cereal. Staple foods are maize, millet, yams, and cocoyams.

A farm plot is arranged with the main crops in the centre, planted in furrows or large square patches. Round the edges are other crops forming a border. For example, a yam plot will be edged first with sweet potatoes, then with groundnuts, and later with maize and *wandzou* peas.

Sweet potatoes are harvested first, then the other crops and finally the yams themselves. A month later the ground is hoed and ridged and melons and maize are sown, followed a little later by beans and gourds. Three months later all these are harvested.

Cocoyam plots are prepared at the time of the yam harvest (beginning of the dry season). The men hoe the patches round which the women plant gourd and bean seeds. The men then put in the cocoyam plants, each one in a little funnel-shaped hole which collects moisture. When the plot is ready, at the beginning of the rainy season, the men add sugar-cane cuttings. The following year cocoyam is replaced by cereals.

On exhausted soil the Bafia sow solanaceæ whose leaves they eat as green vegetables. Finally, they make very large groundnut plots where groundnuts are the sole crop.

Near the homestead the kitchen garden contains all items likely to be needed urgently, including xanthosoma, cassava, and plantains.

Everything is stored either in baskets or granaries over the kitchen, in three-walled granary shelters, or in fenced yam-stores.

The Administration, aiming at the increased exploitation of the country's resources, has given strong encouragement to the people to grow cocoa and rice in addition to the usual food crops. Coffee has also been introduced. The country as a whole already produces more than 1,000 tons of cocoa a year and the production of palm-oil is increasing annually. Experiments with mechanized agriculture, also, have shown that the country should lend itself well to these methods.

A native Provident Society, with an official of the Department of Agriculture as technical adviser, is responsible for the development of farming and stockbreeding. It distributes seeds, and maintains groups of workers who help on the plantations and in the preparation of agricultural produce. The Society also owns lorries for use in the buying-up and distributing of produce.

The Bafia and Yambasa own more domestic animals than do the Banen. These include dogs, goats, sheep, and chickens, and the number of pigs is gradually increasing. In the past dogs were kept mainly for food, though women were forbidden to eat dog-meat once they reached puberty. Today, however, some people are very reluctant to kill them. Goats and sheep are used primarily in ceremonial exchange, though the latter are subject to a food taboo which is still operative among the older members of some of the Bekpa clans. With reference to this taboo (which Tessmann says applies also to the antelope) the old people say, " these animals are the descendants of a Lemande woman who married a Guife man."

TRADE AND MARKETS

Channels for the disposal of the produce of this rich country are fortunately numerous. Thanks to the main Nkongsamba-Yaounde road and to the many roads which pass through or converge on Bafia, the large trading centre, the country is brought very close to Yaounde. From Bafia several roads lead south, one going via Guife (Bafia) across the territory of the Mehele (Yambasa) to the centres of Yangben and Omende in the south, and another passing via Gufan (Bafia) to Yendzing (Yambasa), Bombato, and Balamba. Finally there is a road linking these two in the heart of Yambasa country. Roads from Bafia to Yaounde via Saa and from Bafia to Eseka (Basa) are also being planned.

These roads allow markets to be held periodically at the following places during the cocoa season: Bayomen (Yambeta, Bape, Balom, North Lemande); Bunyabus-sumbi and Ombessa (Yambasa); Bokito (Yambasa, South Lemande); Benyi-Yangben and Keleng (Basso village, a market intended to serve an isolated Babimbi area).

CRAFTS

Bafia technology differs in certain respects from that of the Banen.

Wood-workers use very rudimentary tools—small axes, matchets, knives, and chisels. With these they square the timber from which they make various household articles: bedboards, doors, posts (for building houses), bed and table legs, and handles for iron tools. The Bafia do not make wooden mortars. They do, however, carve human figures.

Bark is obtained from certain large trees, and is cut into wide sheets, dried, and used to line the walls of houses.

In weaving, the Bafia use raffia fibres and cotton. The latter is grown near the homestead around the kitchen-garden. Both men and women weave.

In basket-work, the Bafia use thin strips of raffia-leaves and of oil-palm stems, and also of the bark of certain shrubs (*Triumphetta*), as well as rattan. By a very simple method, they make baskets with or without lids, as well as termite traps. They use the projecting spiral method of basket-work to make covered baskets for holding various household articles. They make wallets and sleeping-mats of flexible basket-work, though the latter may also be made of rigid basket-work, in which thin strips of stems are joined by knotted cords.

Pottery is made by both men and women. Men make pipes; women make cooking-pots. Pipe-making involves the shaping of a lump of clay which is then drawn out and bent sharply near the middle. Cooking-pots are made from rolls of clay placed spirally one above the other and smoothed outside and inside; pressure from above gives the pot its bulging shape; the bottom is closed by being drawn out and lastly the neck is made from another roll of clay.

Blacksmiths today use only old European iron for making tools. The Bafia have never smelted iron ore, probably because there is none in their soil. In the past they obtained ore from the Banen-Eling.

Houses are built by methods very similar to those of the Banen, though there are one or two minor differences. The roof is covered with sheets of raffia-leaves tied to the framework, instead of with mats, the leaves being ridged and sometimes covered with a layer of clay. The walls may have their interstices filled with clay or be lined with overlapping sheets of bark fixed to posts. The walls are then smeared with white clay or, if made of bark sheets, with a paste of crushed char-coal which is thought to prevent damage by termites.

A few old wooden stools are engraved with geometrical designs and cooking pots are slightly decorated by means of a plaited roller.

Dances, in which large circles of men move in an anti-clockwise direction miming, for example, a hunting scene, are of particular interest. These dances are probably relatively old, but others, such as the bicycle mime, are clearly of modern inspiration.

SOCIAL ORGANIZATION AND POLITICAL SYSTEM

GROUPING

In *Die Bafia* Tessmann draws up a complete and detailed list of the component divisions of the Bafia people.[2] Starting with the smallest unit and working upwards he lists the following: Unter-Familie, Familie, Familienverbände, Unter-Sippe,

[2] Tessmann, 1934.

Sippe, Sippenverbände, Unter-Stamm, Stamm, Rasse; an approximate translation would be: sub-family, family, joint family, sub-clan, clan, clan-group, sub-tribe, tribe, race.

Henri Relly of the French Colonial Service, who was several times in charge of the Bafia Sub-division and made a French translation of Tessmann's work,[3] questions the accuracy of Tessmann's list. According to Relly, a varying number of " sub-families " form a joint family and a number of joint families form a village; often the village consists of joint families which are grouped together quite arbitrarily, usually because of their proximity and for administrative purposes. One or more villages compose a clan and several clans make up the tribe. The joint family is the most important social unit and bears the name of its founder; in the village of Dang (Bafia) the name of the joint family or sub-family is preceded by *Bia* or *Ri*, meaning " descendants of." Relly states that before the arrival of the Europeans the only authority recognised by the Bafia was the head of the joint family. Each sub-family lived separately with its dwelling-huts grouped inside an enclosure. Today the " sub-families " are still dispersed in this way and there is a tendency for them to break with the traditional authority of the joint family head, though the " sub-families " making up the joint family still retain a strong feeling of common ancestry.

From the unfortunately rather brief genealogies recorded by Relly, it is clear that what he calls a " sub-family " is not the smallest domestic unit, consisting of a man, his wife or wives, and their children, but a group which includes a grand-father and his descendants. In fact, the " sub-family," according to his terminology, is a group of *bia* or descendants in the male line of one grandfather, that is, all his married sons with their wives and children.

" Village " maps show each joint family living on its own clearly delimited land, dispersed, not clustered together. This was one of the characteristics of Banen society, as it is of the Bafia. Relly has already described this tendency to disperse in order to escape, to a certain extent, from the authority of the joint family head. This authority is still recognized morally, though in practice each elementary family seeks material independence, works for its own keep and tends to be concerned only with its own prosperity. This is in spite of the fact that rights to family land are the same for all, and that certain hunting customs remind people of the respect due to the " elder " and the " father " (head of the joint family). In the realm of marriage, too, there are strict rules intended to prevent the " mixing of blood " and to compel a man to take a wife from outside the joint family.

The Homestead (*mɛɛ, pl. bomɛɛ*)

This consists of a few huts inhabited by the members of a single elementary family linked by close blood relationship—a man, his wives, and children. When a son marries he sets up house nearby, and two brothers may live in neighbouring compounds. The huts (*naa*), which are built round the sides of a square, have sloping roofs and may consist of one or more rooms. This arrangement is so similar to that of the Banen that there is no need to describe it further.

The kitchen hut (*naa megin*) may have several rooms, one for each wife, and each with its own door to the outside.

The stores (*tsak*) for cocoyams, yams, millet, and palm-oil are either special huts which sometimes adjoin the living quarters, or they may be rooms raised above these on a floor covered with packed earth mixed with palm-nut fibres. A small window, secured from the inside, is cut out of the gable. Sometimes stores may consist merely of a simple fence of stakes driven into the ground, and they are then also used to stable goats. Finally, when built as three-walled shelters, with a roof, these stores are also used as meeting-huts for the men (*kepana*).

---

[3] Unpublished MS. in the library of Centrifan, Douala.

RIGHTS OF INHERITANCE AND SUCCESSION

On the death of the family head, there is only one " moral " heir, already chosen by the head during his lifetime. Primogeniture is the general rule, intended to prevent the dispersal of property belonging in fact to the whole family and administered by the eldest member. The father is nevertheless free to choose a younger son if he thinks his eldest son is unfitted for the role of successor.

Five days after a man's death, his chosen heir becomes the new administrator of the family property, which is equally divided among all the male children. If there are no sons the heirs are the dead man's full brothers, or if he has none, then his half-brothers by the same father. If there is no male heir, the dead man's senior wife becomes the guardian of the property until a male child is born, either to one of the deceased's female descendants or to his widow. When this child grows up he will be declared successor to the family head.

LAND TENURE

The customary rules of land ownership are similar to those of the Banen. Land is owned collectively by the clan, and joint and elementary families all have their own plots on this land. Originally palm groves were also owned collectively, but today this is found only in a few villages; individual ownership of palm-trees is now more common and a man will clearly demarcate such property. In villages where bush palms are still collective property, the gathering of palm-nuts is strictly regulated. Each family in turn is entitled to the entire crop produced in a single dry season, other people being allowed to take only enough to eat.

The administrative officer Coquil writes that when a member of the family wishes to make a plantation, the family head allocates a site. This is one of the few remaining vestiges of the family head's authority, but it is an important one. It may happen that, after appropriate negotiations, a family head will allow a stranger to settle on his land. In this case the stranger has a right to the produce of any tree he may plant himself, but the fruit of the palm, avocado, and kola trees already growing on the land remain the property of the family head.

This customary right over the land is not a right of possession. The family head may not sell the land. However, a member of the family may obtain a deed of acknowledgement of land rights over a plantation which he has developed, and when this becomes final, the holder becomes owner of the soil. This law, of European inspiration, and as yet little applied among the Bafia, will hasten the disappearance of customary ownership of land.

MAIN CULTURAL FEATURES

PHYSICAL AND MENTAL CHARACTERISTICS

The Bafia are usually of medium height, thickset, and strong. Neither Bafia nor Yambasa submit readily to chiefly authority, which trait is perhaps shown in the wide dispersal of their dwellings.

ORNAMENT AND DRESS

Originally, the Bafia knew only one method of skin decoration: women and young girls scarred themselves on the arms and thighs with pieces of burning wood. Such scars may still be seen on old women today. Later, both men and women, in imitation of neighbouring peoples, decorated themselves with fine cuts. This custom is now dying out.

Like the Banen, the Bafia pierced their ear-lobes and filed their teeth. Tessmann states that the Bafia said that they did this to distinguish themselves from animals. " Otherwise," they said, " we would resemble pigs or chimpanzees."

L

In the past, Bafia women simply wore a narrow belt of banana fibre supporting a bunch of ferns passed between the thighs. But from earliest times also, it was customary for both men and women to wear a very small loincloth made originally of bark, but later, of course, of European cloth. During the last war, because of the shortage of cloth, bark was again used to a striking extent.

The Bafia, whose country is very small and crossed by the main road to Yaounde, have readily adopted European dress which is now worn by both sexes.

THE LIFE CYCLE

Throughout the Central Cameroons there is an obvious similarity in birth and circumcision customs.

CIRCUMCISION

This is not accompanied by an initiation ceremony. In the old days it took place at the end of adolescence, but today a boy is circumcised much earlier. According to Tessmann, circumcision was introduced fairly recently among the Bafia, and even more recently among the Yambasa, but he does not state the source of this information.

NAMING

Among the Bafia a child is named as soon as it is born, either by its father or by the old woman who presided at the birth. Boys keep the same name all their lives, whereas girls, according to Tessmann, changed theirs at marriage—and every time they went to another man. This " conjugal " name, according to the same author, was only used by the husband and his near relatives, the woman's family continuing to use the name she received at birth. This was the custom as observed by Tessmann: today it is far from being the general practice.

MARRIAGE

Marriage among the Bafia differs completely from the Banen form. Marriage by exchange between clans does not exist. There are two forms of marriage among the Bafia, namely:

  (a) The normal and widespread form involving a payment by the husband to the wife's family.

  (b) Marriage by capture, which was once very fashionable and is now gradually disappearing. There was only one restriction here: the couple could not be blood relations of any degree and they had to belong to different clans. Dr. Anderson writes: " The taboos on marriage with a particular woman could nevertheless be annulled by throwing a bound ram backwards and forwards over the woman's house until it died, a tiring task which ended in joyful feasting on the ram's carcase."

Among the Banen, in former days, if a woman ran away from her husband or was captured in the market, she was not considered to have made a new marriage. Custom required that her father who had himself received a wife in exchange for his daughter, should take back the latter from her lover and return her to her husband. If he failed to do this, he had to compensate the husband by giving him another wife or by returning his own. Among the Bafia, however, the situation is very different. The theft of a woman constitutes a marriage: it is a recognized convention. No one (neither her father nor her husband if she is already married) goes to fetch her back, but the man from whom she has been stolen merely acquires the right to act in the same way towards the captor's wives; in the case of a young unmarried girl, the captor must make peace with her family. In accordance with this custom, women circulated from village to village, passing through the hands of a succession of husbands and leading a very licentious life, as did the men. According to Tessmann, a stolen woman belonged to all the men of her captor's family before belonging to her husband. Children born of this kind of marriage were the property of the captor-husband even if the woman was already pregnant at the time of her capture. A daughter, however, was generally returned to the real husband, or to the woman's father, in order to bring about a reconciliation. Among the Yambasa, daughters born of such a marriage belonged to the captor-husband, who, however, always had to give a portion of any game he killed to the injured husband.

FUNERAL CEREMONIES

The burial ceremony differs little from that of the neighbouring Banen. Among the Bafia, there is the same display of dancing accompanied by chanting, the same squandering of wealth, the same type of grave. Here, however, custom requires that the corpse, lying on its left side, should have its arms folded and its knees drawn up to its elbows.

LOCATION AND PHYSICAL ENVIRONMENT

The Balom call themselves *Fak*. The name " Balom " appears to be a nick-name given to them by the neighbouring Tikar, and that of " Bakwandjim," used on all maps to designate the Balom of the right bank of the Mbam, is also a nick-name given to them by the Bamum.

Balom country is extremely isolated. The Mbam River crosses it from north to south and then, after meeting its tributary the Nun, runs from west to east and thus forms a natural frontier to the country. The Mbam and Nun are big torrent-like rivers, impossible to navigate, hence the isolation of the area, and in the north there is only one place, near the small village of Teta, where the river can always be crossed. Certain other parts are fordable, for a few months only, in the dry season, but in places which can be reached only after half a day's march along narrow tracks and across an uninhabited area. In the south the Nun can be crossed at one point and the Mbam at two, but all are dangerous.

These rivers, about 300 yards wide, broken by rapids and bordered with tsetse-fly-infested forest, cut the country off from the road and from the neighbour-ing Bafia. During the dry season, when the river beds are strewn with rocks and sandbanks, canoes are the only link with the outside world.

In the north, the country of the Balom is separated from that of the Tikar by a forest 20 miles wide—yet another isolating factor. Steep wooded hills come down to the right bank of the Mbam—hills intersected by numerous streams and rising to a height of 1,800 feet form a natural barrier between Balom and Bamum country. The savanna-covered uplands of the left bank are uninhabited as far as the track which follows the first spurs of the Ngolop and Djanti mountains, whose peaks reach a height of nearly 5,000 feet. Numerous little rivers cross the country-side, which is intersected by forest strips, some of which, in the south, are rich in oil-palms.

In this area, so cut off from the outside world, all the villages are situated on a circular track without any link between its eastern and western sections, which are separated by the Mbam, impossible to cross during the greater part of the year. Coquil writes: " This track is the only line of communication, the only link between the various Balom villages: a path along which two men cannot walk abreast. Sometimes it loses itself in the high grass; sometimes, in the forest, it crosses great roots and becomes a slippery path down the side of a gulley. Interrupted by numerous rivers—bridgeless, of course—skirting hills, it is extremely hard to travel, and one can well imagine what efforts are expended by the planters who carry their produce on their heads from Nianzon to Bafia."

TERRITORIAL GROUPING AND DEMOGRAPHY

There is little information regarding the Balom, who, by reason of their great isolation, have never been studied systematically, and it is not possible to list their tribes and sub-tribes. So far, the only demographic data available are the census figures for the Balom villages, given here:

Village					Men	Women	Total
Diuma..	..	..	..	..	41	51	92
Bangong	..	..	..	..	187	223	410
Dǝk ..	..	..	..	..	122	109	231
Kop ..	..	..	..	..	52	66	118
Ba ..	..	..	..	..	125	156	281
Ga ..	..	..	..	..	174	187	361
Nianzon	..	..	..	..	107	78	185
Mpany..	..	..	..	..	125	127	252
M'Puga	..	..	..	..	93	90	183
Boko ..	..	..	..	..	75	76	151
Ngen ..	..	..	..	..	86	85	171
Zo ..	..	..	..	..	107	105	212
Djaka ..	..	..	..	..	149	146	295
Zakan ..	..	..	..	..	67	51	118
Muzi ..	..	..	..	..	115	122	237
Bee ..	..	..	..	..	174	188	362
Gufe ..	..	..	..	..	89	98	187
							3,846

This total of 3,846 shows an increase over the figures of the previous census.

TRADITIONS OF ORIGIN AND HISTORY

The Balom know nothing of their early origins, but say that in the fairly recent past their villages moved gradually from their original sites in the north to a more fertile region. This is especially true of the southern villages, near the left bank of the Mbam. Tradition has it that some of their villages were originally established on Mount Ngolop, but that the inhabitants were driven away during wars with the Tikar and the Babute towards the end of the last century, and at first took refuge on the right bank of the Nun among the Yambeta and the Bape. This is where Dominik found them when he arrived in 1905. Later on they left the area to go north of the Nun to the right bank of the Mbam, where they settled in numerous villages which they named after their families, and these names are still in use today. Some of these villages moved yet again, while others dispersed. In this way some of the small settlements split up, some of the members founding small hamlets on the right bank, e.g., Zakan and Dǝk.

It was at the time of these migrations that Europeans first occupied the country.

LANGUAGE

All existing evidence shows that the Balom speak a language related to that of the Bafia. Tessmann stated that it was merely a dialect of the latter. Certain aspects of their material culture, however, have suggested to the present writer that the Balom may have come from a region much farther north and that they may have borrowed their language from the Bafia.

MAIN FEATURES OF ECONOMY

AGRICULTURE

The Balom are essentially an agricultural people. Coquil, who made several visits to Balom country, states that maize, the staple food, is the most widespread crop, together with a little millet, gourds, and cocoyams. Men clear the forest and burn grass and trees, while women sow, hoe, and weed.   Children and old men, who live in the fields and sleep in shelters made of leaves, watch and protect the crops against the depredations of warthogs and monkeys.

Coquil lists the seasonal activities as follows:

August: new plots prepared; maize sown.

September: weeding and ridging of maize.

October (season of heavy rains): ears of grain are forming.

November–December: maize and millet harvested; women rest, men clear new plots; cocoa harvested and dried.

January–February: old plots cleared; hunting and fishing.

March: maize sown on old and new plots; palm-nuts harvested.

April–May: groundnuts sown; maize plots weeded; palm-nuts harvested.

June: maize harvested.

July: maize harvested; millet sown.

The Balom thus have two maize harvests annually, and one each of millet, cocoa, and palm-nuts.

Cash crops for export have been introduced.   Some, such as coffee, have failed, but others, such as cocoa and cabbage-palm, have been successful and have enabled the Balom to pay their taxes.   Moreover they are stable crops which keep the local population in one place and prevent the breaking-up of villages which results from the Balom system of working a plot for six years and then abandoning it.   Certain villages, such as Ba, Ga, and Djaka, are well grouped and laid out.   The Administration has also tried to develop the local production of raffia, wild honey, beeswax, etc.

TRADE AND MARKETS

Internal trade is almost non-existent among the Balom.   There is not a single bush market in the interior of the country, and only two in the south, close to each other, on the right and left banks of the Mbam.   A few itinerant traders go from village to village selling salt and buying maize, dried fish, and wild honey.

There is no road into Balom country and, until a few years ago, the only way they could dispose of their cocoa and cabbage-palm was by carrying it to Bafia, a journey which involved the difficult crossing of the Mbam.   In order to alleviate the situation, the Administration opened a market at Bayomen, a village near the right bank of the Mbam.   This market serves as a centre for Balom, Bape, Yambeta, and North Lemande produce.

SOCIAL   ORGANIZATION

Coquil states that in the past, the village chief was all-powerful.   Later, however, when the need for new farming land caused villages to break up, the chief's authority diminished in comparison with that of the family heads.   The old form of organization is still found in compact villages such as Ga, where the chief has undisputed authority, but in general individualist tendencies are increasing, and it is sometimes hard to tell whether a particular man has left his village in order to escape the chief's authority, or whether he has gone in search of new farming land.

THE HOMESTEAD

The Balom homestead, like that of all the Central Cameroons peoples, consists of a cluster of huts round a central yard: the husband has a hut, and each wife has one for herself and her children.

Huts are round, with mud walls and conical grass-thatched roofs, supported at the centre by a strong pole.   A partition with an opening at one end divides the hut into two.   The outer room is the kitchen, from which the smoke escapes through a small raised door, and the inner room serves as a bedroom. Immediately under the roof there is a granary, from whose floor are hung drying maize cobs. These huts are well built but dark inside, as they have no windows.

In certain western and northern villages there are huts of the Bamum or Tikar type, rectangular with four-sided straw roofs. Some of these huts, as in the village of Mpany, are decorated with plaited straw. The roofs of these huts serve as granaries.

MAIN CULTURAL FEATURES

PHYSICAL AND MENTAL CHARACTERISTICS

The Balom show very marked negroid characteristics. Their bodies are thickset, with long arms, and the women have very hollow backs.

They are dogged and courageous workers, but very resistant to change and unwilling to accept advice. They accordingly oppose any innovations suggested by the Administration in an attempt to develop their agriculture.

ORNAMENT AND DRESS

Some women are tattooed in the Bamileke manner, on the stomach and chest. They are usually naked except for a bead or fibre belt which supports a cloth passed between the thighs. Men wear either a large loose shirt, similar to that of the more northerly tribes, or a small loincloth.

Like the Bafia, both men and women have the lobe of one ear pierced.

Variously coloured preparations are smeared on the body on special occasions. When a girl reaches puberty her body is smeared with a red powder made of *padouk* wood. At this time, too, one of her nostrils is pierced so that small pieces of bright metal may be placed in the hole.

After the birth of her child, a woman smears her thighs with this same red powder. As elsewhere, white is the colour of mourning, and widows and widowers smear their bodies with clay. They draw a white circle round the arms, thighs, and calves, and another round the head after it has been shaved.

THE LIFE CYCLE

We have already seen how closely Balom social organization resembles that of the Bafia. There is a similar resemblance between the life cycles of the two peoples: they differ only in a few minor details.

MARRIAGE

It seems likely that the Balom borrowed the custom of marriage by capture from the Bafia at a comparatively recent date and that originally the only form of marriage was that involving a bridewealth payment by the husband, with all its consequences. Among the Balom, in marriage by capture, a husband whose wife had been stolen could in fact claim from her parents the return of this payment. If they refused his claim, the children born of his wife's second marriage belonged to him. However, if the child thus handed over in compensation to the first husband was a girl, he was expected to give a present to the captor-husband. This present, also regarded as compensatory, usually consisted of two goats. We have here a custom somewhat different from that of the Bafia: its rules are much more far-reaching.

BIBLIOGRAPHY

Baumann, H., and Westermann, D.
    Les Peuples et les Civilisations de l'Afrique. [Trans. by L. Homburger.]
    Paris: Payot, 1948.

Chauleur, P.
    " Esquisse ethnologique pour servir à l'étude des principales tribus des Territories du
    Cameroun sous Mandat Français." *Bull. Soc. Et. Cam.*, No. 3, 1943, pp. 9–66.

Dominik, H.
    " Die Bapea-Expedition." *Deutsches Kolonialblatt,* 1905, pp. 526–33.

    The purpose of this expedition was to protect the Yambasa against the unruly
    Bapea. The latter's territory was at the time known only through von
    Schimmelpfennig's report of 1901. Dominik's report describes the region
    traversed by the expedition and also certain features of Bati culture. In
    addition, it contains a description of a Bape village. After one month of
    skirmishing with the local people, the expedition had managed to explore
    about 50 sq. kms. of Bape country.

Dugast, I.
    " L'habitation chez les Ndiki du Cameroun." *J. Soc. Afr.*, X, 1940, pp. 99–126.
    " L'agriculture chez les Ndiki de population Banen." *Bull. Soc. Et. Cam.*, VIII,
    1944, pp. 7–103.
    Inventaire Ethnique du Sud-Cameroun, Mém. I.F.A.N. (Centre du Cameroun),
    Série: Populations, No. 1, 1949. See pp. 43–55.

Farelly, M.
    Chronique du pays Banen. Paris: Société des Missions Evangéliques de Paris,
    1948.

    This work, by a missionary, consists of a series of brief sketches which give an
    interesting general account of Banen country. It describes local beliefs and
    the attempts made by the young educated people in the schools to break the
    hold of ancestral custom.

Hoesemann [Major]
    " Ethnologisches aus Kamerun." *Mitteilungen aus den Deutschen Schutzgebieten,*
    1903, pp. 150–182.

    Major Hoesemann was a member of von Schimmelpfennig's expedition, and
    during the period it spent with Chief Somo, he made very accurate observa-
    tions of " Indiki " material culture, illustrated by numerous sketches.

Johnston, Sir H. H.
    A Comparative Study of the Bantu and Semi-Bantu Languages. 2 vols. Oxford
    University Press. Vol. I, 1919; vol. II, 1922.

    The Banen vocabulary, which Johnston calls Indiki (Banyim) is given in vol. I,
    pp. 698–710, as No. 235.

Koelle, S. W.
    Polyglotta Africana. London: Church Missionary House, 1854.

    Banen vocabulary: XXII E 11.

Labouret, H.
    " Sorcellerie et sortilèges chez les Bafia et les Yambasa." *Togo-Cameroun,* avril-
    juillet, 1935, pp. 159–62.

Menzel
    " Streifzüge um Jabassi." *Deutsches Kolonialblatt,* 1907, pp. 455–8.

Millous, P.

"La frontière ethnique soudano-bantou au Cameroun." *L'Anthropologie*, XLVII, 1–2, 1937, pp. 99–101.

Passarge-Rathjens

Article on "Bafia" in *Deutsches Kolonial Lexikon*, I, Leipzig, 1920, p. 112.

Puder [Major]

"Die Bafia- (Bapea-) Expedition." *Deutsches Kolonialblatt*, 1911, pp. 454–7.

An account of the pacificatory expedition which had to be sent out following the death of Commandant Dominik. In 10 days all resistance was broken down. The expedition then marched against the north-eastern Banen, who surrendered after three weeks. The country was henceforward to remain under military occupation.

Tessmann, G.

"Die Völker und Sprachen Kameruns." *Petermann's Geogr. Mitteilungen*, 1932, No. 5–6, pp. 113–20; no. 7–8, pp. 184–90.

Die Bafia und die Kultur der Mittelkamerun-Bantu. Ergebnisse der 1913 v. Reichs-Kolonialamt ausges. Forschungsreise nach Kamerun. Stuttgart: Strecker und Schröder, 1934.

Thorbecke, M. P.

Auf der Savane. Berlin: E.S. Mittler, 1914. See especially pp. 206–18.

Frau Thorbecke accompanied her husband, Professor Thorbecke, on a long scientific expedition, in the course of which she made numerous notes and sketches. On their way from Tikar to Babute country they spent a few days among the Balom, and Frau Thorbecke gives a brief description of the people and their country.

von der Leyen

"Bericht über seine Erkundung des Nun." *Deutsches Kolonialblatt*, 1911, pp. 662–4.

An interesting study of the physical geography of northern Banen, Kibum, and Yambeta country, and southern Balom country (Bakwandjim people).

von Schimmelpfennig

"Bericht über die Expedition von Ngutte II nach Jabassi." *Mitt. aus. d. Deutsch. Schutzgebieten*, 1901, pp. 144–66.

This report gives an account of the expedition's journey through Banen country, from the time it crossed the Mbam in Yambeta country until it entered Basa country along the Nyamtam track. The names of most of the tribes visited by the expedition are listed, together with the names of their chiefs.

von Stein

"Die Jabassi-Expedition, 1908–09." *Deutsches Kolonialblatt*, 1910, p. 499.

von Stein zu Lausnitz

"Eine Erkundungs-Expedition zwischen Wuri und Sanaga." *Deutsches Kolonial-blatt*, 1908, pp. 521–31.

On p. 526 of this report there is an account of the journey among the Bafia and, more particularly, the Yambasa peoples, with a description of the country, its inhabitants, and certain aspects of their material culture.

INDEX

Abo, 90
Administration, 11–12, 36–7, 42, 56, 66, 94, 104, 105, 134
Adultery, 46, 110, 114, 115–16, 124, 145
Age-sets, absence of, 143
Aghem, 11
Agriculture, 26, 61, 97–8, 113, 138–9, 157–8, 165–6; rituals connected with, 47, 48, 81–2, 108, 111, 126–7
Alphabet, Njoya's, 58–9
Altars, 47
Ancestor cult, 47, 81, 126–7
Animals, domestic, 27, 97, 158
Assault, 114, 116
Associations, 38–40, 42, 73–4, 110–13; absence of, 152; boys', 44; religious, 111, 152; secret, 49, 66, 70, 73–4, 128; women's, 47, 113

Baboons, 128
Bafia, 132–3, 154–63
Bafoussam, chiefdom of, 104–6 and 87–131 *passim*
Bafut, 13, 18, 21–2, 45
Bagam, chiefdom of, 103–4 and 87–131 *passim*
Bakoko, 90
Bali, 11, 12, 20, 28, 87
Balom, 132–3, 154, 164–7
Bamessing, people of, 27, 28, 33, 46, 48–9
Bamileke, 53, 55, 87–131, 136
Bamum, 11, 53–86, 87, 136
Banden, 87
Baneka, 87
Banen, 87, 132–54
Bangangte, 87–131 *passim*
Bansaw, Banso. *See* Nsaw
Bape, 132–3, 154–63 *passim*
Basa, 139
Basket-making, 140
Bati, 93, 132
Beadwork, 63
Beer, 26
Bekke, 154–63 *passim*
Bekpa, 154–63 *passim*
Bentkom, 55, 75
Betrothal, 78, 120
Bikom. *See* Kom
Birth, 44, 77, 119, 146–7, 167; statistics, 89
Bornu, 20
Bororo. *See* Fulani
Bridewealth, 45, 78, 120–1, 122, 148, 167
Bum, 11, 12, 13, 18, 21, 41–2
Burial, 46, 78–9, 124–5, 149–50, 163

Canoes, 63
Cattle, 11, 61, 97, 109
Chamba, 11, 20
Chameleons, 64, 78
Charms, 48, 152
Chiefs, chiefdoms, 11–12, 42, 55, 71, 102–3, 94, 108–10, 141, 144, 166
Children, 44, 45, 117
Chimpanzees, 128

Christianity, 25, 33, 48, 56–7, 137, 153
Cicatrization, 119, 161
Circumcision, 44, 78, 148, 162
Clan head, 31, 41
Clans, 31, 41, 66, 141–2, 160; royal, 32, 41
Coffee plantations, 54, 60, 61, 139
Compounds, 29, 34, 65, 100, 142, 160
Coronation ceremonies, 70–1, 109–10
Cotton, 64
Counsellors, 32, 36, 37, 38, 41, 68, 71, 103, 104–5, 141
Crafts, 27, 62–4, 98–9, 140–1
Credit-groups, 28
Crops, 26, 61, 97, 138, 158, 165
Currency, 62
Curses, 144

Dances, 49, 81, 110, 149, 150
Death, 46, 78, 124–5, 149
Divination, diviners, 47–8, 81, 128–9, 152
Divorce, 46, 123–4, 129
Dress, 27, 77, 119, 146, 162, 167
Drums, 75, 108

Ear-piercing, 146, 161, 167
Education, 25, 56–7, 94, 137, 157
Egypt, 82
Elders, 144, 160
Eling, 132–54 *passim*
Elip, 154–63 *passim*
Embroidery, 63
Exogamy, 35, 45

Family, 142; extended, 33; joint, 160
Fire-making, 140
Fishing, 27, 61, 138
Fon, 23, 36–42, 70–1, 102
Food, 26, 61, 138; taboos, 158
Fulani, 11, 20, 23, 54, 55, 97
Fungom, 11, 13, 17, 22–3, 27, 29, 33–4, 35, 43

Germans, 21, 24, 56
God, 47, 48, 80, 126, 151
Granaries, 62, 139, 158
Grave-huts, 125

Hausa, 11, 27, 28, 53, 57, 62, 94
Head, king's, ritual importance of, 81
Horses, 11, 55–6, 62
Hospitals, 25, 137, 156–7
Housing, 27, 62, 65, 98, 141, 142, 166–7
Hunting, 27, 61, 97, 138

Implements, 26, 63, 99, 138, 157
Inheritance, 34, 72–3, 116, 142–3, 161
Iron. *See* Smiths
Islam, 33, 48, 56–7, 94, 153
Itundu, 132–54 *passim*
Ivory, 62, 99, 104, 109, 119

170